P9-DMD-825

BETTMANN PORTABLE ARCHIVE

BETTMANN PORTABLE ARCHIVE

...A graphic history of
almost everything...presented
by way of 3,669 illustrations
culled from the files of
The Bettmann Archive
...topically arranged and
cross-referenced to serve as an
idea stimulator and image finder.

Picture House Press, Inc.

EDITOR:
Otto L. Bettmann

ART DIRECTOR:
Herbert Migdoll

TYPOGRAPHIC CONSULTANT:
Martin Solomon

Picture House Press specializes in the publication of "total" picture books. The Bettmann Portable Archive is the initial volume of a projected series to add up to an Encyclopedia Iconographica.

The Bettmann Portable Archive

First Printing, 1966
Second Printing, 1967
Third Printing, 1973
136 E. 57th St., New York, N.Y. 10022

Manufactured in the United States of America.
Library of Congress Card No. 66-22452

CONTENTS

INTRODUCTION

It has been said that music not performed ceases to exist. The paradox applies to pictures as well. Art not seen loses its meaning. ℂ This is perhaps the reason why Picasso hates drawers and closets. Even if his studios get notoriously cluttered, he insists that his artistic possessions be out in the open. Once they are stored away in a cabinet, they cease to exist for him. ℂ In a picture reference library such as The Bettmann Archive, millions of pictorial items are filed away. What a pity everyone can't see all of them! What a pity they can't all come alive again between the covers of a book or a whole shelf of books like the 211 volume Catalogue of the British Museum. ℂ What I am able to bring you in this volume certainly falls far short of this—a mere sampling, a mere 3,669 pictures. Just as the material of The Bettmann Archive itself had to be limited by rules aimed at the acquisition of items that are essential or prototypal, so too, this book. In compiling it, I felt like a glazier putting windows in a house of pictures, hoping that something of the past, as well as my own graphic philosophy of the past, could be perceived within—by artists, designers and communicators in New York, Yokohama, Stuttgart or Melbourne. ℂ This book then is a ticket to the Archive, an invitation to come in and see. It is, of course, a partial view only that I can offer in this Portable Picture Library. Yet to see partially may still be better than not to see at all. ℂ Its format makes this a "roam" rather than a "read" book. Hence there need be no guilt feelings for skipping text. We would have provided more text for you to skip, but there just wasn't the room. Book pages are not made of rubber—not yet. ℂ Aside from providing a vicarious journey into the past, I envisioned this volume as a permanent professional tool.

The Portable Archive is designed to answer such questions as: "How did it look?" "How was it made?" "What were people's ideas about this or that?" be it marimbas, matrimony or mayonnaise. ℂ But I have never thought of the Archive, or this book which has been drawn from it, as being committed to the mere retrieval of facts or material states of being. More importantly, pictures of the past are stimulants for the imagination and the creative function. An old steel-engraved picture of a hand with pointing forefinger is a directive in the concrete sense: It says, "Go here." "Go there." "Read this." "Don't forget!" It is a graphic image around which a whole cluster of associations can dance, like electrons around a nucleus. So too is a wood engraving from an old bicycle catalogue, a hand-lettered sign or lithographed music sheet. ℂ The process of free association (the artist's stock-in-trade!) which begins to get under way as one examines such pictures often leads to the creative act. And so this book is an offer of beginnings, starting points, for the artist and writer who might otherwise stumble blindly or stare in frustration at that blank sheet of paper. ℂ My hope that this book might fulfill such a function was bolstered when some art directors had a look at my prepublication dummy. As I watched them turn its pages, I could almost hear the meshing of the cerebral gears starting the free association process. ℂ Similarly, the taste of a biscuit soaked in tea led Marcel Proust backward in time on a journey which gave us *Remembrance of Things Past*. Nothing would please me more than to have this book serve as a sort of wet biscuit (not too wet, though) for the designer, an invitation to go back to times past and to be inspired by the unfathomable wealth of our graphic heritage.

HOW TO USE THIS BOOK

General: Follow Bacon's inductive method: Proceed from the general to the specific. If you are interested in a broad field, be it *Astronomy, Erotica, Textiles* or *Vacations,* consult the Table of *Main Categories* on page 5. If you are looking for a specific subject—apple peelers, Gemini, saxophone, quintuplets or Zeus, consult the *Subject Index* at the end of the book, beginning at page 221.

Idea and Image Index:
If you're on the lookout for a more abstract idea—a saying, symbol or situation illustrated humorously or factually, consult the *Idea Index* on pages 6-9. This will refer you to pictures illustrating colloquialisms, sayings, or abstractions like: "Antiquated," "Applause," "Craftsmanship," "Haul," "Jumpy," "Ouch," "Reliability," "Strength," "Too Many Cooks," "Wild," "Worries."

Method of Presentation:
Only an infinitesimal part of the graphic material in The Bettmann Archive is represented in this book. The sampling presented within this limited framework often required reduction or cropping of illustrations. All pictures shown here in miniature form—silhouetted or otherwise edited—are kept in the files of The Bettmann Archive in the form of full-sized photoprints suitable for reproduction.

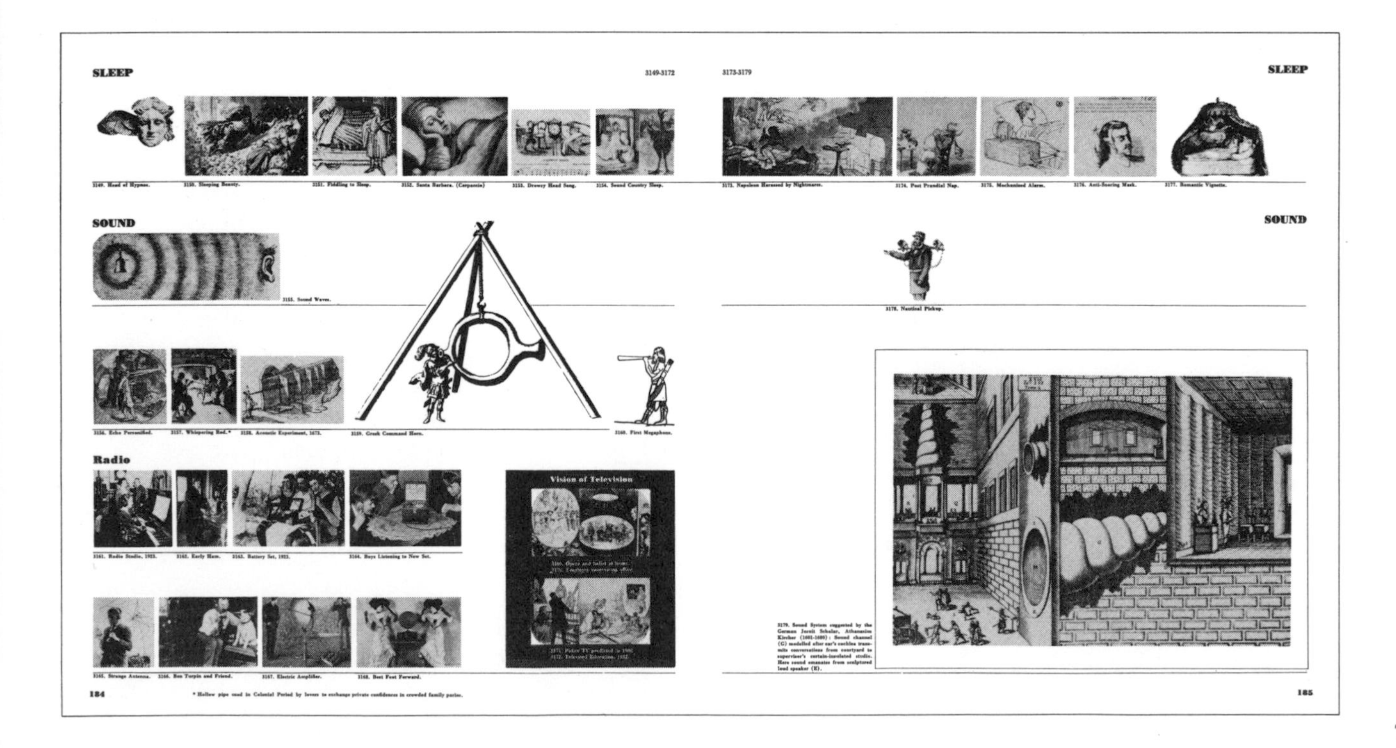
SLEEP 3149-3172
3173-3179 SLEEP
SOUND
SOUND
Radio
Vision of Television
184
185

Typical page spread from The Bettmann Portable Archive: Main categories marked by capital letters; each picture numbered, with range of numbers shown on inside margin at top of each page.

MAIN CATEGORIES

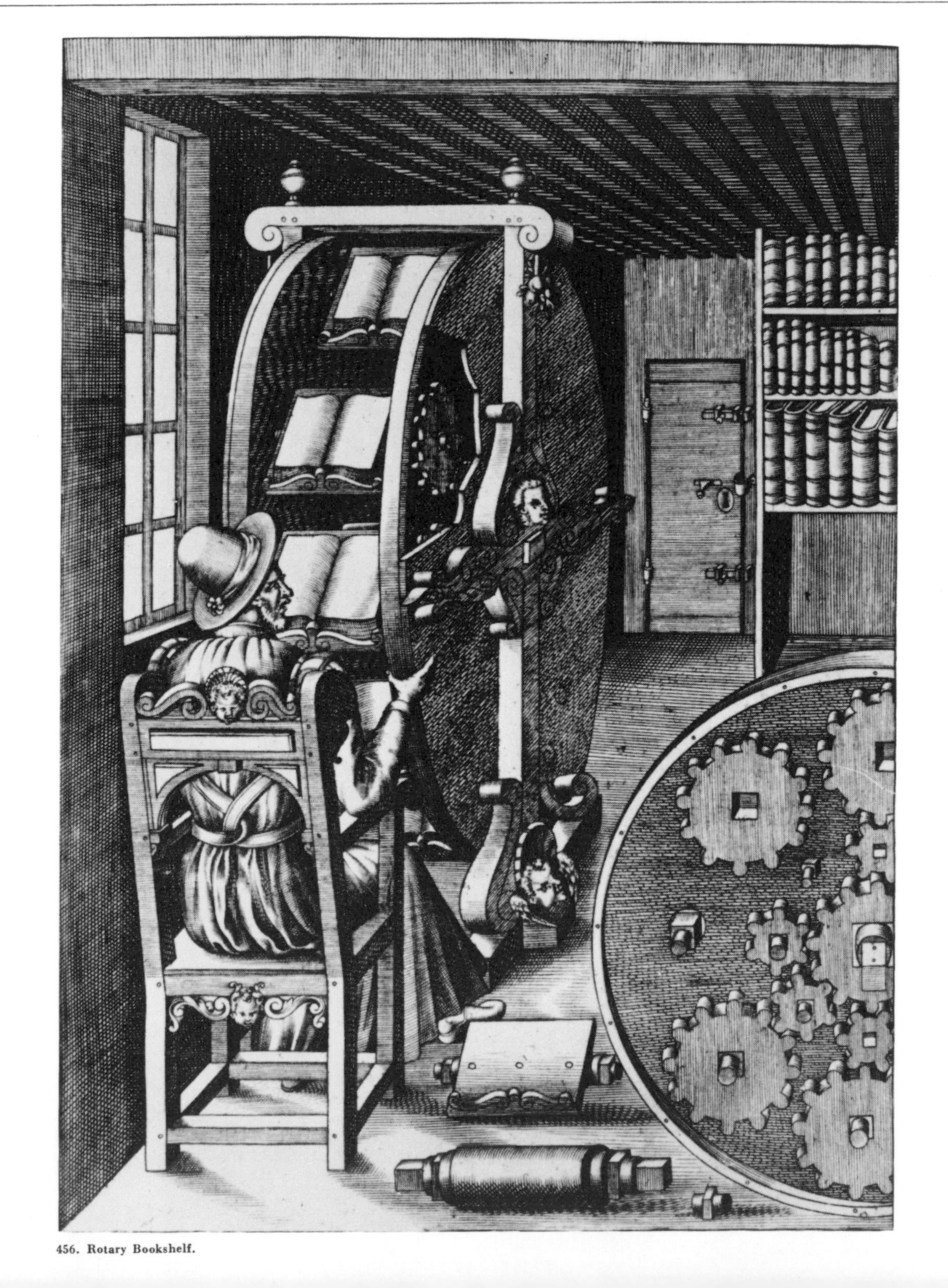

456. Rotary Bookshelf.

This Index refers to symbols, sayings, human qualities, abstractions. For general subject index see page 221.

IDEA AND IMAGE INDEX

For complete, analytical subject index turn to page 221.

1. Monstrous Abduction.

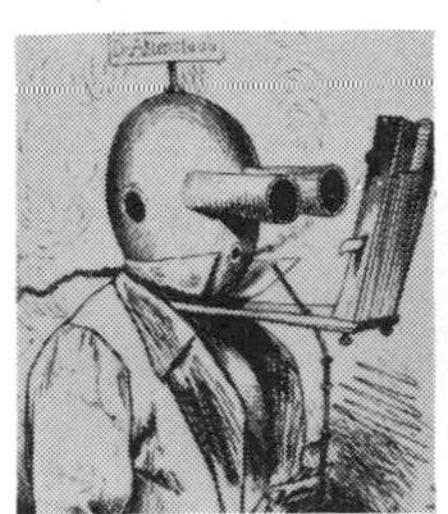

2. Reader's Dust-Protector.

3. Learned Skeleton.

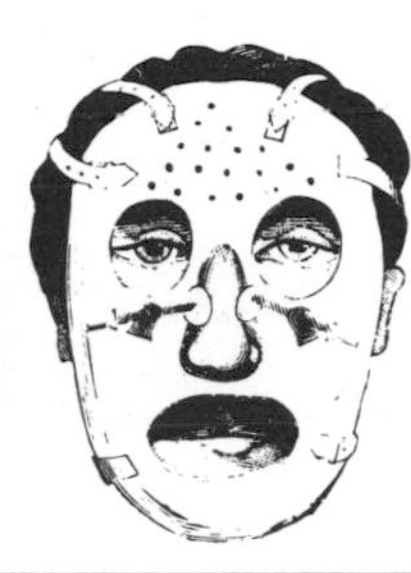

4. Man's Beauty Mask.

5. Heavyweight Bicyclist.

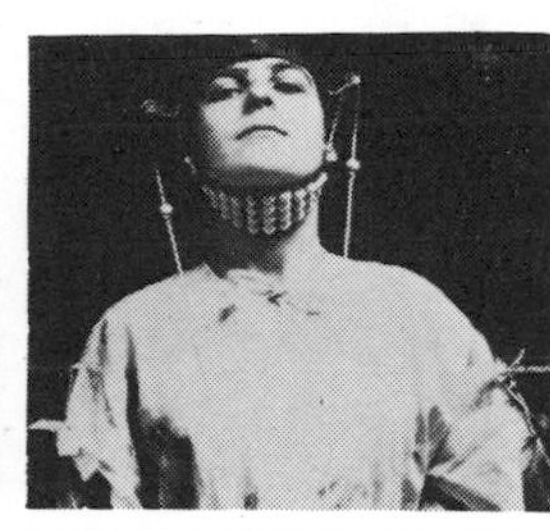

6. Lady's Neck-Stretcher.

7. Railroad Protection Garb.

8. Man-Bearing Tree.

9. King of the Albinos.

10. Pregnant,1552.

11. Inseparable Twins.

12. Nailed Shoes in Perspective.

13. Weird Beard.

14. Toenail-Cutting Machine.

15. Abysmal Miscalculation.

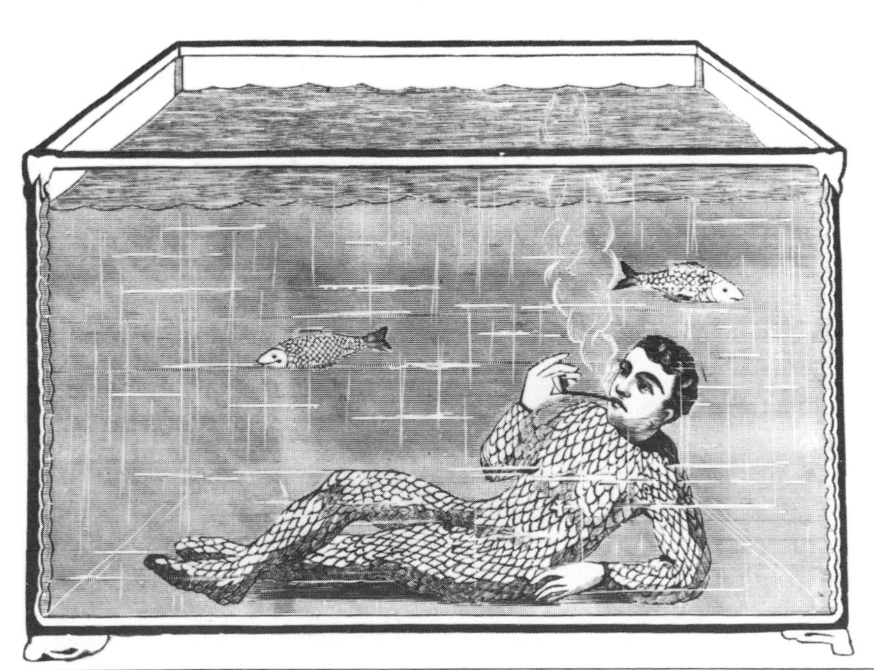

16. A Cool Smoke.

17. Fishy Orator.

18. New York: Poster Wall.

19. 20. 21. 22. 23. Optician's Trademark. 24. 25. 26.

Signs

27. 28. 29. 30.

31.

32. 33.

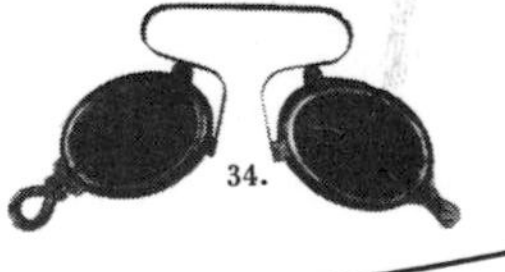

34.

35.

Methods

36. Drumming up Business, 1490.

37. Placard Bearer.

38. Aerial Promotion Predicted, 1882.

39. Walking Ad.

40. Placard Hanger.

41. Paris Kiosk.

42. London Sandwich Men.

43.

44. Brueghel

45. Harvest in Ancient Judea.

46. Prehistoric Man Practices Communal Farming.

47. Tenants Plow Fields of Feudal Lord.

48. Farmer's Tools.

Sowing.

50. Children Pull Peasant's Plow.

51. Threshing.

52. Sifting Feed.

53. Prize Crop.

54. Boy aids in harvest.

merican Farmyard, Winter.

56. Pumpkin Harvest.

57. Corn Husking.

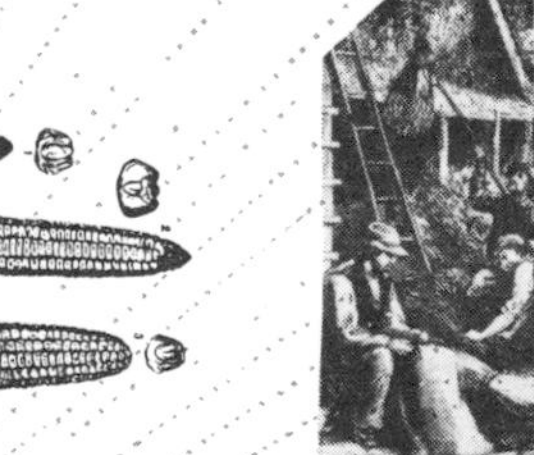

58.

59. Barn with Horsepowered Thresher.

60. Aztec Plants Corn.

61. Corn Grinder.

62. Patent Seed Spreader.

63. Pounding corn in hollow-stump mortar.

Agriculture: continued

64. Farmer Lounging on Steamplow, 1845.

65. Experiment with Mechanical Reaper.

66. Turn of the Crank Sorts Potatoes.

67. Harvesting with Steam Engines on a large Midwest Farm.

68. Oregon Farmhands during Recess.

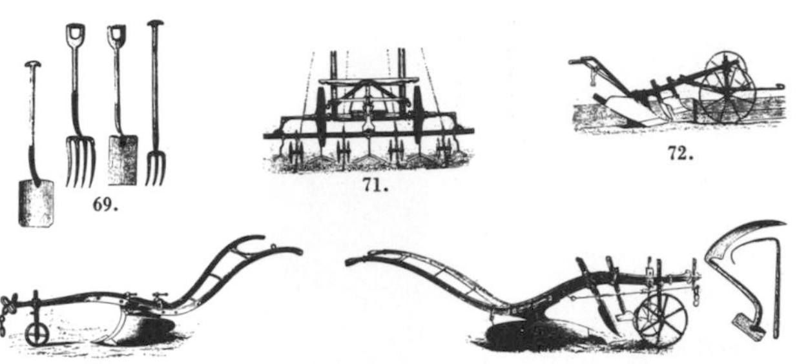
69.

71.

72.

70.

73.

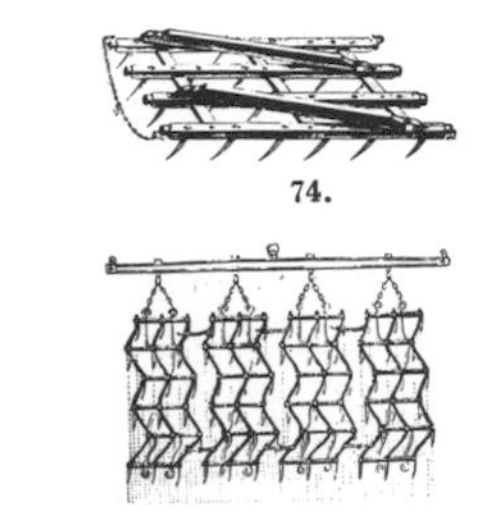
74.

75.

76. 24 Horses Pull Oregon Reaper.

77. Sharpening the Scythe.

78. Ox-Drawn Cutter.

79. Watering Horse.

80. A Full Load.

81.

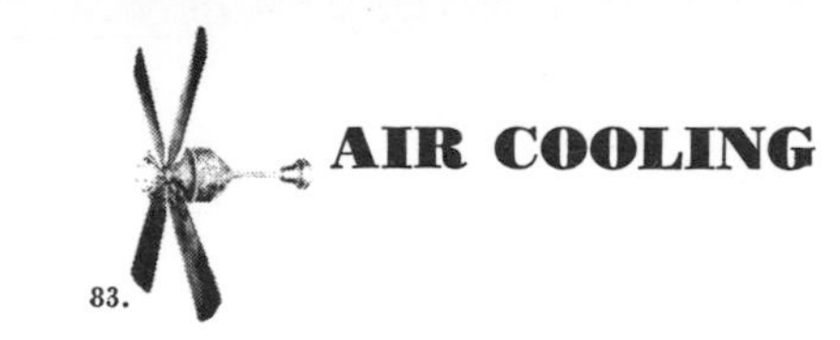

83.

AIR COOLING

82. Ventilated Suit.

84. Slave Fans Pharaoh.

85. Chinese Buys Bags of Wind.

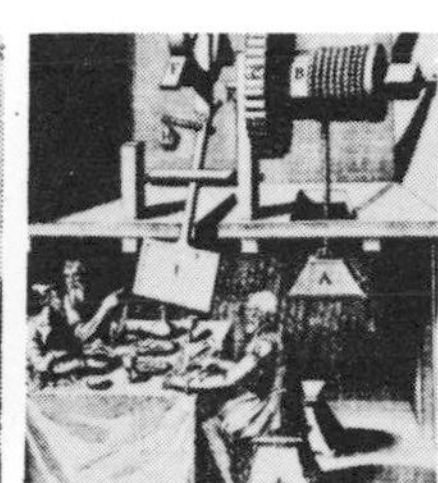

86. Mechanical Fan, 1662.

87. Air Pumped into Mine.

88.

89. Ventilated Chair.

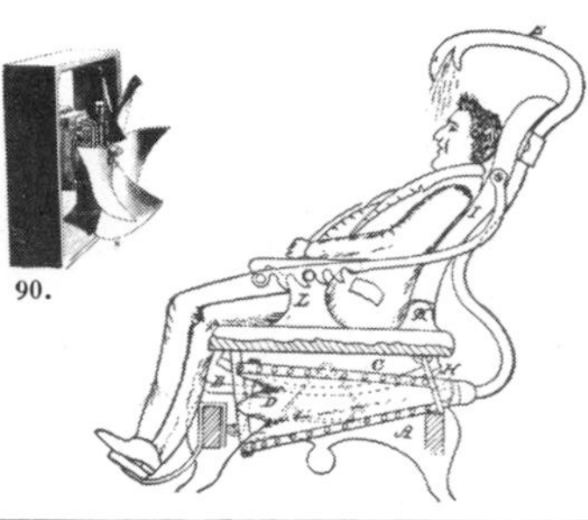

90.

91. Patent, 1869.

92. Cool Air Slot Machine.

93. Water-Cooled Desk Chair.

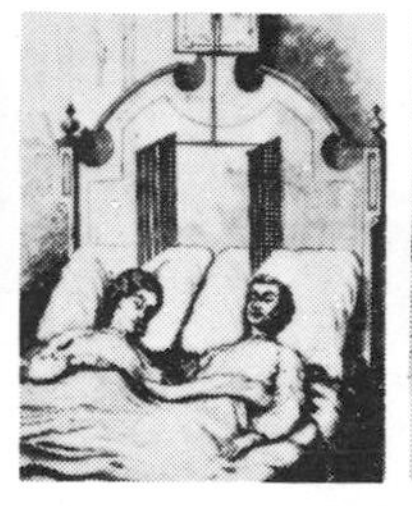

94. Bedroom Cooler, 1880.

95. A Thoughtful Husband,

96. Automatic Fan and Liquor Server.

97. Pedal-Driven Fan.

98. Airy Centennial Exhibit.

ANGELS

99. Raphael.

100. Angels with Laurel Frame.

101. 14th Century Mural.

102. Austrian Baroque.

103. Angelic Choir.

104. Annunciation.

105. Brueghel: Self-Portrait with Critic.

The Nude in Art

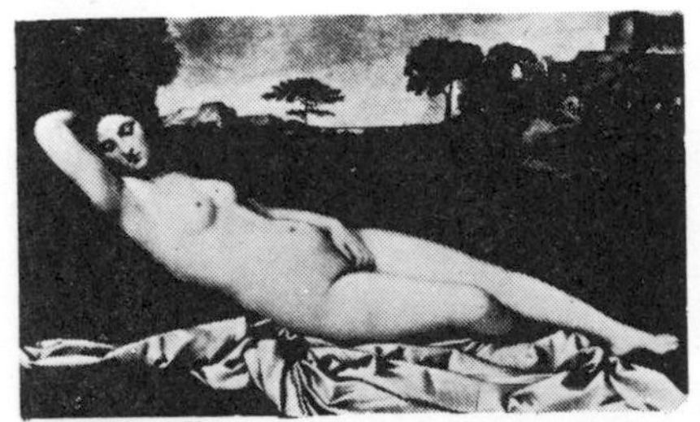

106. Titian: Venus.

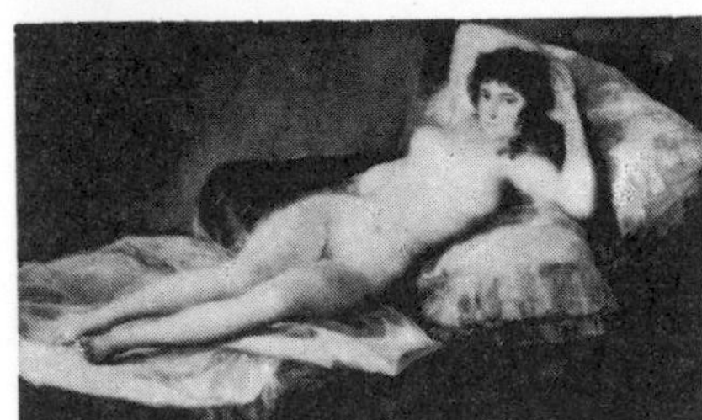

107. Goya: La Maja.

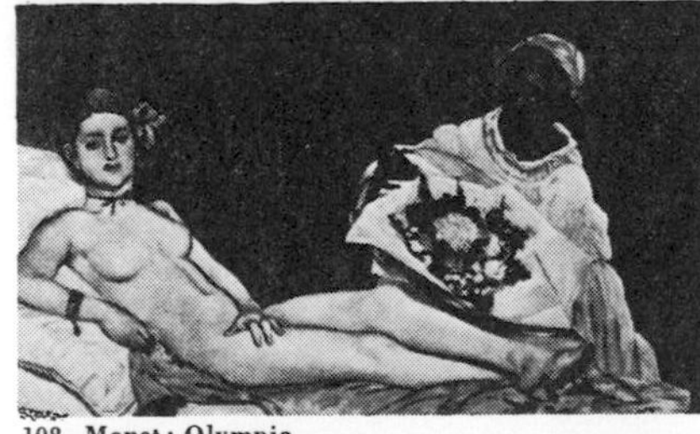

108. Manet: Olympia.

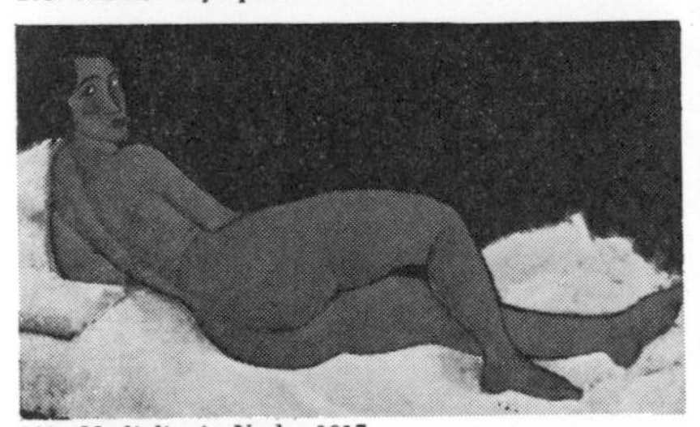

109. Modigliani: Nude, 1917.

110. Matisse: Odalisque.

Details of Great Works of Art

Artists listed by date of birth.

111. 112. 113. 114. 115. 116. 117. 118.

111. Giotto: 1235.
112. Van Eyck: 1360.
113. Piero della Francesca: 1418.
114. Bellini: 1426.
115. Botticelli: 1444.
116. da Vinci: 1452.
117. Durer: 1471.
118. Michelangelo: 1475.

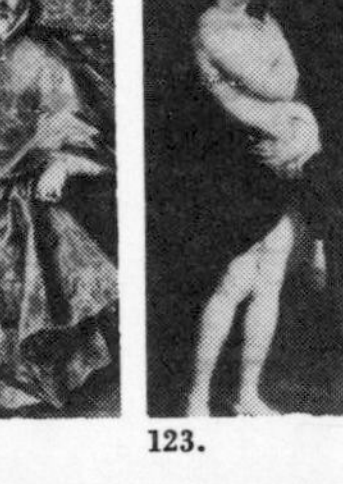
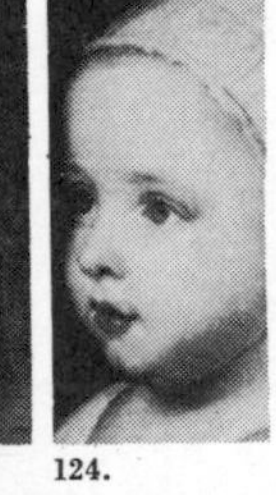

119. 120. 121. 122. 123. 124. 125. 126.

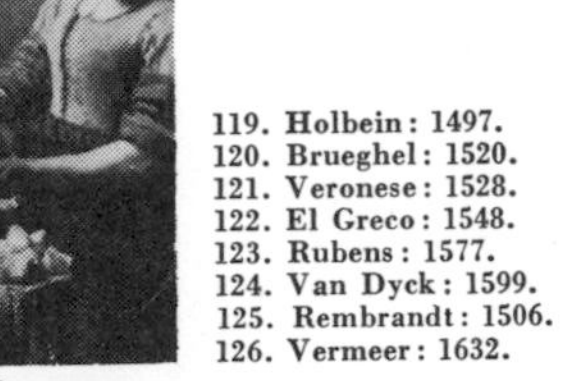

119. Holbein: 1497.
120. Brueghel: 1520.
121. Veronese: 1528.
122. El Greco: 1548.
123. Rubens: 1577.
124. Van Dyck: 1599.
125. Rembrandt: 1506.
126. Vermeer: 1632.

127. 128. 129. 130. 131. 132. 133. 134.

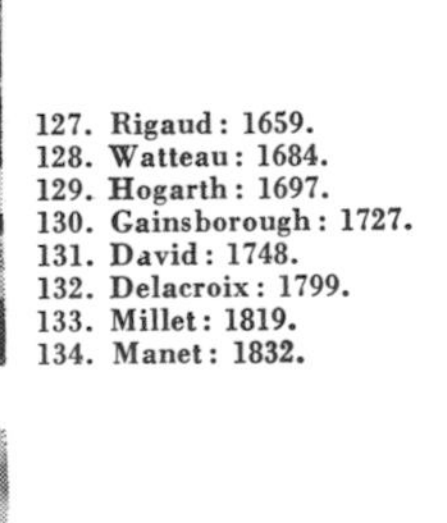

127. Rigaud: 1659.
128. Watteau: 1684.
129. Hogarth: 1697.
130. Gainsborough: 1727.
131. David: 1748.
132. Delacroix: 1799.
133. Millet: 1819.
134. Manet: 1832.

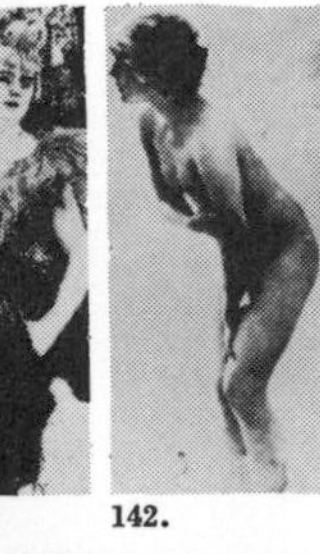

135. 136. 137. 138. 139. 140. 141. 142.

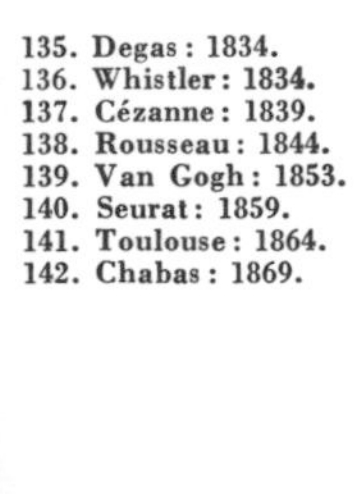

135. Degas: 1834.
136. Whistler: 1834.
137. Cézanne: 1839.
138. Rousseau: 1844.
139. Van Gogh: 1853.
140. Seurat: 1859.
141. Toulouse: 1864.
142. Chabas: 1869.

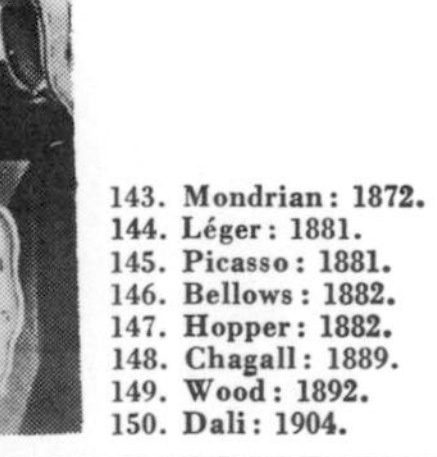

143. Mondrian: 1872.
144. Léger: 1881.
145. Picasso: 1881.
146. Bellows: 1882.
147. Hopper: 1882.
148. Chagall: 1889.
149. Wood: 1892.
150. Dali: 1904.

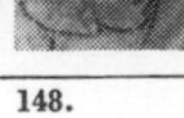

143. 144. 145. 146. 147. 148. 149. 150.

151. Airbrush Artist 1900.

152. Prehistoric.

153. Renaissance Studio.

154. Painter's Apprentice.

155. Copper Engraver 1680.

156. Sculpting a Venus.

157. Art School for the Young.

158. Connoisseur.

159. Draftsmen in Architect's Studio.

160. Patent Drawing Table.

161. Manet Paints in his Boat.

162. The first painter copies nature; the second copies the first. (Daumier)

163. How Whistler Paints three Pictures at once.

164. Artist and Model, 1910.

Artists' Material

165.

166.

167.

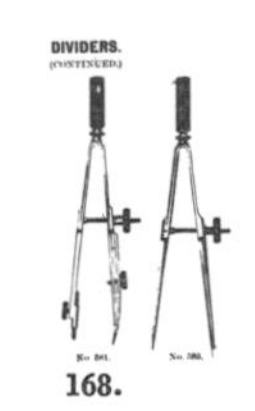

168.

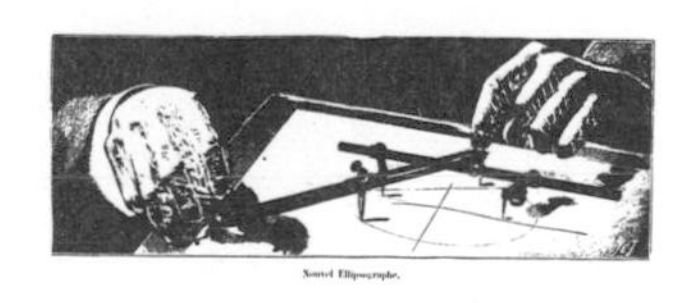

169.

170.

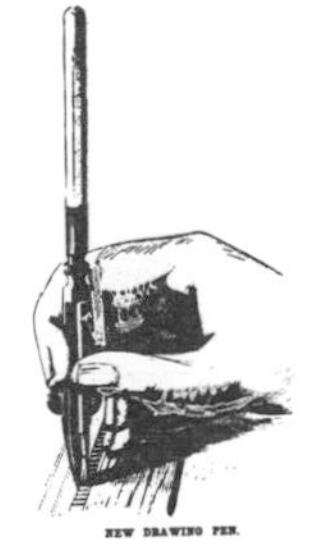

171.

172.

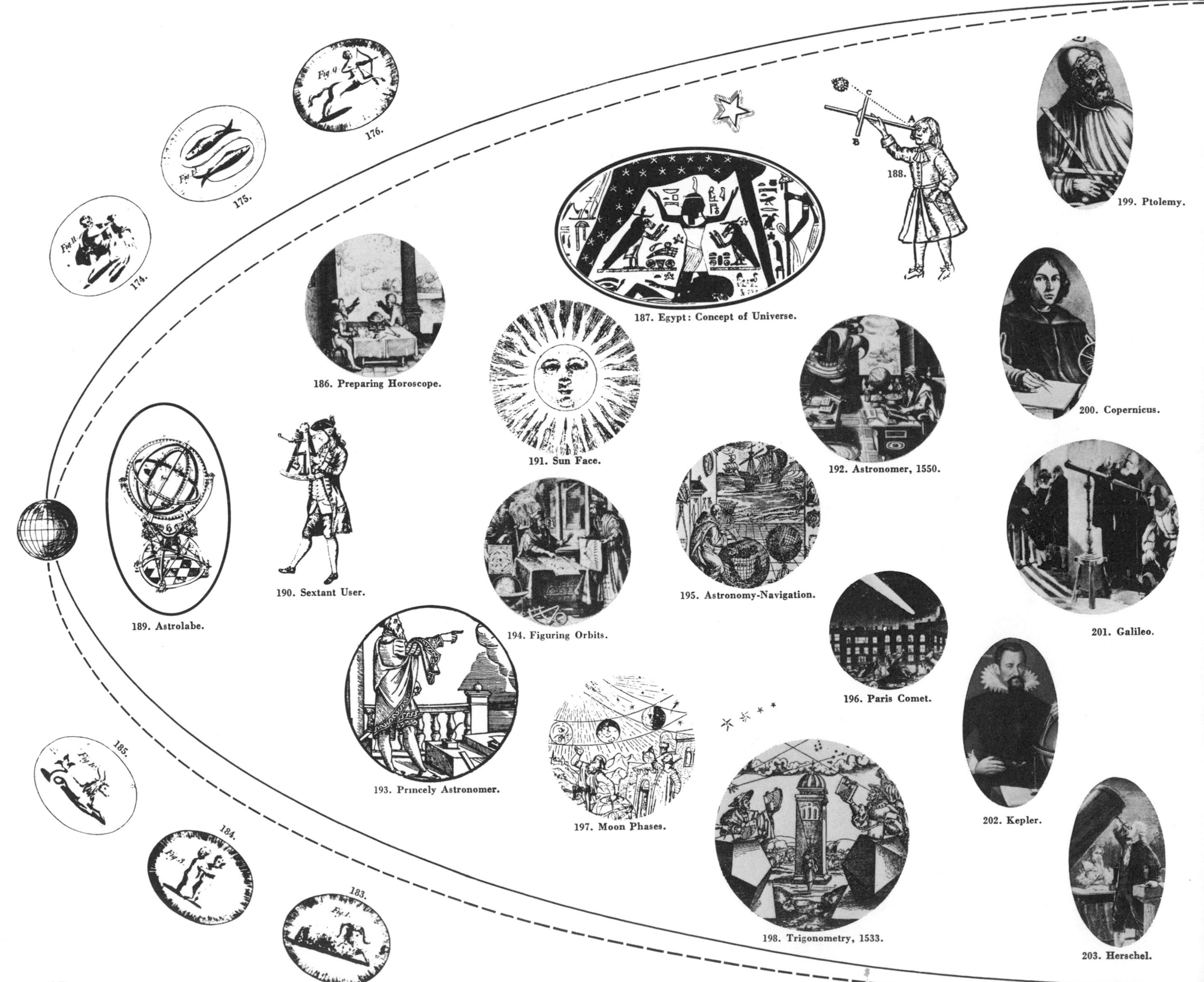

174.

175.

176.

186. Preparing Horoscope.

187. Egypt: Concept of Universe.

188.

199. Ptolemy.

200. Copernicus.

191. Sun Face.

192. Astronomer, 1550.

189. Astrolabe.

190. Sextant User.

195. Astronomy-Navigation.

201. Galileo.

194. Figuring Orbits.

193. Princely Astronomer.

196. Paris Comet.

197. Moon Phases.

202. Kepler.

185.

184.

183.

198. Trigonometry, 1533.

203. Herschel.

173.

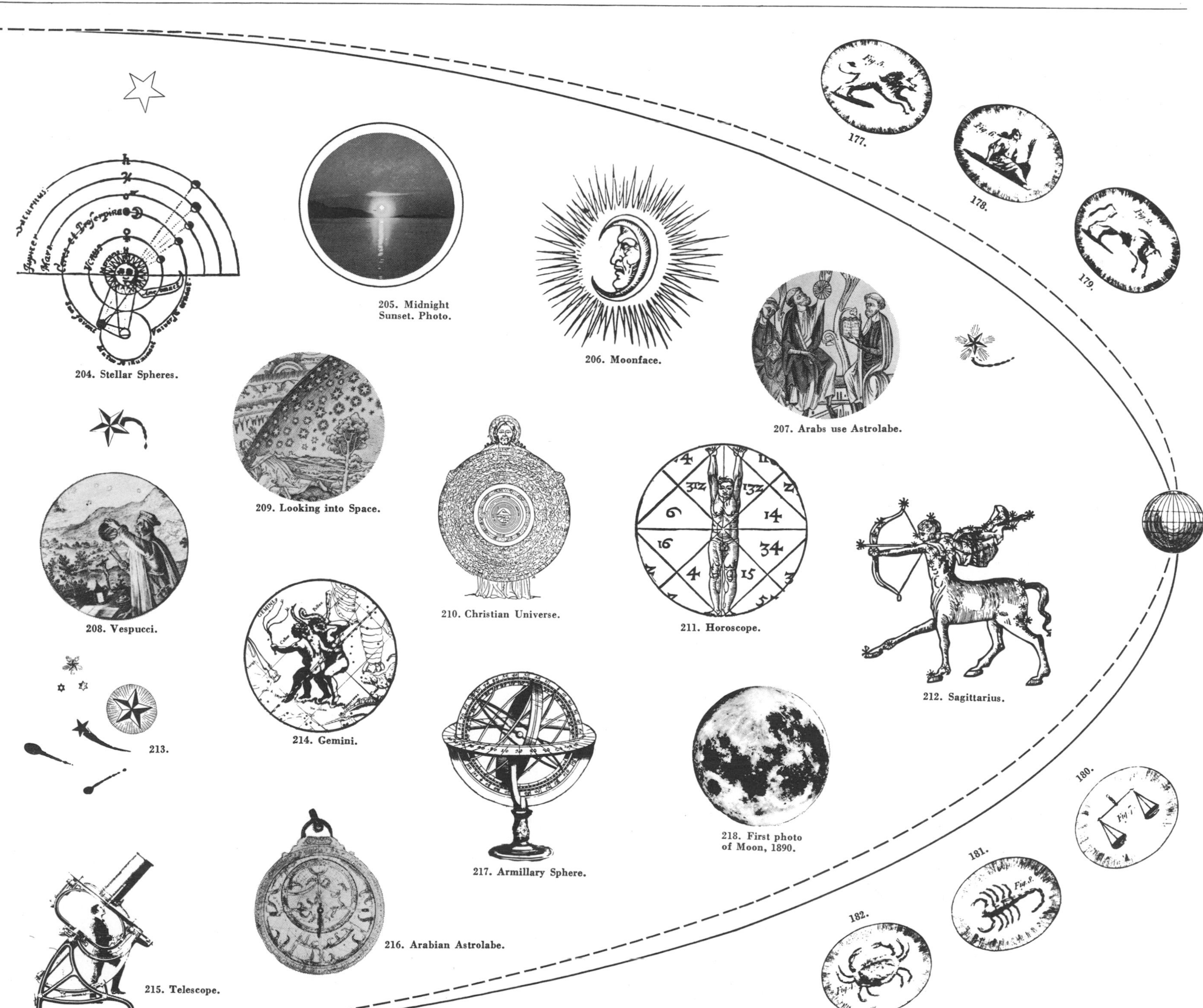

177.

178.

179.

204. Stellar Spheres.

205. Midnight Sunset. Photo.

206. Moonface.

207. Arabs use Astrolabe.

208. Vespucci.

209. Looking into Space.

210. Christian Universe.

211. Horoscope.

212. Sagittarius.

213.

214. Gemini.

215. Telescope.

216. Arabian Astrolabe.

217. Armillary Sphere.

218. First photo of Moon, 1890.

180.

181.

182.

220. Rembrandt's sketch of Raphael's Castiglioni portrait made when the painting was auctioned off in 1639 for a price of 3500 guilders.

219. Gavel.

221. Hard Sell.

222. Wife Auction.

223. Thomas Rowlandson: The Book-Auction. Water Color.

224. Poster.

225. Frame.

226. Model T and Guest.

Beginnings

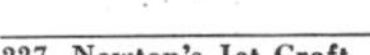

227. Newton's Jet Craft.

228. Walking by Steam.

229. Trevithick's Street Diligence, 1801.

230. Old London Steam Coach.

231. The Horse-Driven Automobile. *

Pioneers

232. Henry Ford Machine Shop, Bagley Ave., Detroit.

233. Chain-Driven Motor Truck, ca. 1906.

234. Sightseeing Bus, 1910.

235. Early Laundry Trucks, 1915.

236. Petrocycle.

237. Benz Victoria, 1893.

238. Electric Hansom Cab.

239. Paris Taxi, 1899.

240. Daimler's Scooter.

241. First Duryea Car, 1893.

Early Custombuilts

242. Italian Royal Family.

243. Sultan's Car.

244. Newport Socialites, 1904.

245. Pearl White with Rolls Royce.

*Cartoon ridiculing Alexander Graham Bell's prediction that "the horse will always be the principal motive power of transportation."

Parade of Models

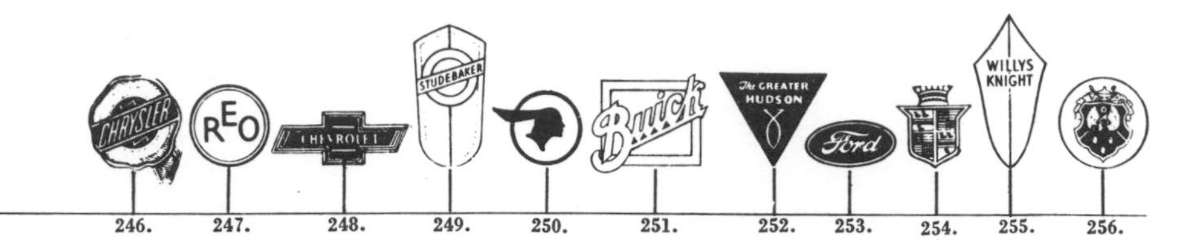

246. 247. 248. 249. 250. 251. 252. 253. 254. 255. 256.

257. Cadillac, first G. M. Car, 1908.

258. Duesenberg.

259. Franklin, 1902.

260. Abbott, 1910.

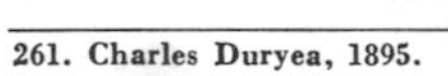

261. Charles Duryea, 1895.

262. Auto-Cycle French, 1900.

263. Edison in Electric, 1909.

264. J. M. Studebaker in Studebaker.

265. Wood's Electric, 1908.

Racing

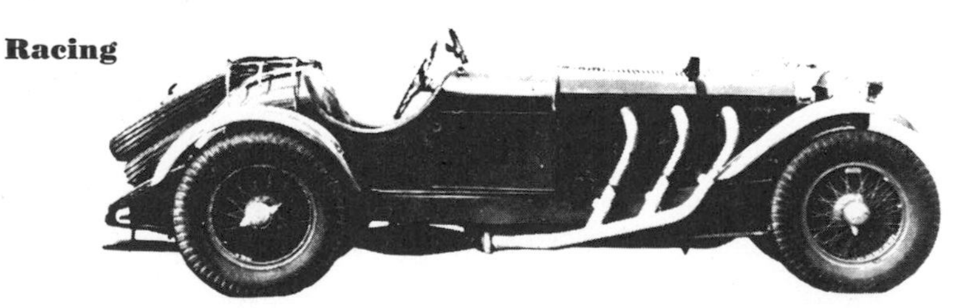

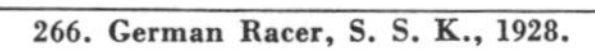

266. German Racer, S. S. K., 1928.

267. Simplex, 1912.

268. Vanderbilt Cup Race, 1904.

269.

270. Paris-Berlin Race, 1904.

271. Indianapolis Poster.

272. Champ: Jenatzki, the French racing demon, first to reach a speed of 100 m.p.h.

Automobiles: continued

273. Leisure Program for Unemployed Horses.

The Automotive Life

274. "Get Out and Get Under."

275. Magazine Cover, 1909.

276. Filling Up with Gallon Can.

277. Driver's School, Paris.

278. Country Road Harassments.

279. Winton Car Stuck in Mud, 1904.

280. Ready for the Wrecker.

281. In Case of a Downpour. Ad, 1904.

282. Traffic Jam on 42nd Street, New York, 1917.

283. Robot Horse.

284. Array of Tin Lizzies.

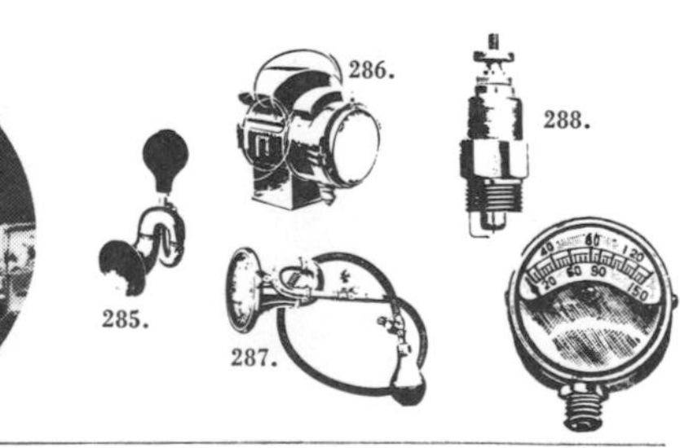

285. 286. 287. 288. 289.

290. Ready for Road Repair.

291. Exceeding Speed Limit.

292. Duster.

293. Winton Car after Mudbath. Iowa, 1904.

294. Cranking Up.

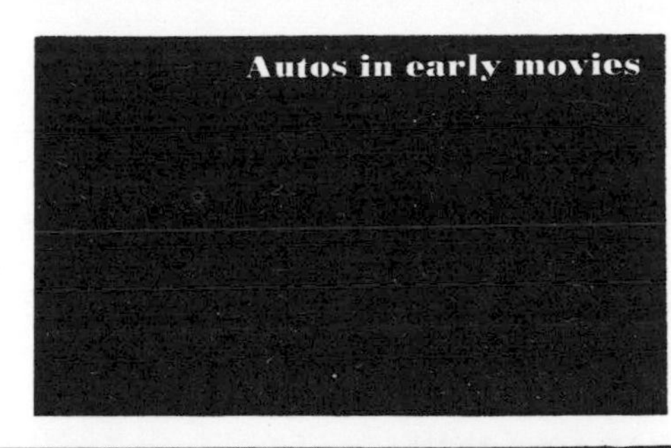

Autos in early movies

295.

296. 297. 298. 299.

300. 301. 302. 303.

304. 305. 306.

307.

308.

309.

310.

311.

For complete, analytical subject index turn to page 221.

BREAD AROUND THE WORLD

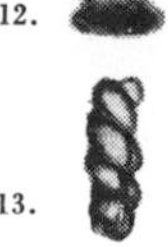
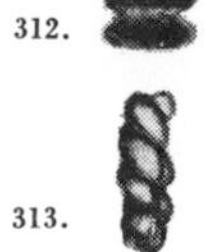

312.

313.

314.

315.

316.

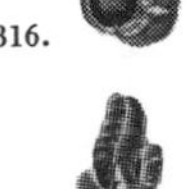

317.

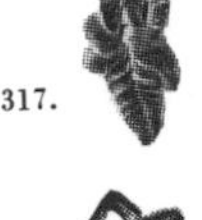

318.

319.

320. Production contest between the bakers and butchers of the City of Nuremberg. Bakers (left) turn out bread in assembly line fashion. Butchers (right) try in the "wurst" way to beat them. 17th century woodcut.

321. Giant cake baked for the soldiers of the army of King August the Strong of Saxony assembled in maneuvers near Dresden, 1730. More than 3600 eggs and 126 cans of milk were needed to produce this piece of pastry. The knife to cut it (insert left) was 10 yards long.

322. Roman Bakeshop.

323. Spice Cookies. 324.

325. Tortilla Baking.

326. Muffin Stove on Wheels.

327. Medieval Bakery, City of Cracow.

328. 17th Century French Patisserie.

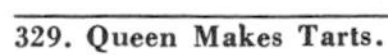

329. Queen Makes Tarts.

330. Salvation Army Girl.

331. Mechanized Bakestove.

332. Victorian Housewife Prepares Pie.

333. Bake Mold.

334. Lower East Side Bagel Bakery, circa 1900.

335. Home Baking, 1900.

336. Pie Baking in Backyard Dutch Oven.

337. Peasant's Bread.

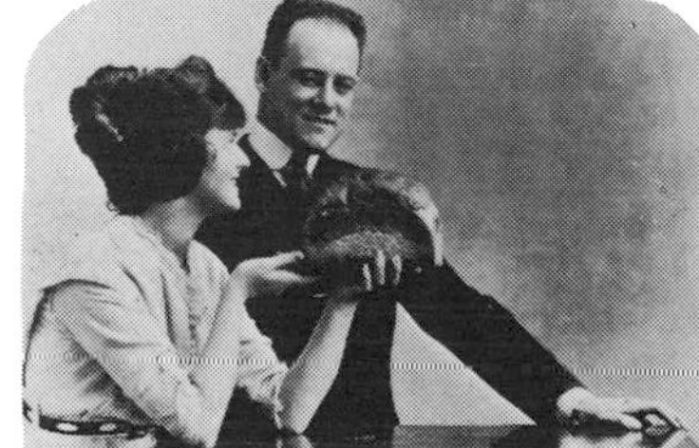

338. Housewife's Pride: Home-Baked Bread.

339. Load of Loaves.

340. Giant Loaf and Bagel Bread.

341. Florentine.

342. Biblical.

343. Mint, 1480.

344. Wampum Shown to Indian Chief.

345. Medieval Bank. Lady Accepts Deposit.

346. Lampoon Against Money Forgers, 17th Century.

347. Usurers.

348. Pleasant Task.

349. California Bank, 1879.

350. Depositors.

351. Teller's Window.

352. Handout.

353. Clerks at Work.

354. Safe Deposit.

355.

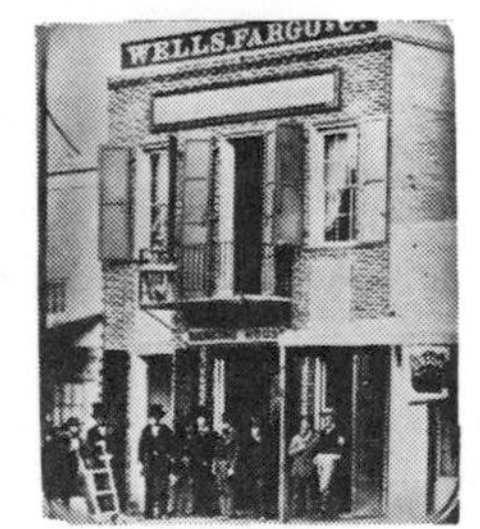

356. Bank Building, 1850.

357. Cashier's Window, California Bank, 1900's.

358. Printing Money, U.S. Printing Office.

359. Boys Making Deposits, ca. 1900.

360. 40 Million $ Check (Panama Canal).

COINS

361. Greek.

362. Medieval.

363. Brokerage House Symbol.

TOY BANKS

364.

365.

366.

367.

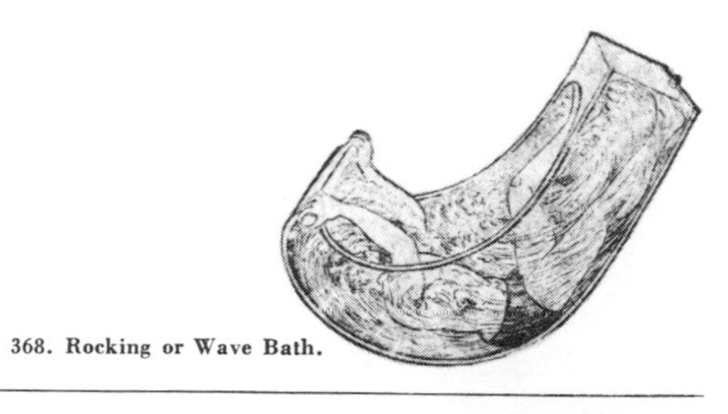
368. Rocking or Wave Bath.

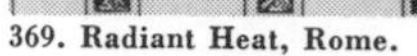
369. Radiant Heat, Rome.

370. Roman Bath.

371. Bag Bath, 1614.

372. Knight Bathed.

373. Shampoo, 15th Century.

374. Mixed Bathing.

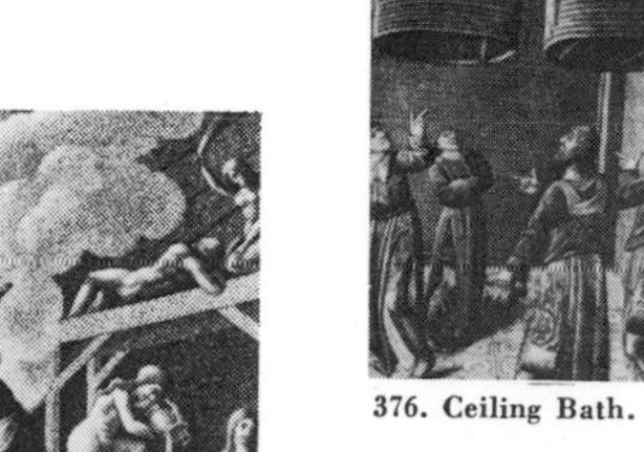
375. Finnish Sauna.

376. Ceiling Bath.

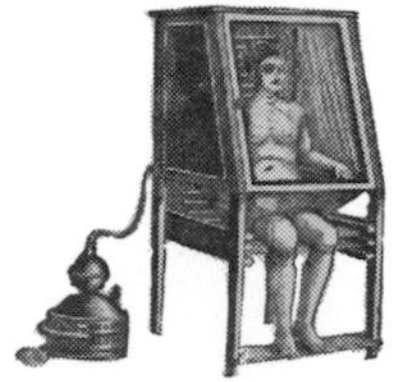
377. Sweating It Out.

378. California Miner's Camp.

379. Improvised Steam Bath.

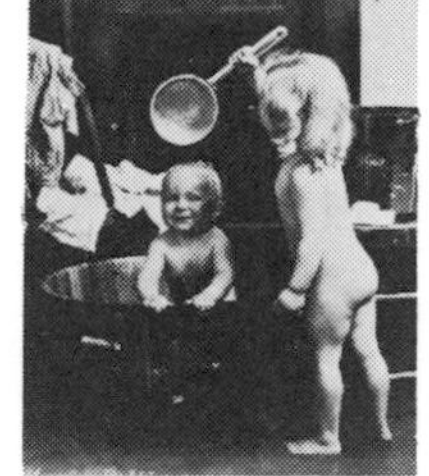
380. Ladle Shower.

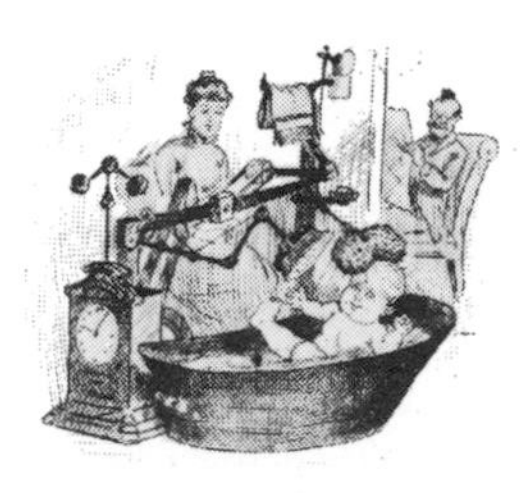
381. Baby-Bathing Machine.

382. Saturday Night.

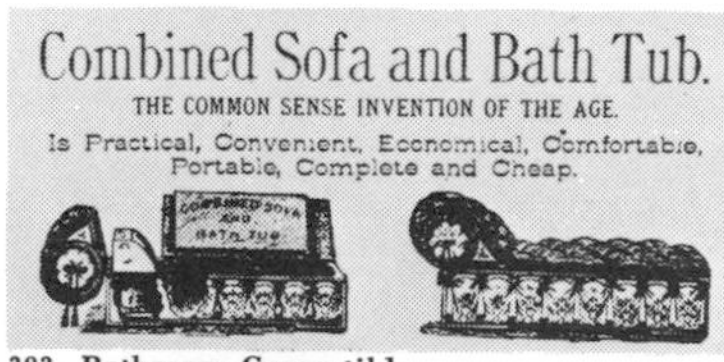

383. Bathroom Convertible.

384. Crystal Tub, 1810.

385. Boot Bath.

386. Shower. (Daumier)

387. Pedal Shower.

388. Drying Up.

389. Ornate Gay Nineties Bathroom.

390. After the Bath. (Forain)

391. Shower Gadget.

392. Gilded Age Mahogany Bathroom.

393. Foot Bath.

BATHING SUITS

394. Whispering Waves.

395. Pair of Mack Sennett Beach Beauties.

396. English Beach.

397. Beach Beauty Contest, 1910.

398. Family Group.

399. The Latest in Seaside Fashions, 1906.

400. Riviera, 1900.

401. Polka Dot.

402. Newport, 1910.

403. Yes?

404. Yes!

405. Society Girl, Crabbing.

406. Stripers.

407. Solace.

408. Annette Kellerman.

409. Ad, 1890.

410. Cop Arrests for Indecent Exposure.

411. Zippy Girls Sliding.

412. Coney Island Competition, 1897.

413.

414.

415. Children on the Beach. Amateur Photo from Family Album of the early 1900's.

416. Dieppe, French Seaside Resort, at the Beginning of the 19th Century.

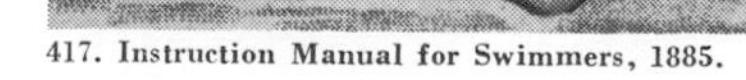

417. Instruction Manual for Swimmers, 1885.

BELLS

418. Girl Bell-Swinger.

419. Glockenspiel.

420. Carillon.

421. Bell Tower.

422. Hand Bell.

423. Group of Swiss Bell Ringers, 1860.

424. Giant Bell, Moscow.

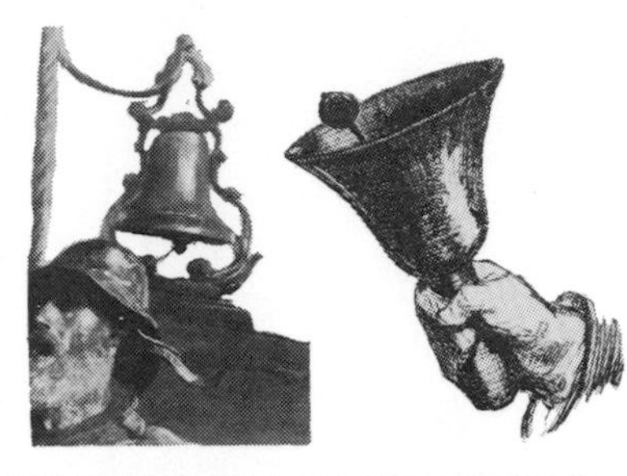

425. Ship's Watch.

426. Dinner Bell.

BILLIARDS

427. Lady Practicing Billiards.

428. Louis XIV and his Court during Match.

429. A Finicky Player.

430. Smoke-filled Poolroom.

431. Tense Moment during a Billiard Game.

432. Trade Sign, San Antonio, Texas.

BLACKSMITHS

433. Prehistoric Ironmongers.

434. The Forge of Vulcan.

435. Anvil

436. The Village Blacksmith.

437. Sculpture, 1400.

438. Hot Iron.

439. A Lady Blacksmith.

440. Yankee Smithy.

BOOKS

441. The Compleat Bookman.

442. Monk in Scriptorium.

443. Alexandrian Library.

444. Children's Library, New York 1900.

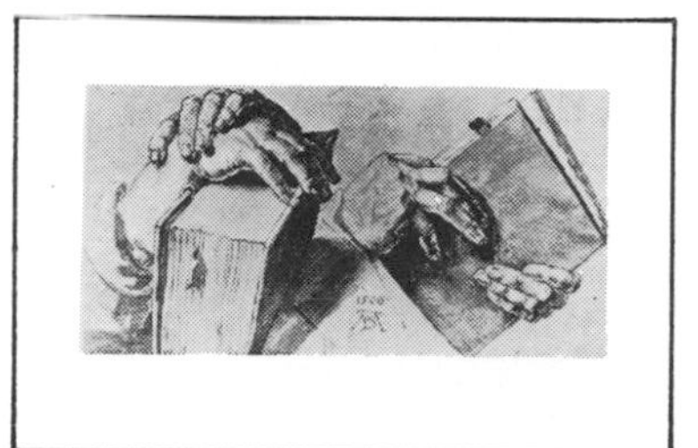

445. Durer: Hands Holding Bible.

446. Book Burning during Reformation.

447. Paris Library, 1842.

448. Bookstall, 1650.

449. Storage of Papyrus Rolls.

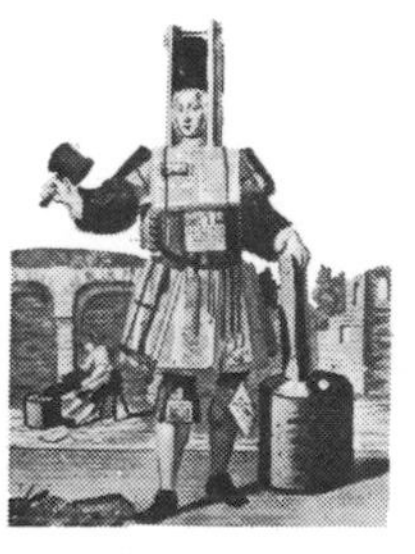

450. Binder with Tools.

451. Bookbindery, 18th Century.

452. Bindery Press.

Reading

453. Avid Reader.

454. Florentine Scholar in his Study.

455. Jew Reading.

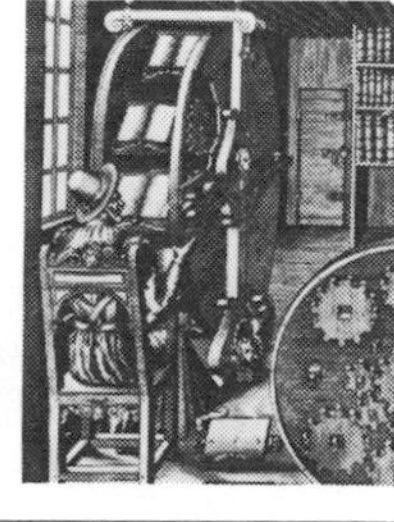

456. Rotary Bookshelf.

457. Dishwasher's Book Harness.

458. Dunk and Read.

459. Boy Bookseller on Train.

460. Reading Stand, 1890.

Art of the Book

461. Medieval Miniature.

462. Pages from 42-line Gutenberg Bible.

463. Shelf.

464. Cartouche.

465. Hornbook.

466. Primer.

467. Alger Title Page.

468. Dime Novel.

469.

470. Bride Preparing for the Wedding, Russia.

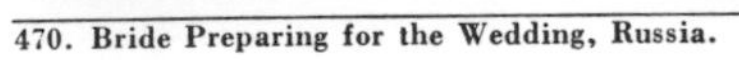

471. Caught Kissing her Groom.

472. Society Bride.

473. Nuptial Kiss.

474. Hollywood Bride.

475. Young Man Catches his Bride, Russia.

476. Admiring Wedding Jewels.

477. Victorian Bride.

478. Wedding Gown.

479. The Wedding Ring.

480. Ready for Altar.

481. Wedding Dreams.

482. The Bride's Underwear: $4.75.

BRIDGES

483. Rope Bridge, Peru.

484. Wooden Bridge, Vermont.

485. Marble Bridge, China.

486. Civil War Viaduct.

487. Eads Bridge, St. Louis.

488. Cable Workers, Brooklyn Bridge.

489. Medieval Bricklayers.

490. Hod Carriers, 1023 A.D.

491. Asphalt Use, Babylon.

492. Building Pyramids.

493. Masons, 1450.

494.

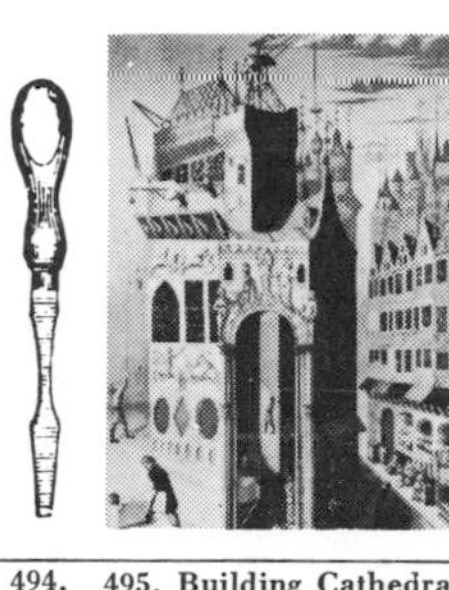

495. Building Cathedral.

496. Decorating Wall.

497. Roofer at Work.

498. Stonemason, 1790.

499. Chiselling.

500. Housebuilding, 1840.

501. Skyscraper Vision.

502. Construction of Clapboard House.

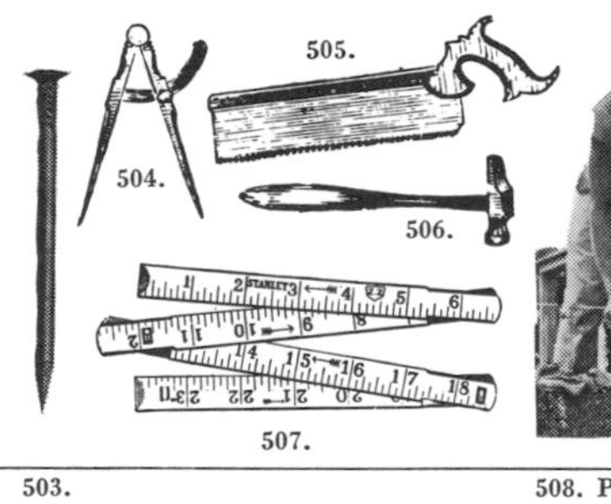

503. 504. 505. 506. 507.

508. Professional.

509. Inspired Amateur.

Architectural Styles

510. Greek. 511. Roman. 512. Indian. 513. Baroque. 514. Castle. 515. Mosque. 516. Cathedral. 517. Abbey. 518. Gingerbread Era. 519. Gilded Age.

520. Classicism.

521. American Colonial.

522. Newport Mansion.

523. Clapboard Front.

524. Skyscraper, New York.

525. Skyscraper, Chicago.

526. Building operations in the 17th century. Carpenters erecting a wooden structure. An anachronistic representation of the building of Noah's Ark. Copper Engraving.

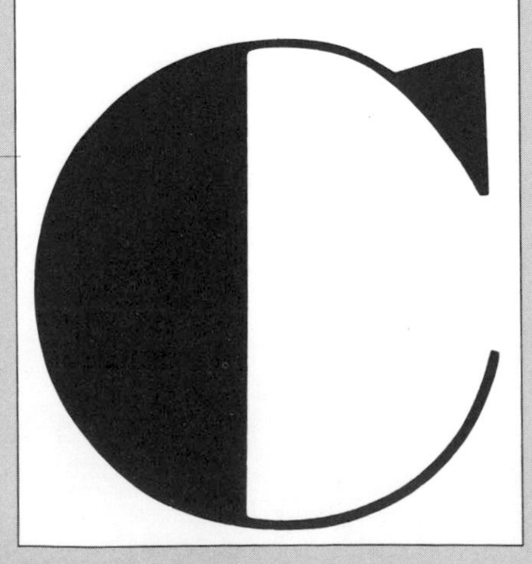

For complete, analytical subject index turn to page 221.

CARRIAGES

527. Chinese Rickshaw.
528. Tent on Wheels, 600 A.D.
529. Medieval Wheelwright.
530. Egyptian Fixing Chariot Tire.
531. Roman Chariot: Relief.
532.
533. Roman Circus.
534. Grecian Girls in Chariot.
535. London Hansom Cab.
536. Tipsy Passenger Enters London Cab.
537. Sports Carriage with Coachman.
538. Two-Wheeled Sedan Chair.
539. Outing in Pleasure Carriage.
540. English Mail Coach en Route.
541. Boy Tends Horse.
542. Solid Wheeled Pleasure Cart (Spain).
543. 18th Century Royal Carriage.
544. Rx for Creaking Wheels.
545. California Mail Coach.
546. Helping a Lady to Alight.
547. Mail Coach Timetable, New York.
548. French Empire Mail Coach.
549. "Step-Up" for Carriage Travelers.
550. Mail Coach.
551. Raising a Fallen Horse, New York City.
552. Aristocrat's Coach with Footmen.
553. Performers Brought to Circus in Giraffe-Drawn Carriage.
554. Couple during Sunday Outing.
555. Parisian Lady. (Toulouse-Lautrec)
556. Four-in-Hand Coach Party.
557. Spoked Wheel
558. Wind-Wagon.

575. Wm. Ramsay.

576. Mme. Curie.

577. Radium Discovered.

574. Langmuir.

570. Dalton's Table.

571. Faraday.

572. Liebig, Giessen.

573. Mendeleev.

566. Renaissance.

567. Boyle.

568. 18th cent.

569. Lavoisier.

565. 16th cent. Alchemist.

560. Woman Druggist.

561. Schwartz Explodes Gunpowder.

563. Man in Retort.

564. Alchemist. (Brueghel)

562. Monk-Chemists.

Alchemy to Atom

578. Atomic Bomb.

559. Egyptian Cosmetician-Chemists.

Dress

579, 580. American Colonial. 581. Dress Reform. 582. Brothers. 583. Boy Actor. 584. Girl, 1880. 585. Little Lord Fauntleroy. 586. Sunday Best, 1890. 587. Girl with Mother. 588. Teenager, 1905. 589. Babes in the Woods.

Babies

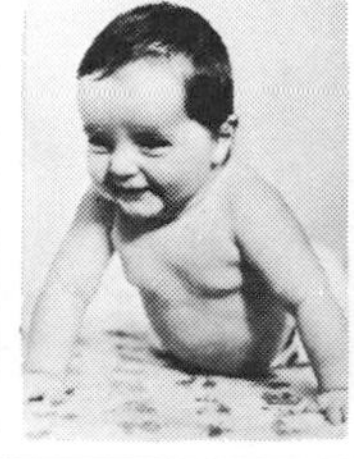

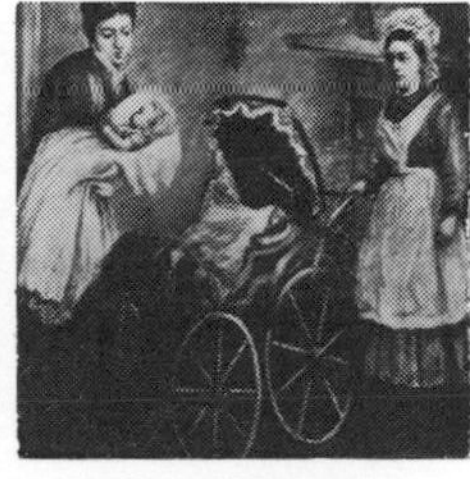

590. Circus Freak. 591. Bear Rug Baby. 592. Sucker. 593. Abducted by Eagle. (Edison Movie) 594. Ready for Outing. 595. Advertising, 1890. 596. Indian Mother. 597.

Games and Toys

598. Hobbyhorse. 599. Doll Carriage. 600. Tricycle. 601. Victorian Children Jumping Rope. 602. Cat's Cradle, New Guinea. 603. Blindman's Buff.

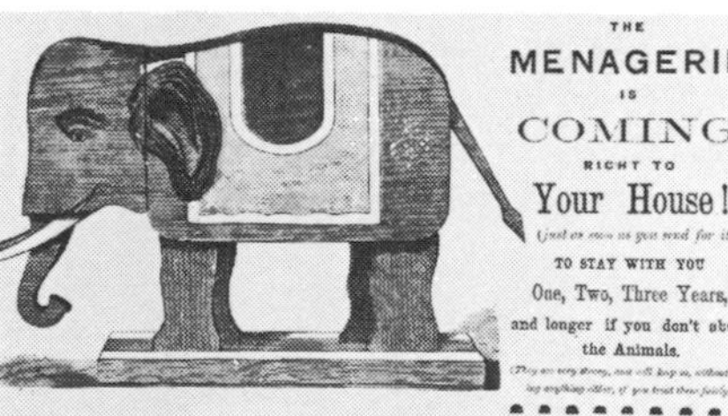

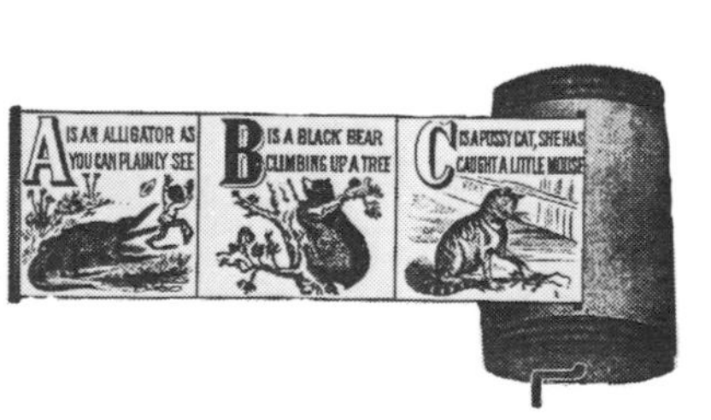

604. Christmas Advertisement. 605. Doll. 606. Hobbyhorse. 607. Couple: Dutch Dolls. 608. Store Window. 609. Jack. 610. Rollout Primer.

611. Motif.

612. Lighted Tree, 1605.

613. Candled Pyramid.

614.

615. Gifts, U. S., 1870.

616. Family, 1852.

617.

618. Family Reunion after Civil War.

619.

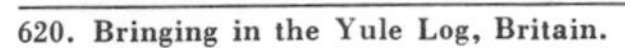

620. Bringing in the Yule Log, Britain.

621. St. Nicholas Spreads Nuts.

622. Parade of Lusty Celebrants.

623. Under Mistletoe.

624.

625. Fessiwig's Ball.

626. Small Town Carolers.

627. Stirrings.

628. Family Dinner, 1868.

629. Arrival of Christmas Coach.

630. Photographing Santa Claus.

631. Holiday Border.

632.

633. Night Before Christmas.

634. Christmas Night.

635. New England.

636. Christ is Born.

637. The Holy Family. German Woodcut.

638. Following the Star.

639. Della Robbia.

640. Bosch.

641. Bellini.

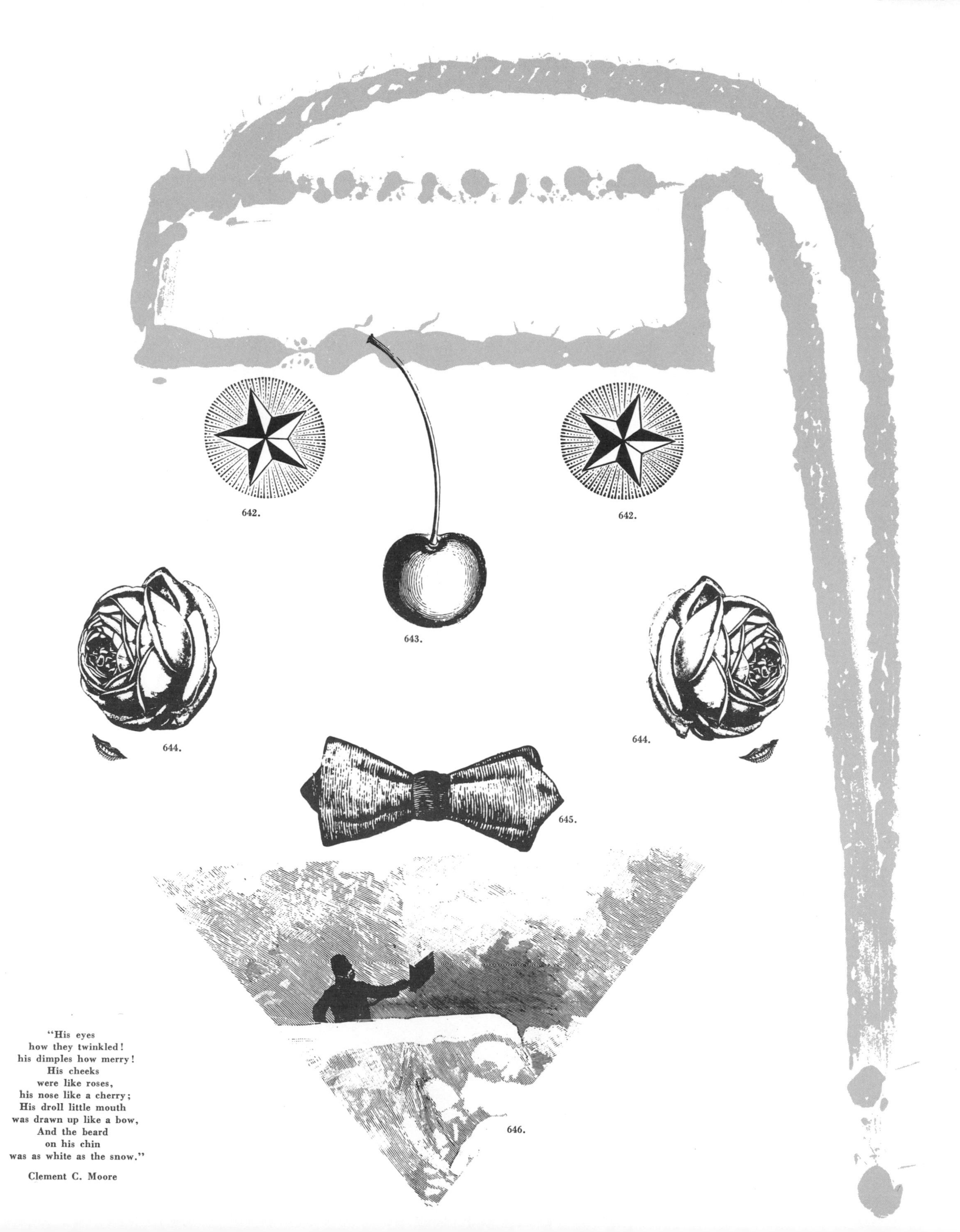

642.

642.

643.

644.

644.

645.

646.

"His eyes
how they twinkled!
his dimples how merry!
His cheeks
were like roses,
his nose like a cherry;
His droll little mouth
was drawn up like a bow,
And the beard
on his chin
was as white as the snow."

Clement C. Moore

BARNUM'S
The Barnum & Bailey Greatest Show on Earth
CONEY ISLAND
WATER CARNIVAL
RINGLING BROS
CIRCUS
THE CHILDREN'S FAVORITE CLOWN
CANNON Ball
"LOYAL"
THE BARNUM & BAILEY GREATEST SHOW ON EARTH
DESCENT DABSALON
EPAUGH & SELLS BROTHERS
IN ACTS OF INFINITE VARIETY
MILWAUKEE'S
BUFFALO BILL
DR. CARV
WILD WEST.
JUMBO
I AM COMING
THE ULTIMATUM OF HUMAN POWER.
$10,000 CHALLENGE
THE GREAT AND ONLY
JAS. ROBINSO
BELGIUM
647.
648.
649.
650.
651.
652.
653.
654.
655.
656.
657.
658.
659.
660.
661.
662.
663.
664.
665.
666.
667.
668.
669.
670.
671.
672.
673.
674.
675.
676.
677.
678.
679.
680.
681.
682.
683.
684.

685.
A Pachyderm's Gratitude: Elephants like lots of water and many little boys have earned a ticket to the Big Show by carrying water for the elephants. One of these incidents is here pictured when a dozen little fellows who had performed such noble work, took their pay in rides on one of the big elephants.

CLOCKS

686. Hourglass.

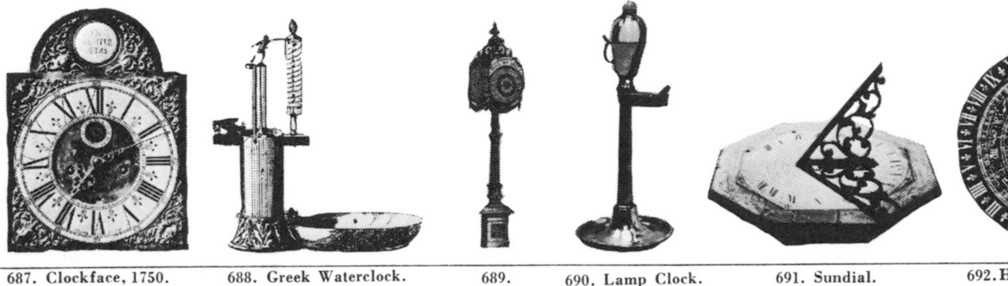
687. Clockface, 1750. 688. Greek Waterclock. 689. 690. Lamp Clock. 691. Sundial. 692. Hampton Court, 1540.

693. Regulator. 694. Time Zones. 695. Victorian. 696. Cuckoo. 697. Mantle, 1810. 698. Mantle, 1890. 699. Alarm.

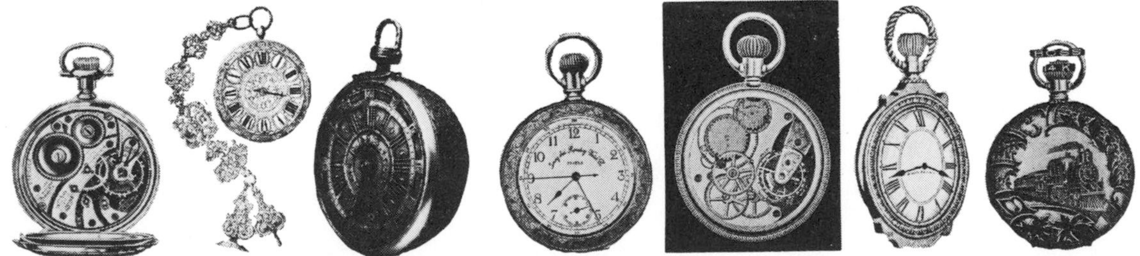
700. Watchworks. 701. Aristocrat's. 702. Nuremberg Egg. 703. Face, 1900. 704. "Short Wind" 705. Sign. 706. R. R. Watch.

707. Colonial Clockshop. 708. 17th Century Horologist. 709. Show Window. 710. Craftsmanship.

CORSETS

711.

712. Winding Up the Lady.

713. Made to Measure.

714. A Little Tighter.

715. Test of Strength.

ASK YOUR MERCHANTS TO ORDER THEM AT ONCE.
The B. V. D. SPIRAL Bustle.
716.

717. Trying on Falsies.

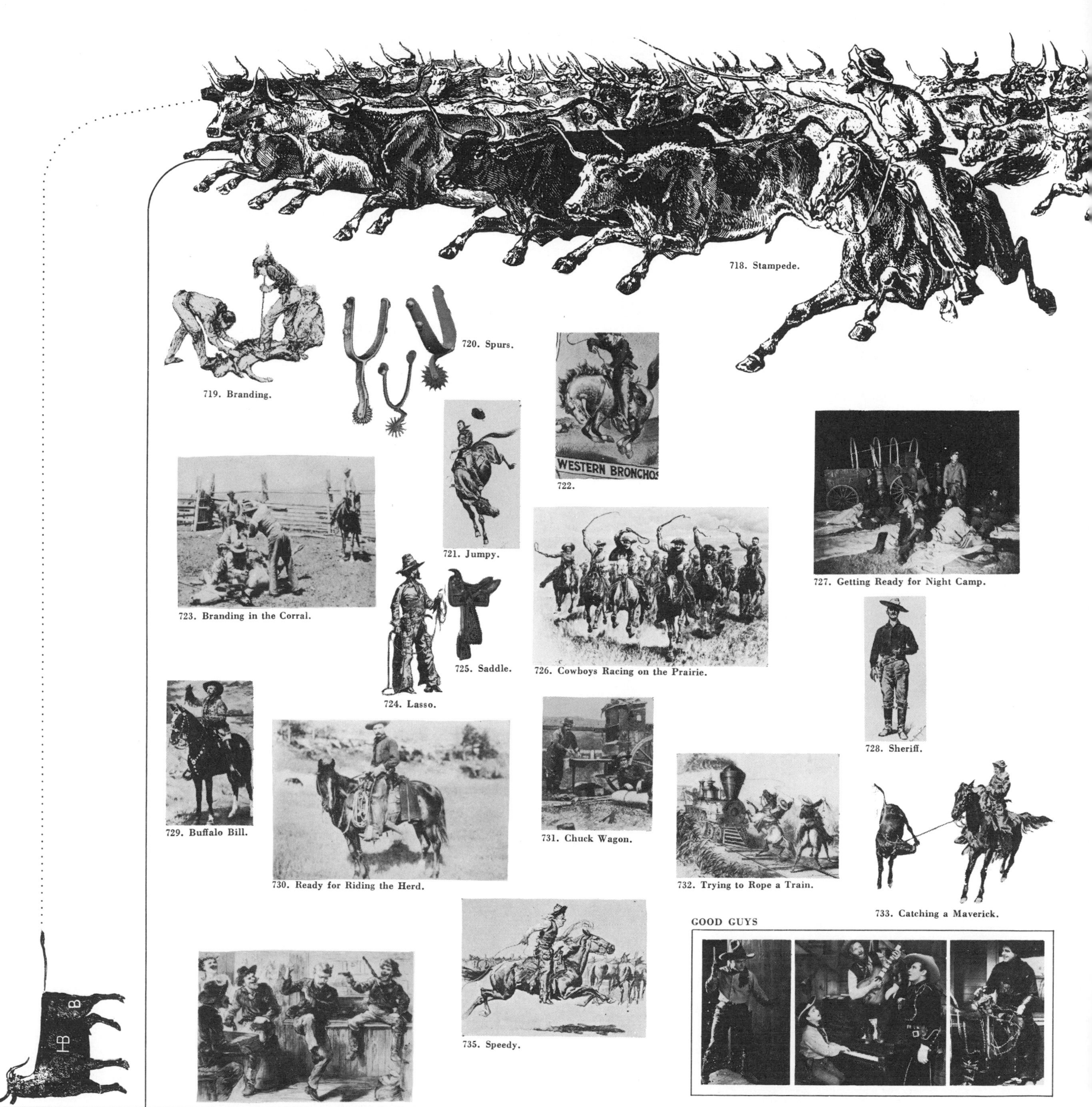

718. Stampede.

719. Branding.

720. Spurs.

721. Jumpy.

722.

723. Branding in the Corral.

724. Lasso.

725. Saddle.

726. Cowboys Racing on the Prairie.

727. Getting Ready for Night Camp.

728. Sheriff.

729. Buffalo Bill.

730. Ready for Riding the Herd.

731. Chuck Wagon.

732. Trying to Rope a Train.

733. Catching a Maverick.

734. Making a Greenhorn Dance.

735. Speedy.

GOOD GUYS

736.

737.

738.

CRIME AND PUNISHMENT

739.

740.

741.

742.

743.

744.

745. 746. 747. 748.

740.
Medieval Murder.
741.
At Gunpoint.
742.
Police Apprehending Thief.
743.
New York City Violence.
744.
Western Bank Robbery.
745-748.
Paraphernalia of N.Y. Police

749.

750.

751.

752.

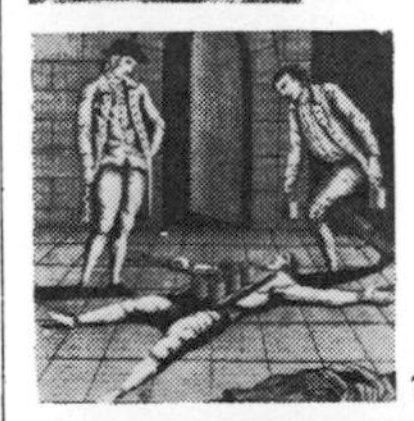
753.

754.

749.
Behind Bars.
750.
Debtor's Prison.
751.
The Black Hole of Calcutta.
752.
English Prison Yard.
753.
Pressed for Confession.
754.
American Prison Yard.

755.

756.

757.

758.

759.

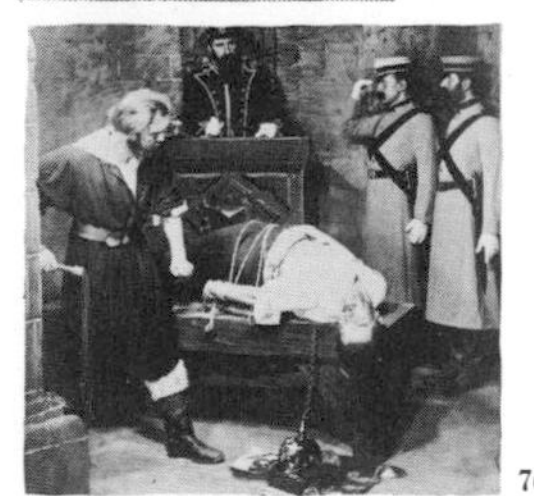
760.

755.
Prisoner on the Rack.
756.
Broiled Alive.
757.
The Dunking Stool.
758.
Tarred and Feathered.
759.
Whipping Adulteress.
760.
Torturing a Nihilist.

761.

762.

763.

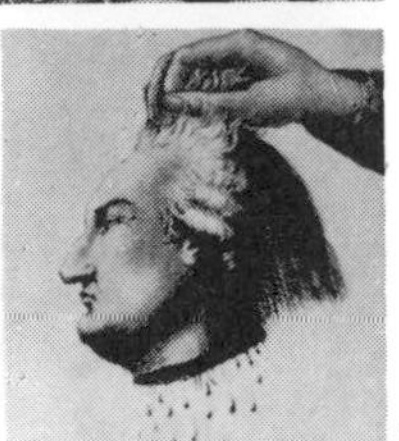
764.

765.

766.

767.

761.
Woman Dragged by Millstone.
762.
Walking the Plank.
763.
Louis XVI Guillotined.
764.
King's Severed Head.
765.
Ready for the Gallows.
766.
Springing the Trap.
767.
Electrocution.

768.

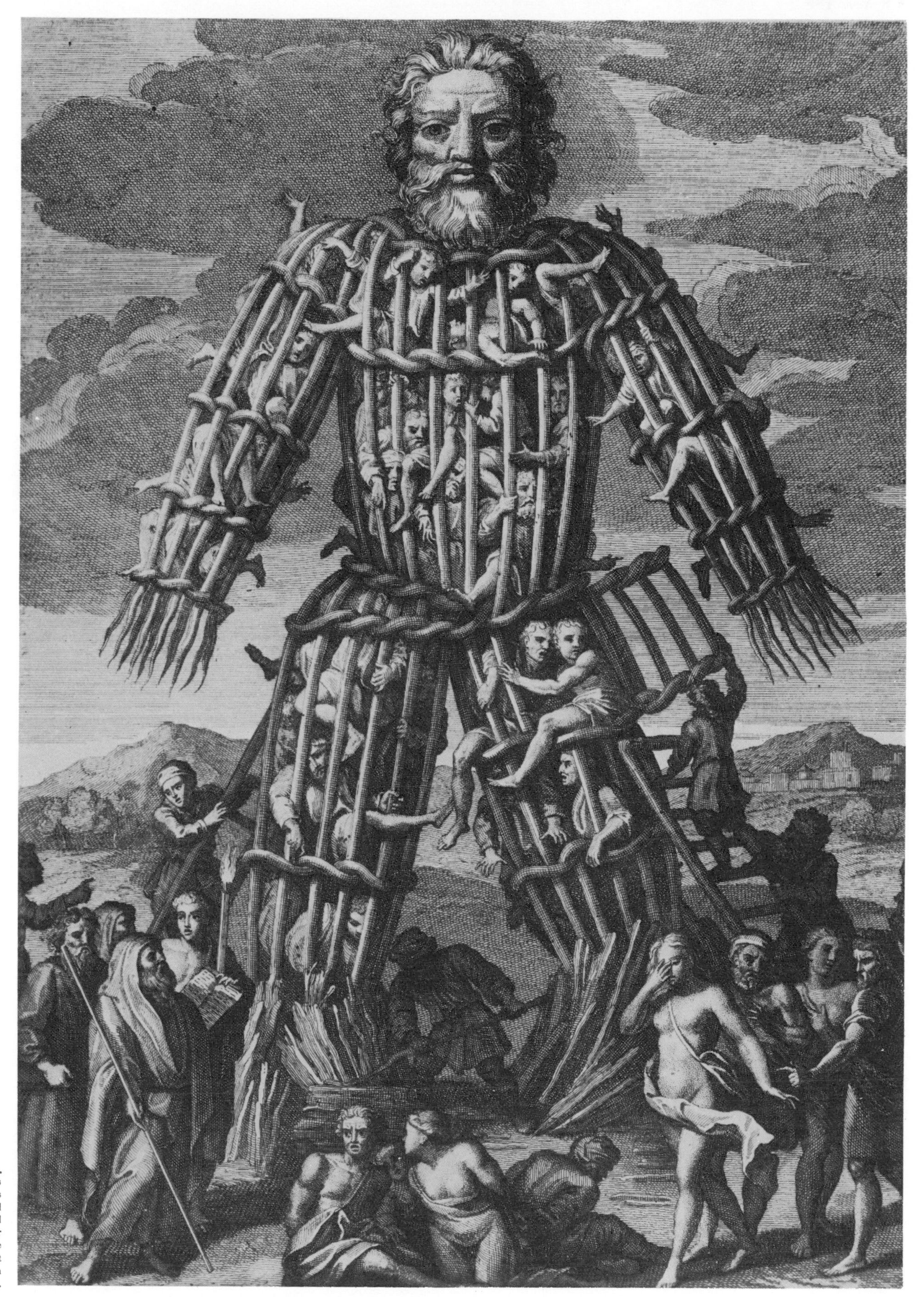

769.
Gallic extermination colossus made of twigs. Criminals and other evildoers were herded into these structures and burned alive. According to Caesar the Druids supervised these executions in the belief that the Gods would accept them with favor as human sacrifices.

770. Walking Machine.

771. Racing: Critical Curve.

772.

773. High Bike Race.

774. Homemade Bike.

775. Balanced Troupe.

776. Man.

777. Woman.

778.

779.

780.

781.

782. Couple: Team.

783. Contraption.

784.

785. Boys.

786. High Bicyclist.

787. Racer.

788.

789.

790.

791.

792.

793.

794.

795.

796.

797.

798.

799.

800.

HILL

YIELD

For complete, analytical subject index turn to page 221.

801. Background: Palace of Trajan, Reconstruction.

802. Empire Dancers.

803. Etruscan.

804. Bacchanalian Dance.

805. Roman Relief.

806. English Dancing Master.

807. Theatrical.

808. Ball Paré.

809. Virginia Reel, Colonial.

810. Christmas Bustle.

811. The Waltz. (Rowlandson)

812. Imperial Vienna.

813. Waltzing.

814. Viennese Ballroom.

815. Quadrille: Follies Bergère.

816. The Jitterbugs of 1850.

817. Polka Mania.

818. Turkey Trot.

819. Grizzly Bear.

820. Fox Trot—Cheek to Cheek.

821.

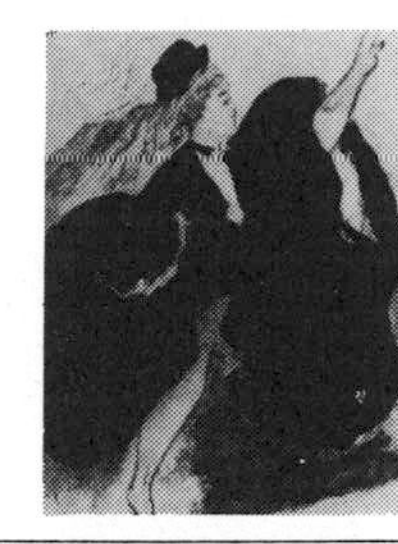

822. Cancan.

Folk Dancing

823. Australian Native

824. Dervishes.

825. Harvest.

826. Highlanders.

827.

828. Russian Village Dance.

829. Mid-19th Century Square Dance.

Ballet

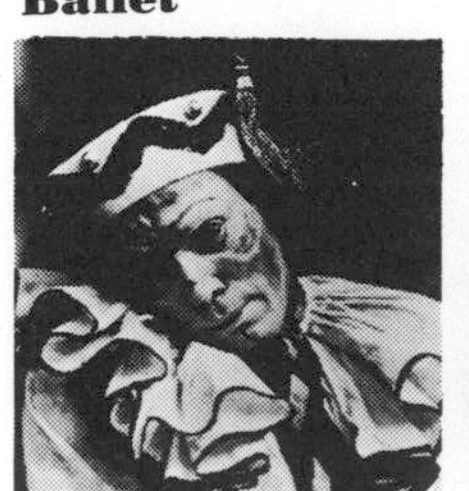

830. Nijinsky.

831. Degas.

832. Karsavina.

833. Fokina.

834. Grisi in Peri.

835. Paris Ballet, 1854.

836. Vaudeville.

837. Spanish.

838.

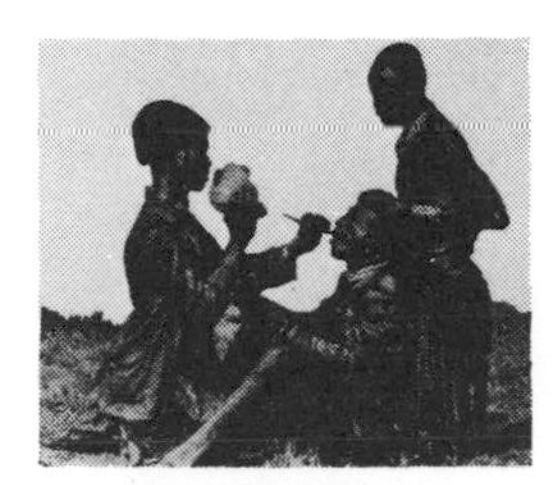

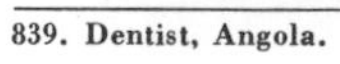

839. Dentist, Angola.

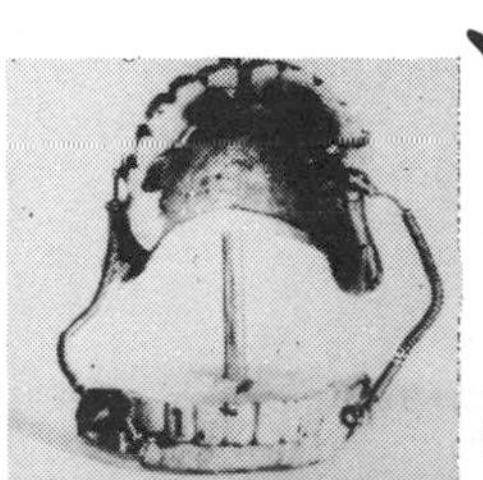

840. Washington's Dentures.

841.

842. A Helpful Wife.

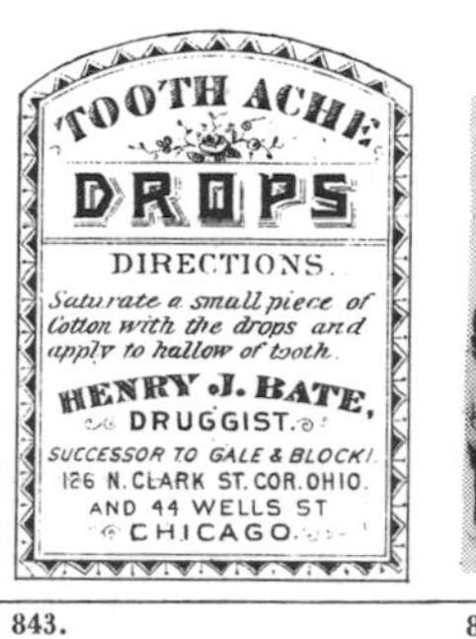

843.

844. Dentist on Horseback.

845. Toothbreaker.

846. "You got the wrong one!"

847. Dental Ad, 1905.

848.

849.

850. Devils of Tooth Decay.

851. American Dentist Uses Parlor as Office, 1840.

852.

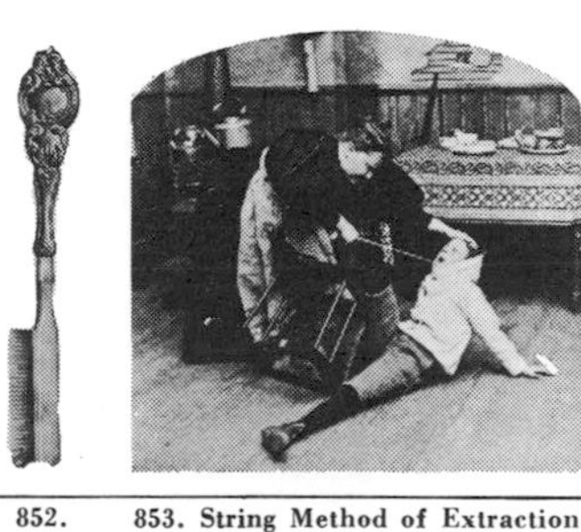

853. String Method of Extraction.

854. The First Electric Drill.

DEVILS

855.

856.

857.

858.

859.

860.

861.

862.

863.

DIVING

866. Brooklyn Bridge

864. Borelli, 1680.

865. Leather Suit, 1460.

867. Ezra Lee, 1776.

868. Ship's Repair.

869. Paris Diver emerges with Dummy from Seine River.

870. Diver in Robot Suit.

871. Alexander the Great Probes the Sea in Transparent Diving Bell. Miniature, 1420.

DREAMS

872. Helena and Dream Goddess.

873. Sleepwalker

874. Dream of Nude-Girl-Companion.

875. Daydreaming.

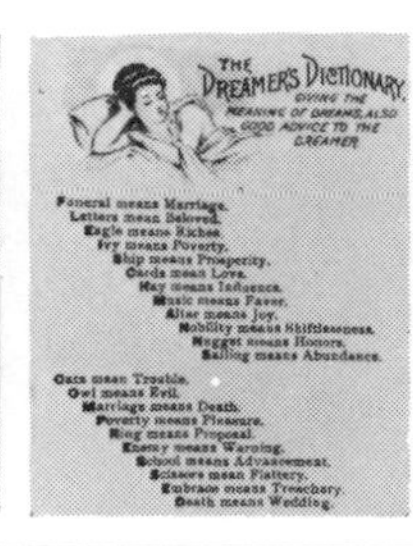

876. Interpreting Dreams.

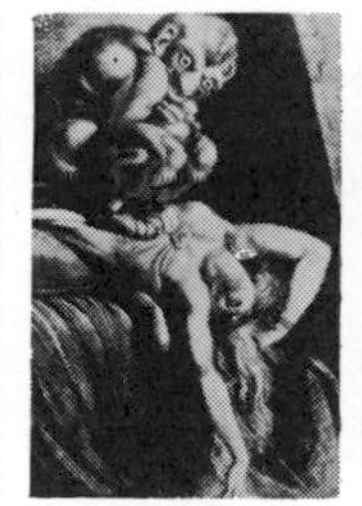

877. Incubus.

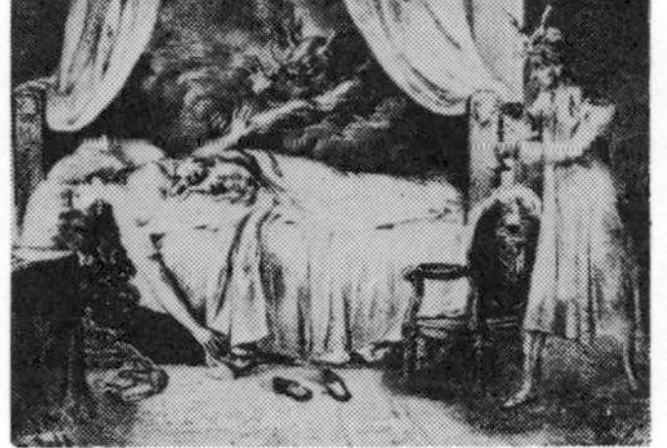

878. Scream of the Nightmare Dreamer.

DRESSMAKING

879. Medieval Guild Sign.

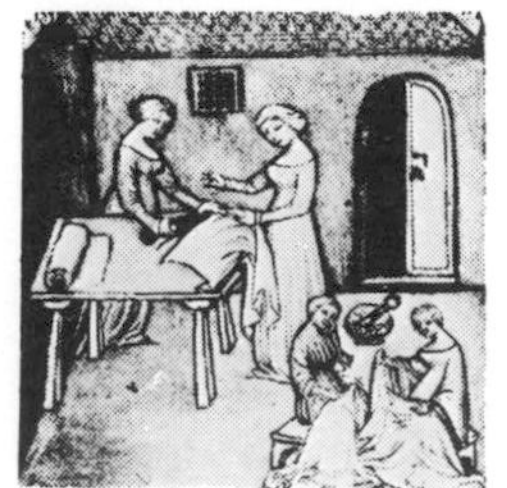

880. Verona Dress Shop, 1450.

881. Pattern.

882. Seventh Avenue Workshop.

883.

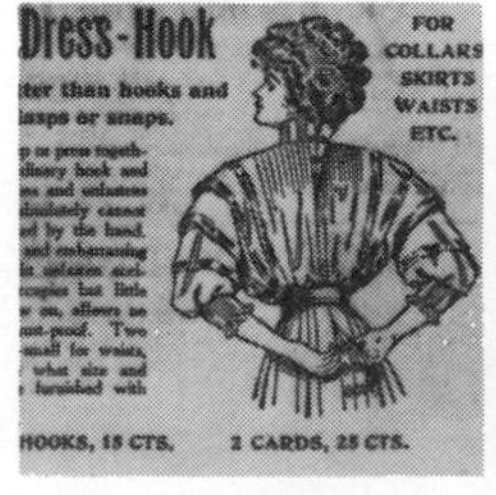

884. B. Z. (Before Zipper).

885. School for Pattern Makers.

886.

887. Pinning Up.

888.

889. Coffee Server, 1700.

890. Plantation, Brazil.

891. A Turkish Coffee House.

892. Coffee House, Restoration Period.

893. Literary Coffee Club.

Coffee

894. Addicts, 1810.

895. Grinding by Hand Mill.

896. Store Grinder.

897. Open Air Coffee Counter, N. Y.

898. Cafeteria: Coffee-Making Machine.

Tea

899. Apes Help in Tea Harvest.

900. 18th Century Family at Tea.

901. Label for China Tea.

902. English Family United at Tea Time.

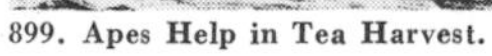

903. Seltzer.

904. Ice Cream, 18 Flavors, Paris, 1805.

905. Crank-Turned Freezer.

906. Ice Cream Parlor, N. Y.

907. Fashionable Couples

913.

914. Syrup.

Soft Drinks

908. Soda Fountain.

909. English Ice Wagon.

910.

911. Soda Fountain.

912. Ice Cream Parlor.

Beer

915. Egyptian Brewer.
916. King Sips Beer through Reed.
917. Mug.
918. Medieval Brewer.
919. Gambrinus.
920. "Prosit."
921. Tankards.
922. Bowery Bar.
923. Ale Wife.
924. Good Old Gemuetlichkeit.

Wine

925. Harvest. (Cossa)
926. Cooler.
927. Italian Wine Harvest.
928.
929. "Your Health."
930. Connoisseur.
931. Bon Vivant.
932. Stag Affair.
933. A Hearty Toast.
934. Flaming Youth.
935. Liquor Store, 1840.
936. Slipper Drink.

Liquor

937. English Distilling Vat.
938. Liquor Label.
939. Along the Bar.
940. Secret Booze Making.

Tavern

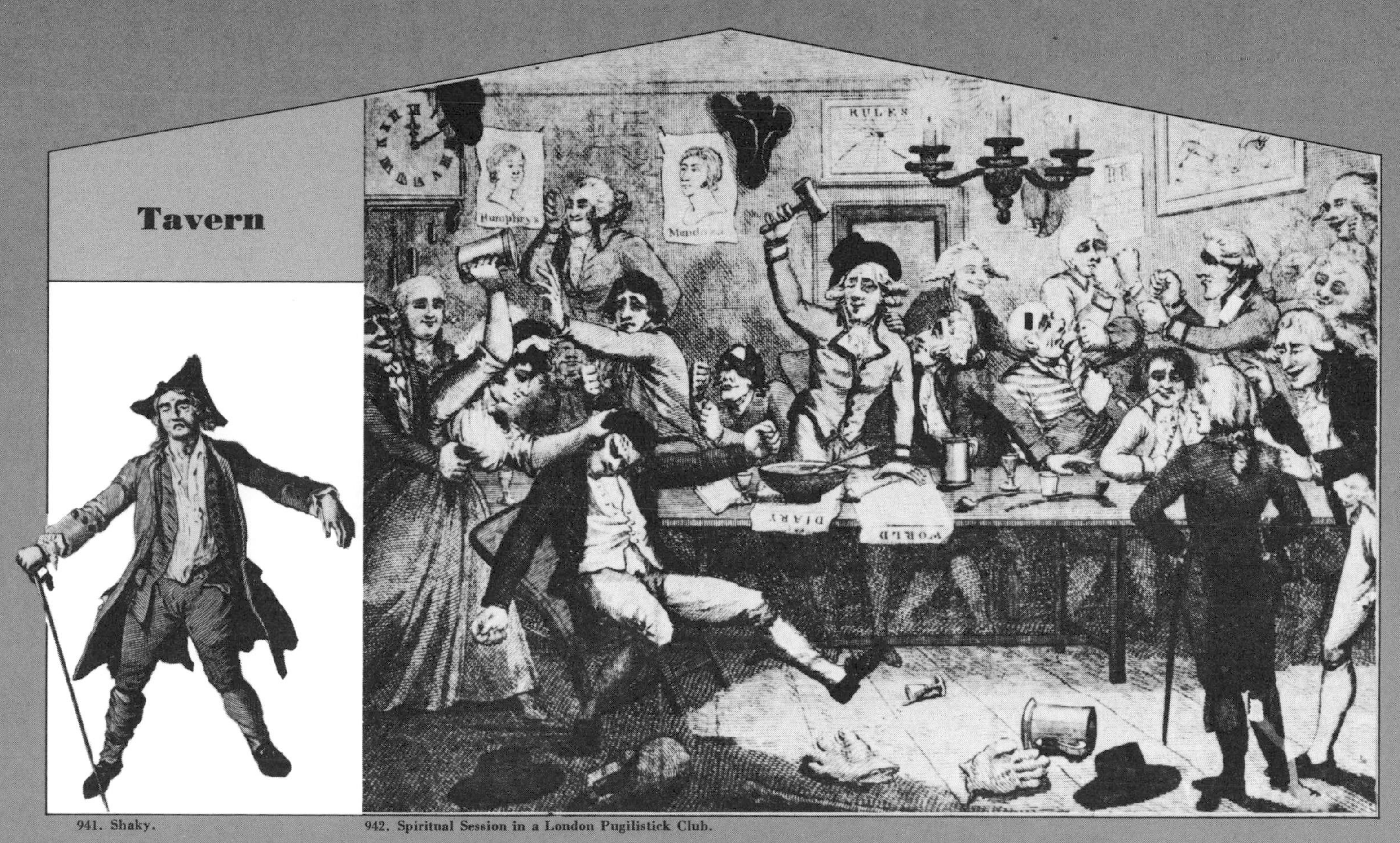

941. Shaky.

942. Spiritual Session in a London Pugilistick Club.

For complete, analytical subject index turn to page 221.

943. Renaissance Knife Engraved with Table Song.

944. Serving One's Fellow Man.

945. The King's Server.

946. Gargantuan Appetite.

947. Licking the Plate.

948. Cardinals Served

949. Ravenous Eater (Cruikshank).

950. Dinner Party.

951. American Family Meal.

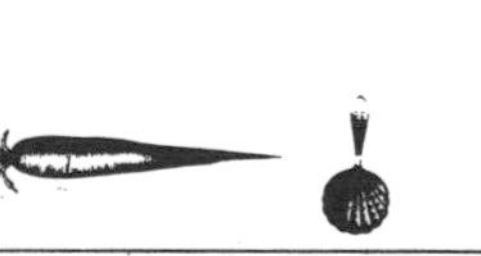

952. 953. 954. 955. 956. 957.

958. The Bean Eater. (Le Nain)

959.

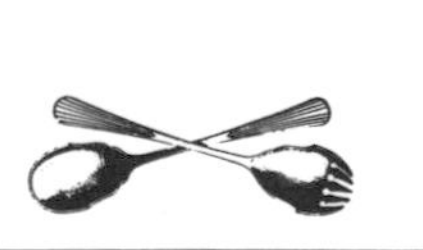

960.

961.

962.

Restaurants

963. Service.

964. The Gourmet.

965. Dinner at the Club.

966. Singing Waiter.

967. "Doing the Best I Can, Mister."

968. Viennese Coffee House.

969. Host.

970. Victorian Serving Counter.

971. San Francisco Eatery, 1890.

972. Romans Gorging Food.

973. A French Chef.

974. Good Food Here. 975.

976. A New Breed of Waiter.

977.

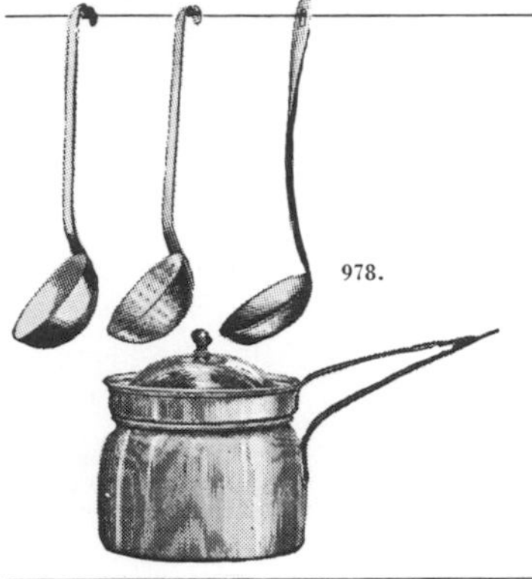

978.

979.

Kitchens

980. Cavemen Prepare Meal.

981. Indians Broil Fish.

982. Hostelry Kitchen in the French Provinces, ca. 1780.

983. Family Gathered in Colonial Kitchen.

984.

985.

"Her dress was always clean and neat,
Her face was never nasty;
She always wash'd her hands before
She made an apple pasty."

986.

987.

988. Fireplace Cooking.

989. U. S. Housewife, ca. 1880.

990. Well Equipped Shaker Kitchen.

991. Dismayed Housewife Faces Dishes.

992. A Hot Cook.

993.

994.

995.

996. Prairie Meal.

997. Mixing Cake Batter.

998. Busy Kitchen before Holiday.

999. Kitchen with Water Pump.

1000. Slum Kitchen.

EGYPT

1001. Gold Pectoral Representing Spirit of King Tutankhamen.

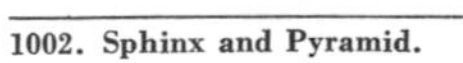

1002. Sphinx and Pyramid.

1003. Nefertiti.

1004.

1005. Papyrus Scroll: The Book of Death.

1006. Mother's Hairdo.

1007. Archers.

1008. Sphinx.

1009. Scribes Recording King's Command.

1010. Osiris on Throne.

1011. Wildcat in Papyrus Thicket.

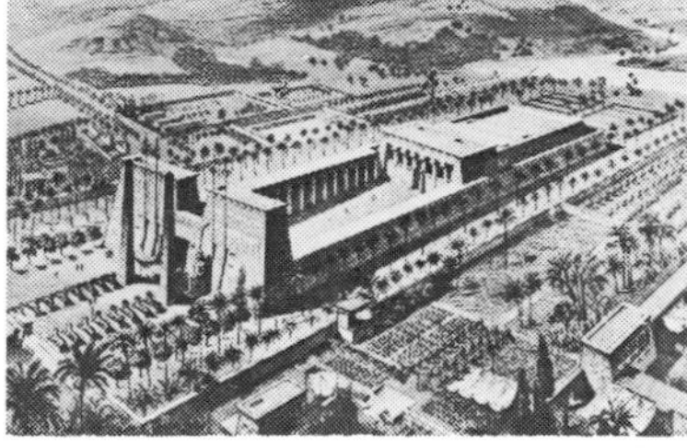

1012. Reconstruction of the Temple at Edfu.

1013. Female Musicians.

1014. Excavation, 1895.

EIFFEL TOWER

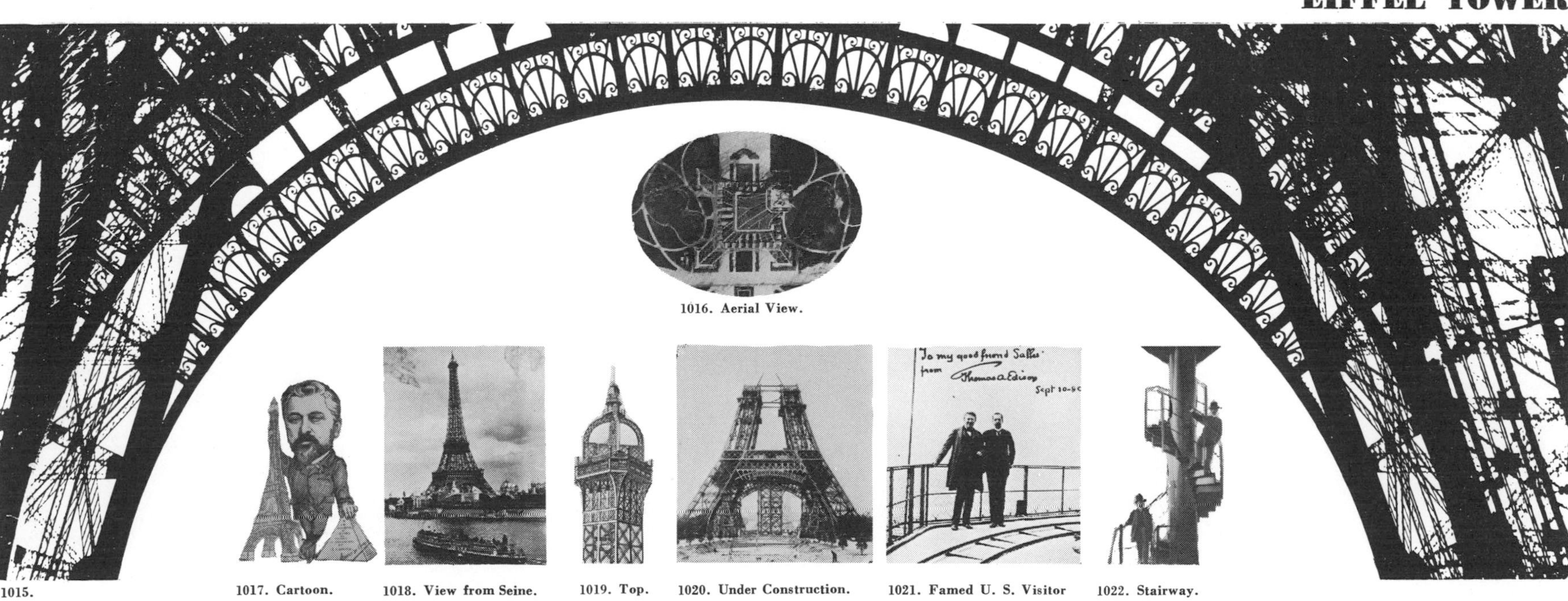

1016. Aerial View.

1015.

1017. Cartoon.

1018. View from Seine.

1019. Top.

1020. Under Construction.

1021. Famed U. S. Visitor

1022. Stairway.

1023.

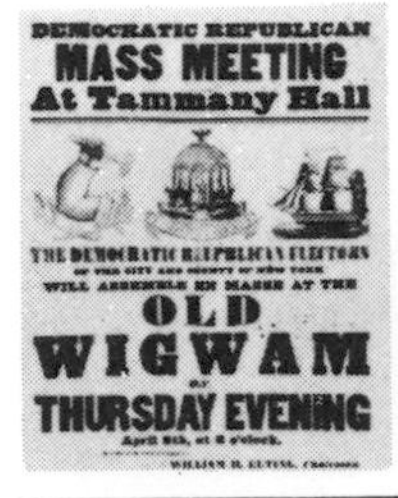

1024. Poster, 1835

1025. Workingmen's Torchlight Parade.

1026. Tippecanoe's Log Cabin Campaign, 1840.

1027. Johnson Campaigning.

1028. Lincoln Boosters.

1029. Torch Bearer.

1030. Campaign of 1859.

1031. Douglas Debate.

1032. Campaign of 1840.

1033. Civil War Veterans Campaigning for Hayes.

1034. Keep the Ball Rolling—Harrison and Tyler.

1035. Greeley Baby-Kissing.

CAMPAIGN BUTTONS

1036. All out for Garfield, 1880.

1037.

1038.

1039.

1040.

1041. Voting, Wyoming.

1042. Handshake Machine.

1043. New Voters, 1867.

1044. Electioneering.

1045. Convention, 1928.

1046. Taft Poster, 1907.

1046.

1047.

1048. Galvani Discovers Animal Electricity.

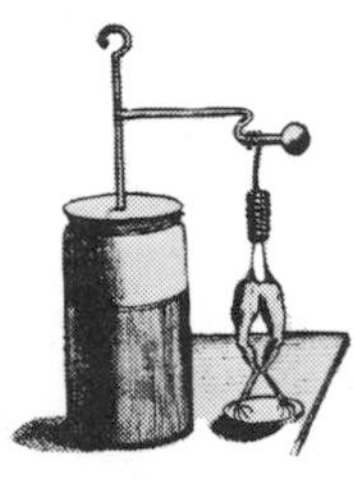

1049. Frog's Legs.

1050. Friction.

1051. Napoleon and Volta.

1052. Poster for Electric Dealer.

1053. Edison in Laboratory.

1054. Experimenter, 1900.

1055. Giant Galvanometer.

1056. Electrical Generator.

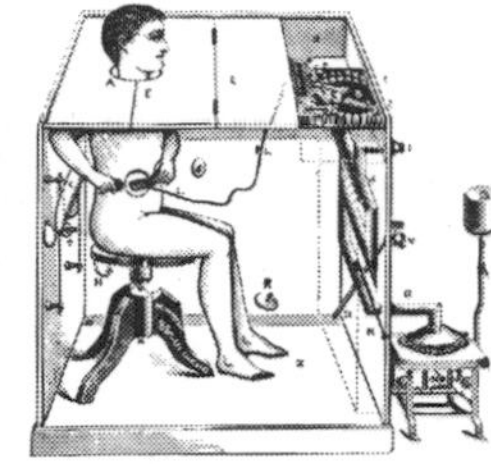

1057. Electro-Therapy Bath.

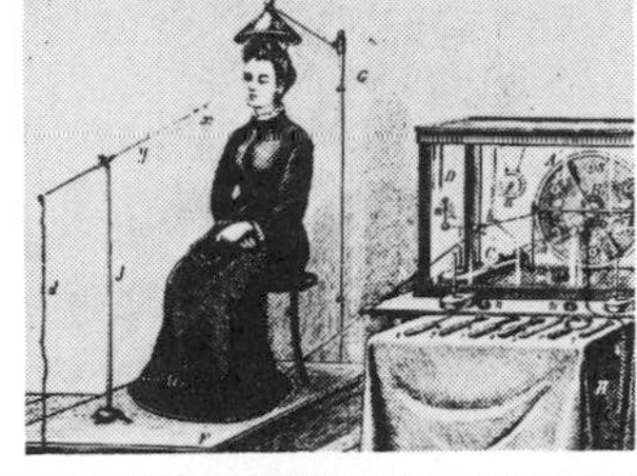

1058. Treating Headache by Electricity.

1059.

1060. Winding Armature.

1061. Ore Detector.

1062. Lightning in Laboratory Test.

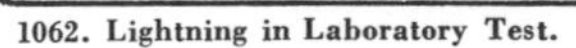

1063. Edison's First Power Station.

1064. Cranking Dynamo.

1065. Storage Battery Powerhouse.

1066. Wiring.

1067.

ELEVATORS

EMBALMING

1068. Medieval Lady Lets her Boy Friend Down.

1069. Elevator-Carriage.

1070. Hydro-Elevator.

1071. Victorian Cab, 1883.

1072. Electric Climber.

1073. Escalator, 1903.

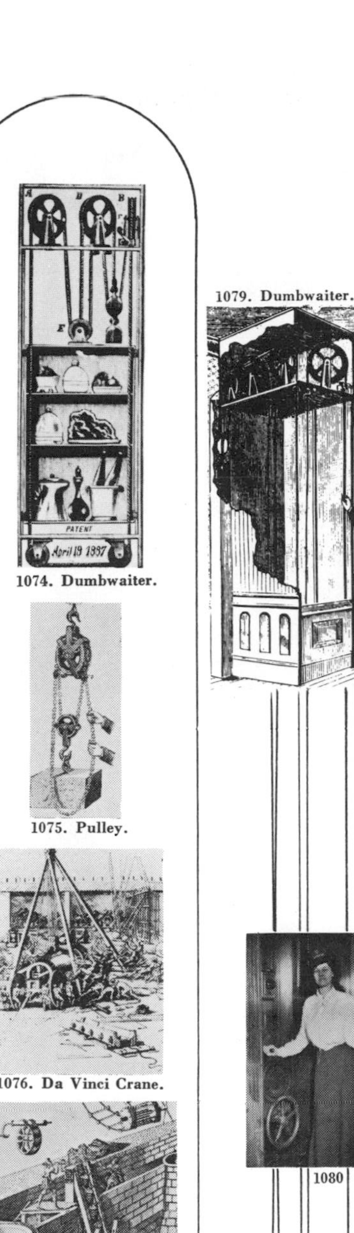

1074. Dumbwaiter.

1075. Pulley.

1076. Da Vinci Crane.

1077. Conveyor Belt.

1078. Pulley.

1079. Dumbwaiter.

1080 Operator

1079.

1081.

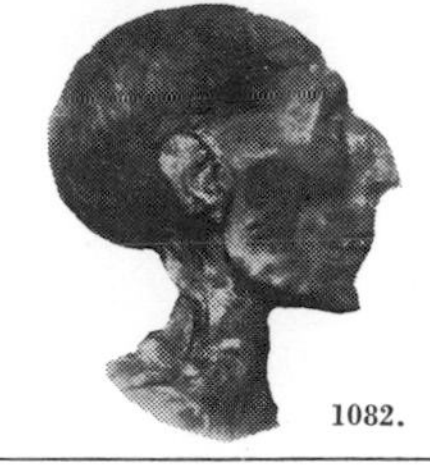

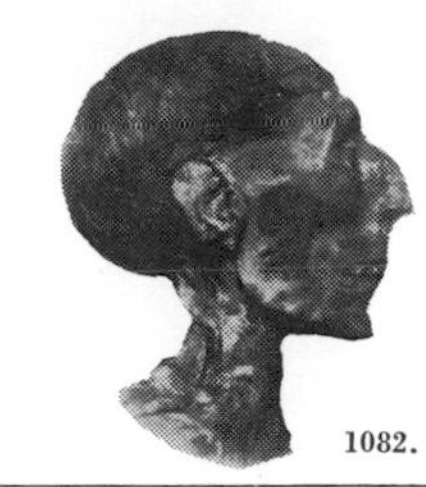

1082.

1083. King Embalmed.

1084.

1085.

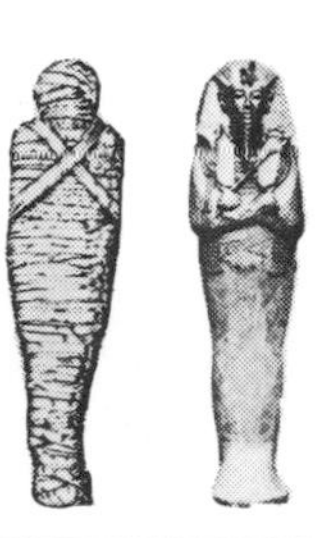

1086.

1087.

1088. Electric Embalmer.

1089. Civil War Embalmer's Tent.

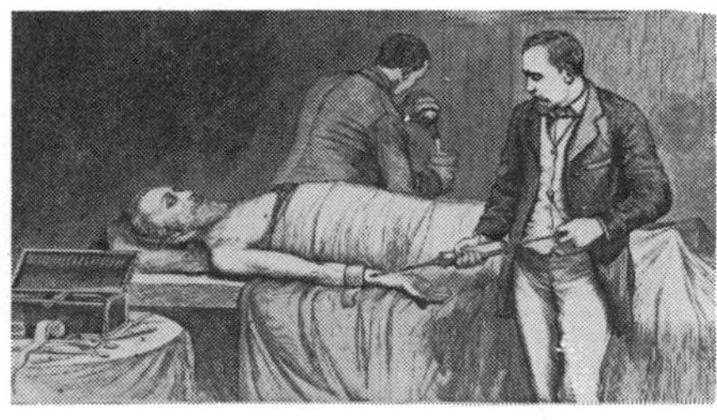

1090. President Garfield Embalmed.

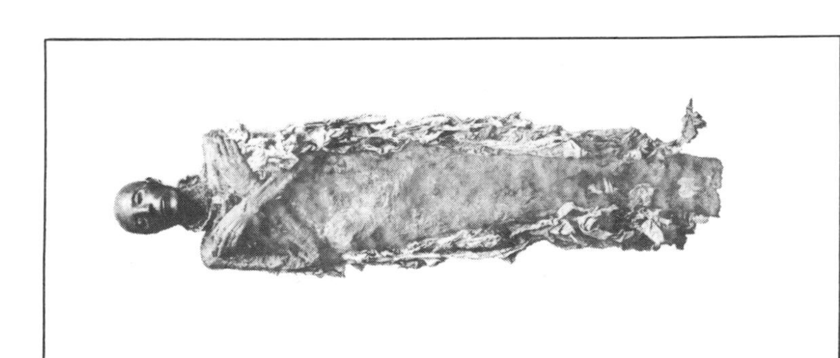

1091. The Mummy of King Seti II.

EROTICA

1092. Galen: Sex Education.

1093. Roman Relief.

1094. Sin. (Bosch)

1095. Greek Vase Scene.

1096. Hermaphrodite.

1097. Royal Copulation.

1098. Peeping Tom, 1630.

1099. An English Bordello.

1100. Piano Teacher.

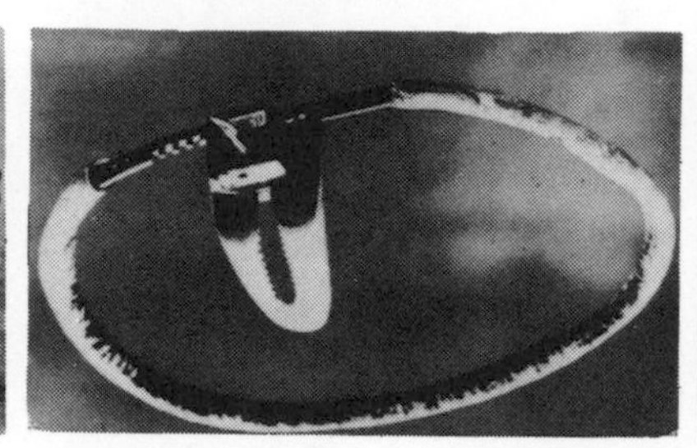
1101. Medieval Chastity Belt.

1102. Adam and Eve.

1103. Young Love (Maillol).

1104. Mutoscope.

1105. Postcard.

EYES

1106. Trade Card.

1107.

1108.

1109.

1110.

1111.

1112.

1113.

1114. Descartes: Vision.

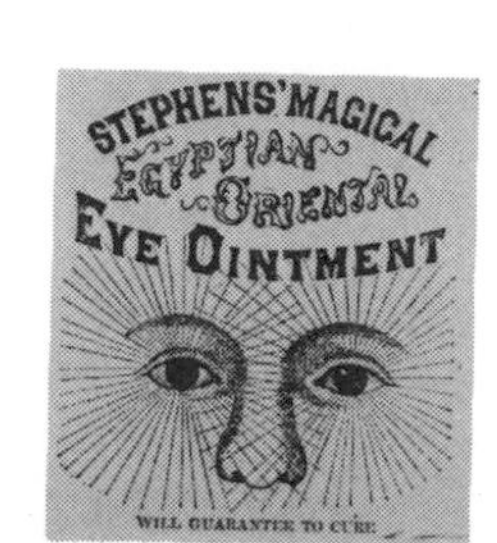

1115. Ocular Lotion.

1116. Bespectacled Joker.

EXPRESSIONS

1117. 1118. 1119. 1120. 1121. 1122. 1123. 1124. 1125. 1126. 1127. 1128.

1129. 1130. 1131. 1132. 1133. 1134. 1135. 1136. 1137. 1138. 1139.

EYE-GLASSES

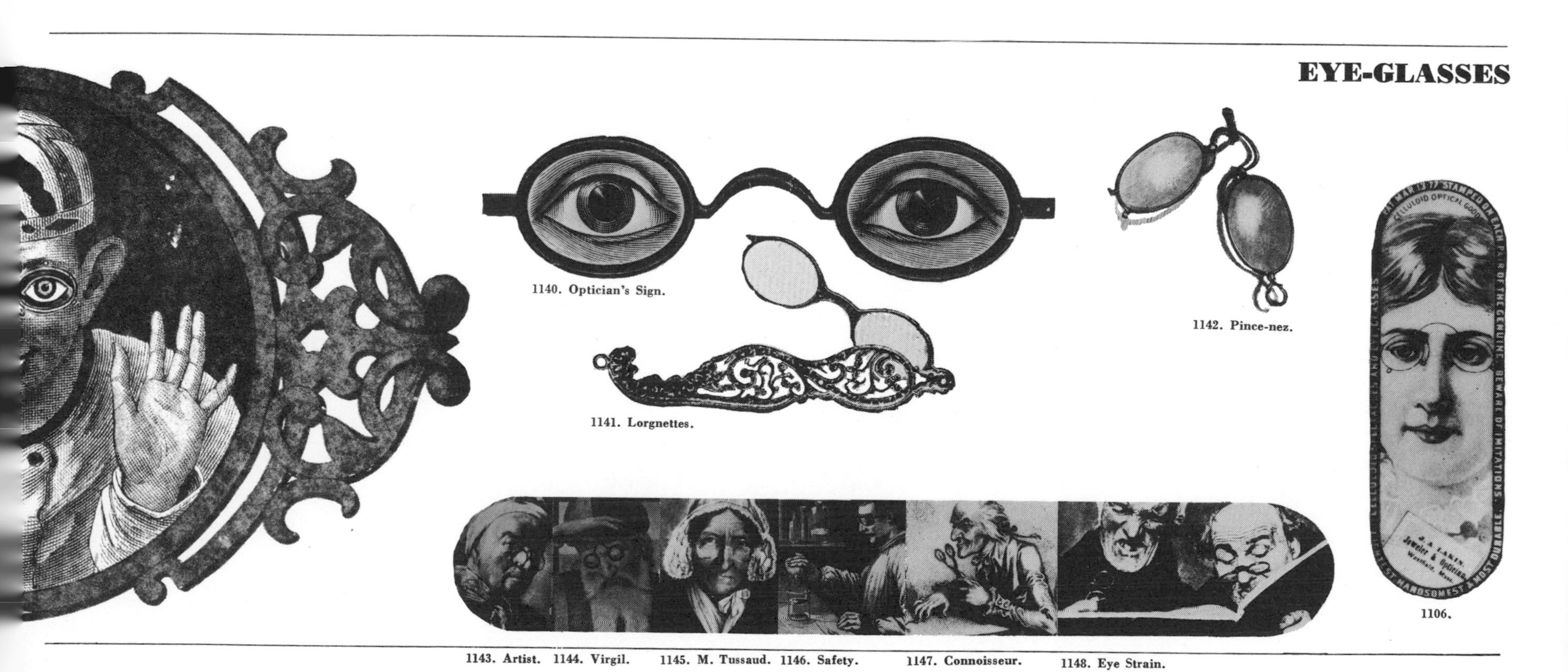

1140. Optician's Sign.

1141. Lorgnettes.

1142. Pince-nez.

1106.

1143. Artist. 1144. Virgil. 1145. M. Tussaud. 1146. Safety. 1147. Connoisseur. 1148. Eye Strain.

For complete, analytical subject index turn to page 221.

1149. Middle Class. 1150. Royalty.

1151. Silhouette of American Family, 1839.

1152. Mother's Birthday.

1153. Trouble.

1154. Biedermeier Family.

1155. Virginia Planter, 1845.

1156. Prosperous New Yorker.

1157. Father Reading Aloud.

1158. European Middle Class, 1850's.

1159. Swiss Family Musicale.

1160. Old Folks at Home.

1161. Status.

1162. Frontier.

1163. Suspended Family.

1164.

1165.

1166.

1167.

1168.

1169.

1170. Family.

1171.

1172.

1173. Sampler.

1174. Parents repose thanks to "Glass Covers for Noisy Children."

FASHIONS

Women's Fashions

1175. Egypt. 1176. Greece. 1177. Medieval Queen. 1178. 1179. Elevated Lady. 1180. Venice. 1181. Rococo Belle. 1182. Empire Fashion. 1183. Bustle. 1184. Victorian Formal. 1185. Coquette. 1186. Gibson Girl.

HOLLYWOOD FASHIONS

1187. Society, 1890. 1188. Lillian Russell. 1189. Cleo de Mérode. 1190. On the Way to Work, 1909. 1191. Shirtwaist. 1192. Party Dress. 1193. Designs of the 1920's. 1194. 1195.

Accessories

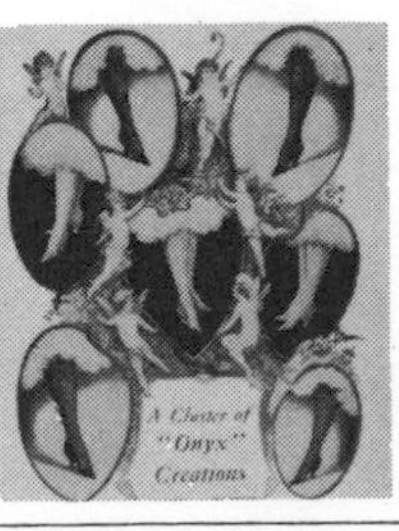

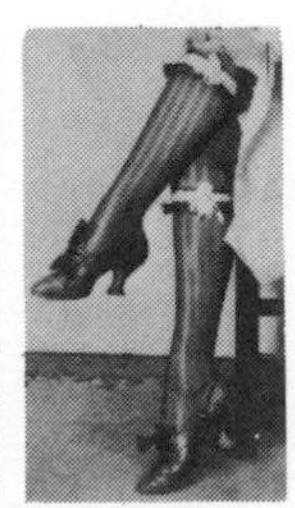

1196. Fixing Garter. 1197. Coquette. 1198. Gloved Parisienne. 1199. Getting Dressed. 1200. Handkerchief Ad. 1201. Admirable. 1202. Hosiery Ad, 1900. 1203. Patterned Hose. 1204. Stripped.

Men's Fashions

1205. Perspective. 1206. 1207. 1208. 1209. 1210. 1211. 1212. 1213. 1214. 1215. 1216. 1217.

Tailoring

1218. Verona Tailorshop.

1219. Medieval Tunics.

1220. Cross-legged Tailor.

1221. Dandies, Beau Brummel Period.

1222. Cutter.

1223. Measuring.

1224. Retail Shop, 1870's.

Accessories

1225. Putting on Tie.

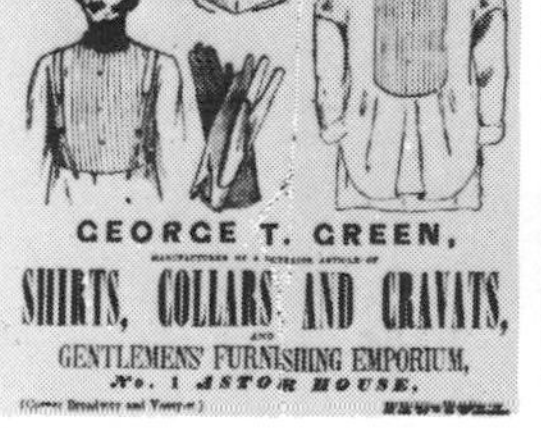

1226. Gentlemen's Accessories.

1227. Pointed Tie.

1228. Trouser-Raising Device.

1229.

1230. Privacy Collar.

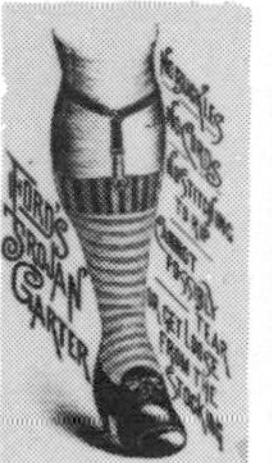

1231. Garter Ad.

1232. Suspenders.

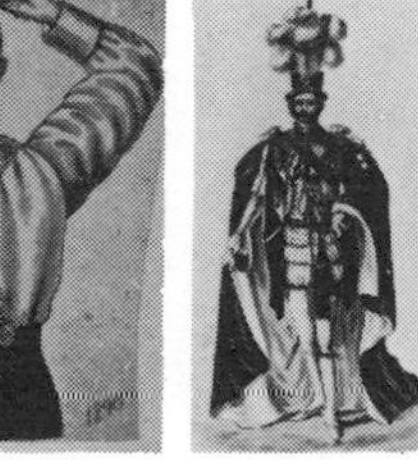

1233.

1234. Collier's Fashion Ad, 1905.

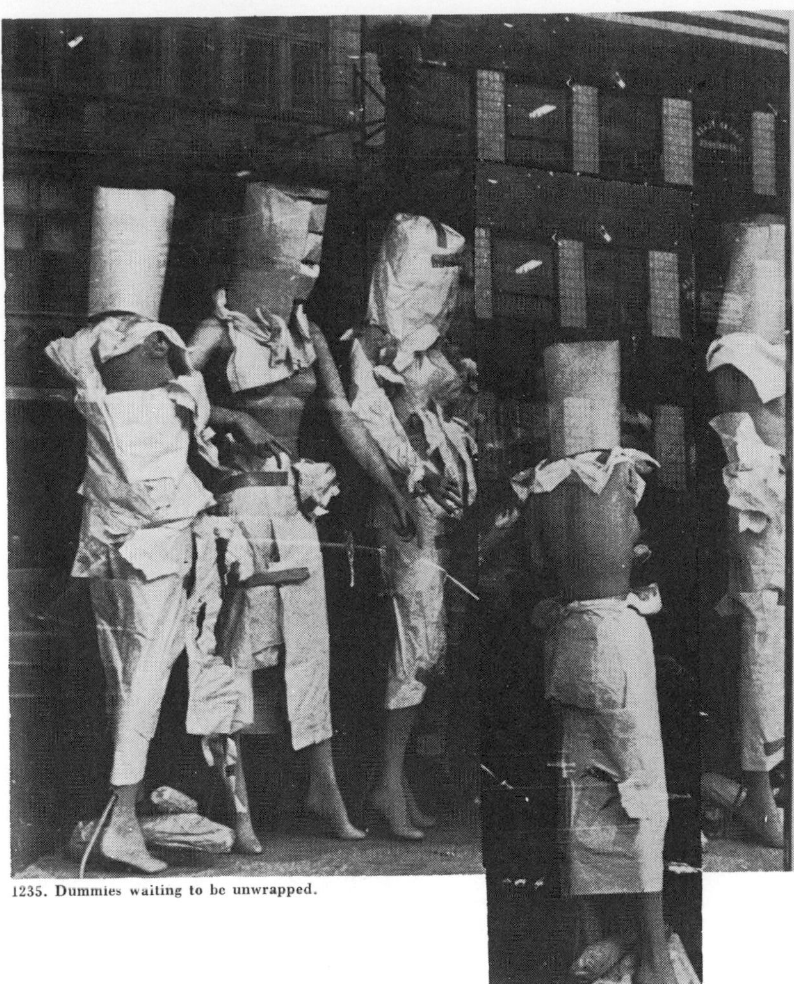

1235. Dummies waiting to be unwrapped.

Photo by Herbert Migdoll.

FIGUREHEADS

1236.

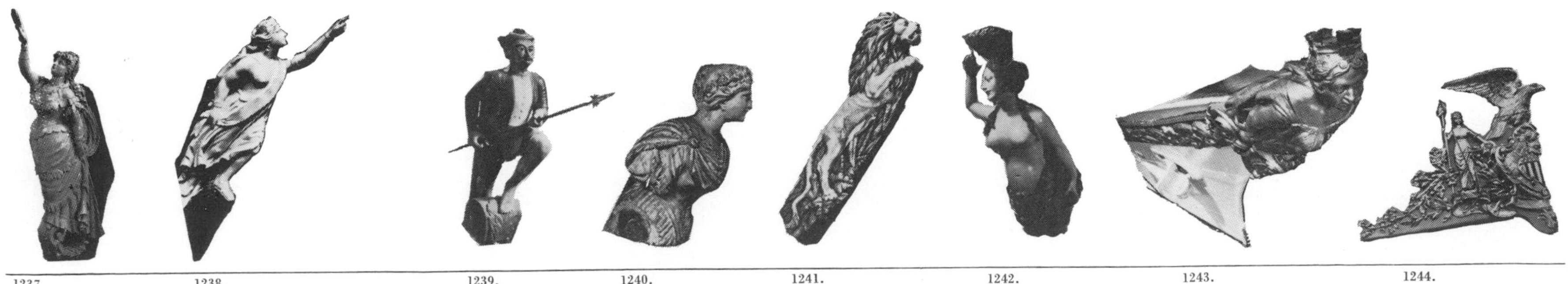

1237. 1238. 1239. 1240. 1241. 1242. 1243. 1244.

1245. "A Fire Engine steaming hot with readiness for public duty."

1246. Fire Extinguisher.

1247.

1248. Bucket Brigade, Old New York.

1249. Hand Pump.

1250. Alarm.

1251. Chicago in Flames.

1252. Female Fireman.

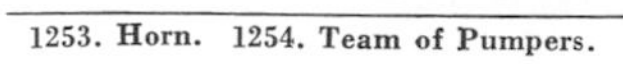

1253. Horn. 1254. Team of Pumpers.

1255. Third Alarm, N. Y., 1870.

1256. Ready for Action.

1257. Hat.

1258. Horse-Drawn.

1259. Fire Prevention.

1260. Prairie Fire.

1261. The Life of the Fireman.

1262. Fire Bucket.

1263. Front of a Firehouse.

1264. Fourth of July Fireworks Poster.

1265.

1266.
Adding Machine. Pascal, 1642.

1267.
Hot-Air Balloon. Montgolfier, 1783.

1268.
Vaccination. Jenner, 1796.

1269.
Punch Card Loom. Jacquard, 1801.

1270.
Steamboat. Fulton, 1803.

1271.
Locomotive. Stephenson, 1814.

1272.
Tele graph. Morse, 1832.

1273.
Reaper. McCormick, 1834.

1274.
Revolver. Colt, 1836.

1275.
Sewing Machine. Howe, 1846.

1276.
Elevator. Otis, 1853.

1277.
Typewriter. Sholes, 1868.

1278.
Airbrake. Westinghouse, 1868.

1279.
Telephone. Bell, 1876.

1280.
Phonograph. Edison, 1877.

1281.
Linotype. Mergenthaler, 1885.

1282.
Automobile. Daimler, 1887.

1283.
Kodak. Eastman, 1888.

1284.
Airplane. Wright Brothers, 1903.

1285.
Radio Tube. De Forrest, 1915.

1286.
Television Tube. Zworykin, 1934.

1047.

1048. Galvani Discovers Animal Electricity.

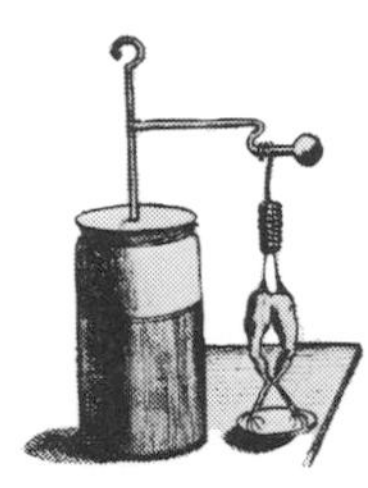

1049. Frog's Legs.

1050. Friction.

1051. Napoleon and Volta.

1052. Poster for Electric Dealer.

1053. Edison in Laboratory.

1054. Experimenter, 1900.

1055. Giant Galvanometer.

1056. Electrical Generator.

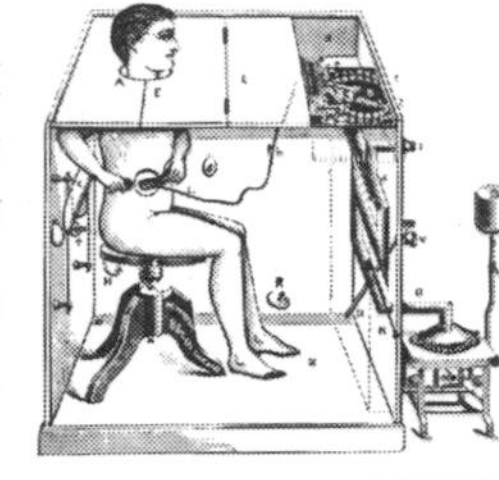

1057. Electro-Therapy Bath.

1058. Treating Headache by Electricity.

1059.

1060. Winding Armature.

1061. Ore Detector.

1062. Lightning in Laboratory Test.

1063. Edison's First Power Station.

1064. Cranking Dynamo.

1065. Storage Battery Powerhouse.

1066. Wiring.

1067.

ELEVATORS

1068. Medieval Lady Lets her Boy Friend Down.

1069. Elevator-Carriage.

1070. Hydro-Elevator.

1071. Victorian Cab, 1883.

1072. Electric Climber.

1073. Escalator, 1903.

1074. Dumbwaiter.

1075. Pulley.

1076. Da Vinci Crane.

1077. Conveyor Belt.

1078. Pulley.

1079. Dumbwaiter.

1080 Operator

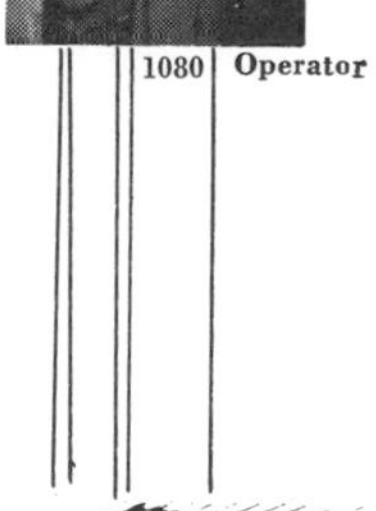

1079.

EMBALMING

1081.

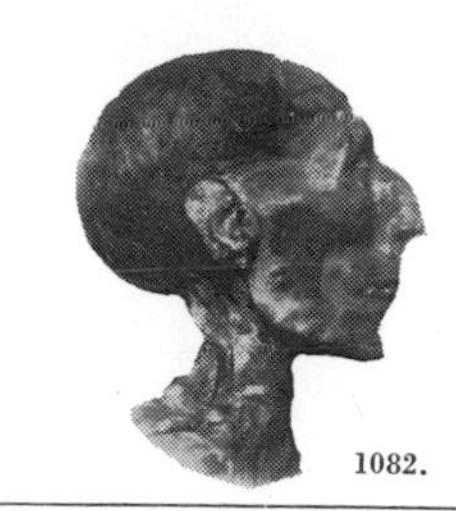

1082.

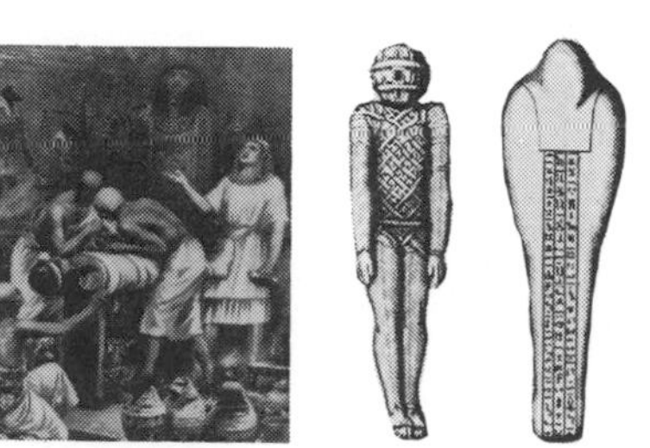

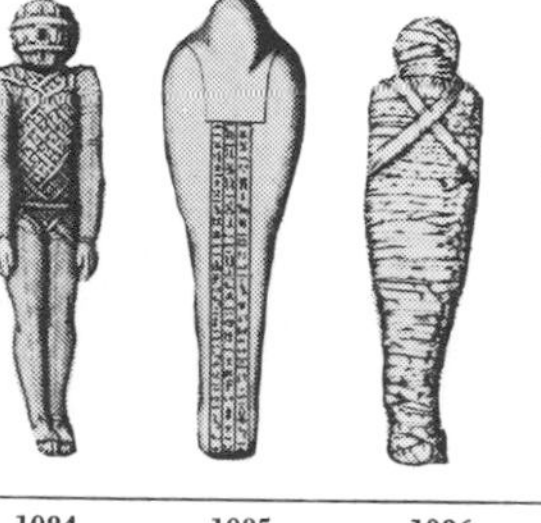

1083. King Embalmed. 1084. 1085. 1086. 1087. 1088. Electric Embalmer.

1089. Civil War Embalmer's Tent.

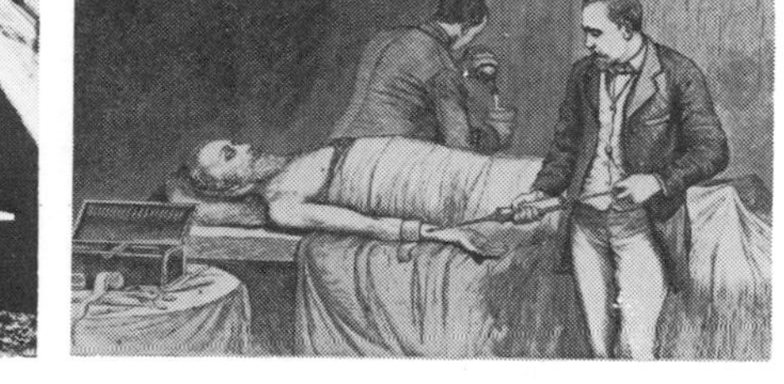

1090. President Garfield Embalmed.

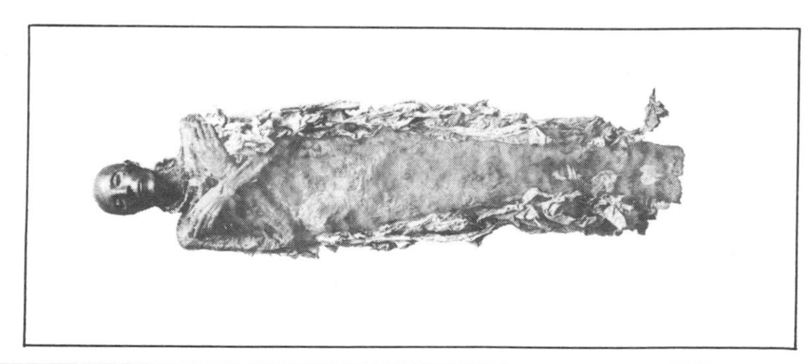

1091. The Mummy of King Seti II.

FRAMES

1341. 1342. 1343. 1344. 1345. 1346. 1347. 1348. 1349. 1350. 1351. 1352.

FRANKLIN

1353.

Yours most affectionately
B Franklin

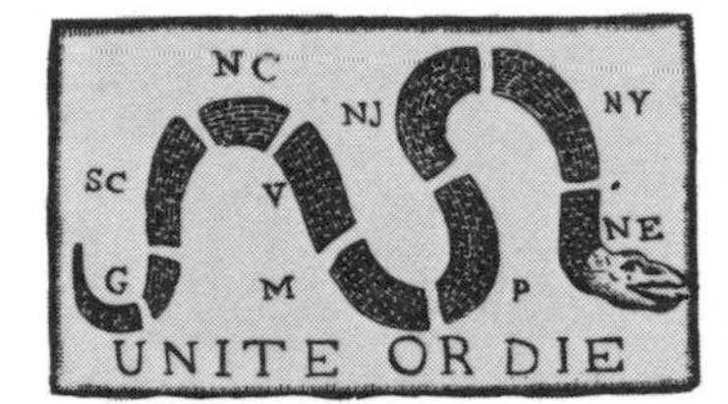

1354. Cartoonist.

1355. Printer.

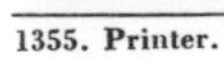

1356. Inventor.

1357. Defender of Liberty.

1358. Musician.

1359. Statesman.

1360. Diplomat.

FREAKS

1361. Pig Nose.

1362. Chang and Eng Poster.

1363. Barnum's Famed Albinos.

1364. Marco Polo's Headless Race.

1365. Pigmentation. 1366. Wonder Birth.

1367. Elephantiasis.

1368. Monster. Chronicle of 1492.

Problems and Prospects of Picture Retrieval

Ideally, picture retrieval should work in the following manner (and perhaps one day it will): The picture user in search of "Melba eating Melba toast" will teletype his coded request to an electronic picture research pool. After a few minutes' wait, a Western Union messenger will arrive with a fat envelope containing pictures of Melba eating Melba toast, dry, buttered or with marmalade! Only a digit here and there has to be changed should the request happen to be for "Thomas Jefferson eating spaghetti," or a reproduction of Leonardo da Vinci's "Mona Lisa." However, the computer might breathe a little more heavily when fed a request for a *profile view* of the famous lady with the enigmatic smile. ¶ This Pictorial Futurama is not offered facetiously. We're getting there. Systems have already been developed that have cut picture research time from days to seconds. Even so there will always be room in this field for the personal touch, taste, visual awareness and a Holmesian gift for sleuthing. ¶ To help in such pursuits and to speed up the retrieval of pictures—the right pictures—The Bettmann Archive has developed a visual index (below). Every picture that gains a permanent place in the Archive is photographed and reproduced in miniature on a file card. These cards record a careful analysis of subject matter. Beyond this an attempt is made to extend cross references beyond the obvious, to search out associative values. For example: A battle scene can have implications beyond the mere action shown. It can exemplify strategy, leadership, attack, ballistics. An illustration from Goethe's "Faust" can go beyond mere literary history. The Witches' Sabbath from this book is cross-indexed under "merrymaking" and has served as an embellishment for many a party invitation. Likewise, a request for a history of the chemical synthesis of living tissue might lead us to Homunculus, Goethe's little man made in a retort. And, Atomic Explosion has among its predecessors the work of that mysterious medieval monk, Barthold Schwartz, the purported inventor of gun powder. He is shown in one of the Bettmann prints hovering over an alchemist's crucible out of which smoke billows upward in the form of a devil. ¶ In analyzing pictures not only their literal contents but their symbolic, ancillary uses are a prime consideration. This has lead to a substantial enrichment of the number of available images. ¶ To build up a system of this sort requires expertise as well as budgetary support, and the pictures themselves have to be worthy of the time and effort taken to assimilate them. It stands to reason therefore that the Bettmann Archive had to establish rather stringent "entrance" requirements: First of all, a picture must be clearly reproducible. Even rare items are of little value if they cannot stand up in reproduction. Conciseness and quick readability are other musts. Ideally, pictures must go to the heart of the subject without gratuitous digressions or editorializing. As I often explain it to my younger helpers groping for the answer to the key question in our field: What is a good picture?—"An art director or editor buys a picture the way a housewife buys a steak. It's the meat that counts; the fat only adds to the poundage." ¶ The Bettmann index helps to fill requests for pictures that epitomize, pictures that amuse, pictures that dismay, pictures that stimulate associations. ¶ Yet not every request can be filled. Life is just too multifarious to be depicted in its every aspect. Not even ten million pictures could capture its diversity and meaning. This being the case, we have to take solace in the fact that in our work day, reminiscent of a picture quiz program, we sometimes win and sometimes lose. Many pictures we would like to have are simply unobtainable, not because of any lack of zeal on our part, but rather because they were never taken, drawn, painted or engraved. And so we have to limp along without a picture of Melba eating Melba toast, or Jefferson eating spaghetti, or Mrs. Charles the Great on a restive white steed. It's hard enough to retrieve the retrievable, let alone what wasn't there in the first place.

NO. C. 58/25

DESCRIPTION Gossaert, Jan(called Mabuse) ca. 1478-1533. St. Luke painting madonna. Vienna Art Historical Museum. Detail showing guiding hand of St.Luke sketching portrait of madonna on a piece of parchment. He uses a chiseled silver point stylus (forerunner of lead pencil).

INDEXED UNDER
Gossaert, Jan
Artist at work
Silver point
Parchment
Date file 1475-1525
Angel
Devotion

THE BETTMANN ARCHIVE

Typical card from The Bettmann Visual Index with picture analysis and indication of cross references.

977.

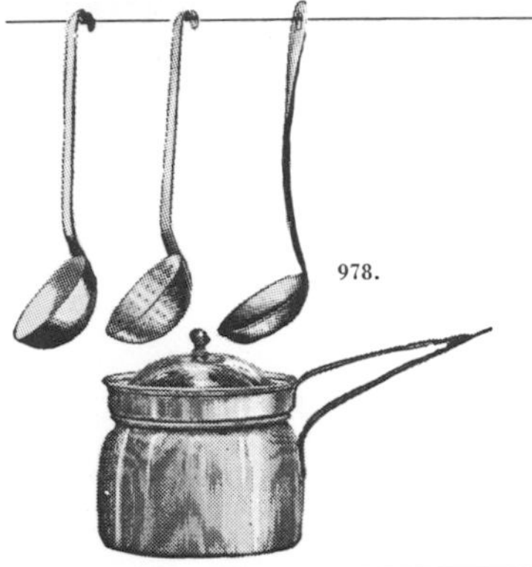

978.

979.

Kitchens

980. Cavemen Prepare Meal.

981. Indians Broil Fish.

982. Hostelry Kitchen in the French Provinces, ca. 1780.

983. Family Gathered in Colonial Kitchen.

984.

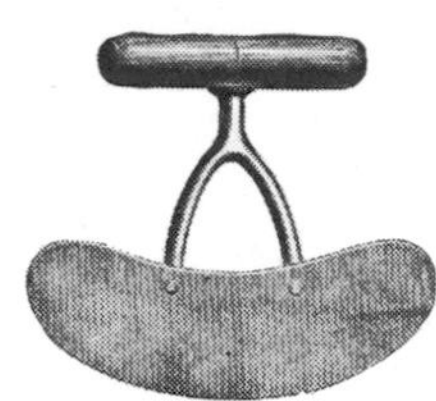

985.

986.

"Her dress was always clean and neat,
Her face was never nasty;
She always wash'd her hands before
She made an apple pasty."

987.

988. Fireplace Cooking.

989. U. S. Housewife, ca. 1880.

990. Well Equipped Shaker Kitchen.

991. Dismayed Housewife Faces Dishes.

992. A Hot Cook.

993.

994.

995.

996. Prairie Meal.

997. Mixing Cake Batter.

998. Busy Kitchen before Holiday.

999. Kitchen with Water Pump.

1000. Slum Kitchen.

EGYPT

1001. Gold Pectoral Representing Spirit of King Tutankhamen.

1002. Sphinx and Pyramid.

1003. Nefertiti.

1004.

1005. Papyrus Scroll: The Book of Death.

1006. Mother's Hairdo.

1007. Archers.

1008. Sphinx.

1009. Scribes Recording King's Command.

1010. Osiris on Throne.

1011. Wildcat in Papyrus Thicket.

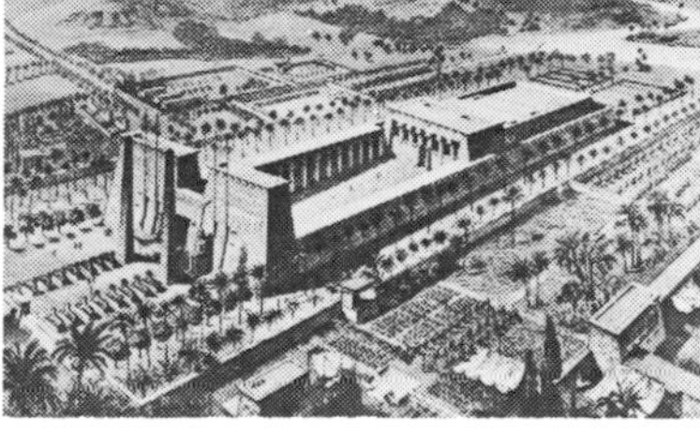

1012. Reconstruction of the Temple at Edfu.

1013. Female Musicians.

1014. Excavation, 1895.

EIFFEL TOWER

1015.

1016. Aerial View.

1017. Cartoon.

1018. View from Seine.

1019. Top.

1020. Under Construction.

1021. Famed U. S. Visitor

1022. Stairway.

1405.
Lillian Russell

1406.
Guide.

1407.
Toast.

1408.
Beachers.

1409.
Beavers.

1410.
Top Hats.

1411.
Supine.

1412.
Foreigners.

1413.
Floating.

1414.
Military Mission.

1415.
Macabre Duet.

1416.
Runners.

1404. Ferris Wheel at Chicago Columbia Exposition, 1893.

1417. Cogwheel.

GLASS

1419.

1420. Roman.

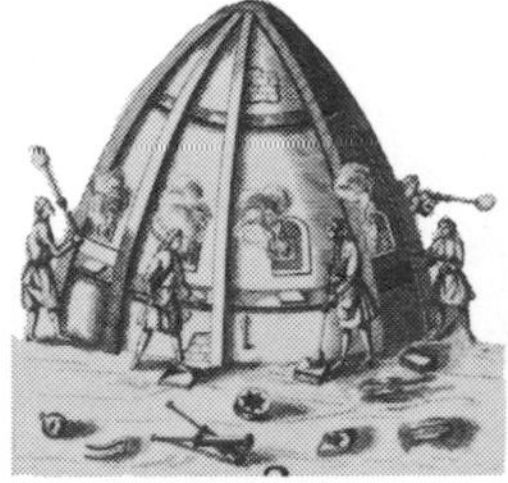

1421. Glass Furnace, 1530.

1422. Annealed Glass Packed.

1423. Glazier's Shop: Picture Framing.

1424. Blowers at Work.

1425. Child Labor in Glass Factory, 1870.

1426. Renaissance Goblet.

GLOBES

1427.

1428.

1429.

1430.

1431.

1432.

1433. Geographer. (Rembrandt)

1434. Mercator, Dutch Map Maker.

1435. Sky Globe.

GHOSTS

1436.

1437. English Graveyard Apparition.

1438. King Maymon, 1600.

1439. Scaly Underworld Character.

1440. Conjuring up Woman in White.

1441. Barnum Spectacle.

1442. Christopher Marlowe's Faust.

1443. Monster-Riding Ghost.

1444. Midnight Visitor.

1445. Winged Gremlin.

1234. Collier's Fashion Ad, 1905.

1235. Dummies waiting to be unwrapped.

Photo by Herbert Migdoll.

FIGUREHEADS

1236.

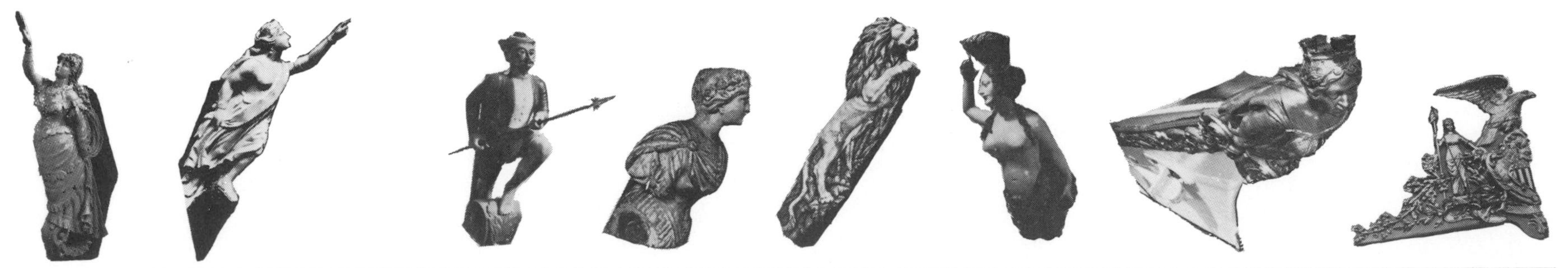

1237. 1238. 1239. 1240. 1241. 1242. 1243. 1244.

1245. "A Fire Engine steaming hot with readiness for public duty."

1246. Fire Extinguisher.

1247.

1248. Bucket Brigade, Old New York.

1249. Hand Pump.

1250. Alarm.

1251. Chicago in Flames.

1252. Female Fireman.

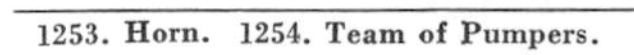

1253. Horn. 1254. Team of Pumpers.

1255. Third Alarm, N. Y., 1870.

1256. Ready for Action.

1257. Hat.

1258. Horse-Drawn.

1259. Fire Prevention.

1260. Prairie Fire.

1261. The Life of the Fireman.

1262. Fire Bucket.

1263. Front of a Firehouse.

1472. Hoplite.

1473. Head, 1600 B.C. 1474. Helen Abducted. 1475. Venus. 1476. Apollo. 1477. Back View. 1478. Laocoön. 1479. Discobolus. 1480. Socrates. 1481. Aristotle. 1482. Pericles. 1483. Oedipus and Sphinx.

1484. Parthenon.

1485. Piraeus, Harbor of Athens.

1486. Olympia Temple District.

1487. Caryatids.

1488. Lyre Player.

1489. Slave Market.

1490. Women Bearing Sacrifices.

1491. School Scene.

1492. Greek Phalanx.

1493.

GYMNASTICS

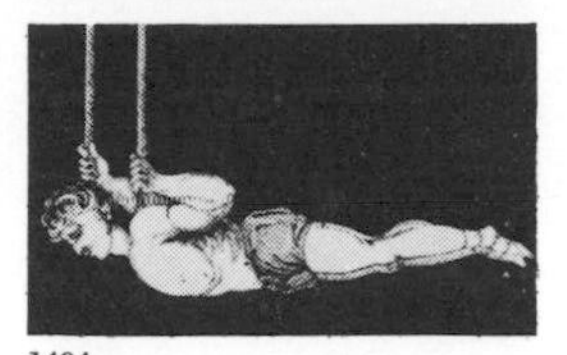

1494.

1495.

1496. Feat of Balance.

1497. High School Athletic Team, 1900.

1498. American Gym, 1860.

1499. Clubs.

GUNS

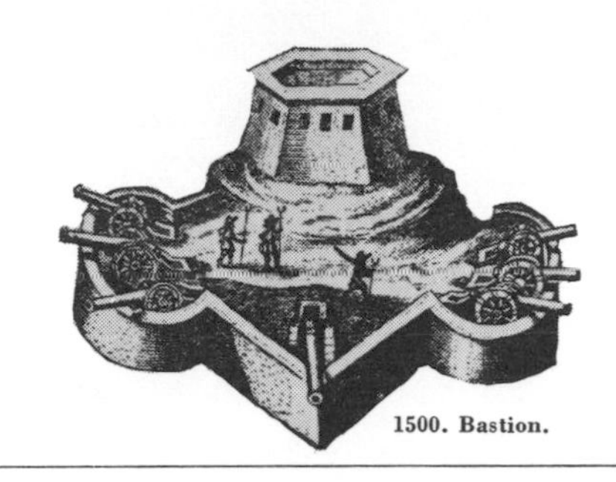

1500. Bastion.

1501. U.S. World War I.

1502. Cannon Used in Battle of New Orleans.

1503. Revolutionary War.

1504. Outlaw's Holster.

1505.

1506. English, 1850.

1507. 17th Century Siege Gun.

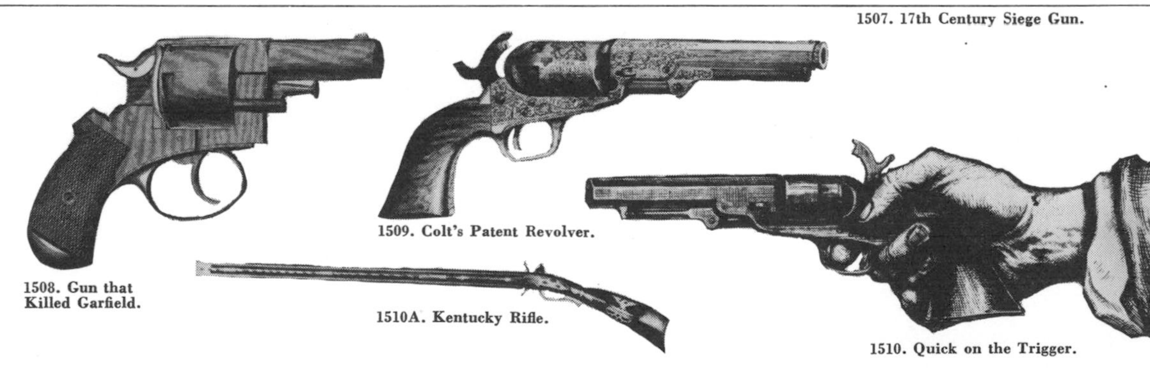

1508. Gun that Killed Garfield.

1509. Colt's Patent Revolver.

1510A. Kentucky Rifle.

1510. Quick on the Trigger.

GRINDING

1511. Amor Sharpens Arrow.

1512. Nose to Grindstone.

1513. Itinerant.

1514.

1515. Arabs.

1516. Swedes.

1517. Italian.

1518. Factory.

For complete, analytical subject index turn to page 221.

1149-1174

1149. Middle Class. 1150. Royalty.

1151. Silhouette of American Family, 1839.

1152. Mother's Birthday.

1153. Trouble.

1154. Biedermeier Family.

1155. Virginia Planter, 1845.

1156. Prosperous New Yorker.

1157. Father Reading Aloud.

1158. European Middle Class, 1850's.

1159. Swiss Family Musicale.

1160. Old Folks at Home.

1161. Status.

1162. Frontier.

1163. Suspended Family.

1164.

1165.

1166.

1167.

1168.

1169.

1170. Family.

1171.

1172.

1173. Sampler.

1174. Parents repose thanks to "Glass Covers for Noisy Children."

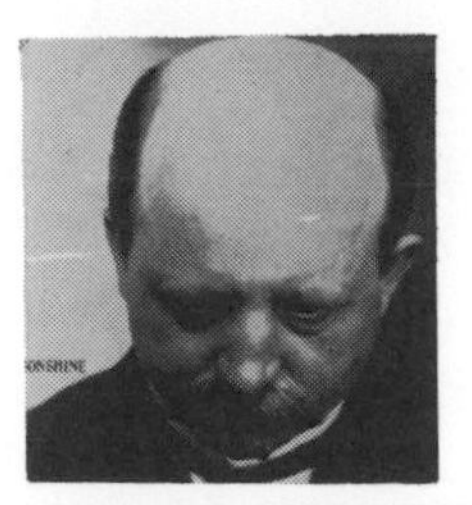

1536. Billiard Ball.

1537. Towering Wig.

1538. Pumpkin Haircut.

1539. Grenadiers Grooming Pigtails.

1540. Receding Hairline.

1541. Amazing Tonic.

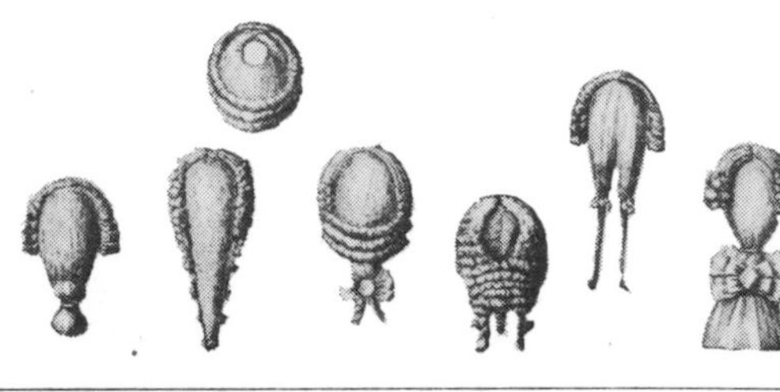

1542. Types of 18th Century English Wigs.

1543. Cave Shave.

1544. Haircutter. Greek Clay Figure.

1545. Tweezers, Kenya.

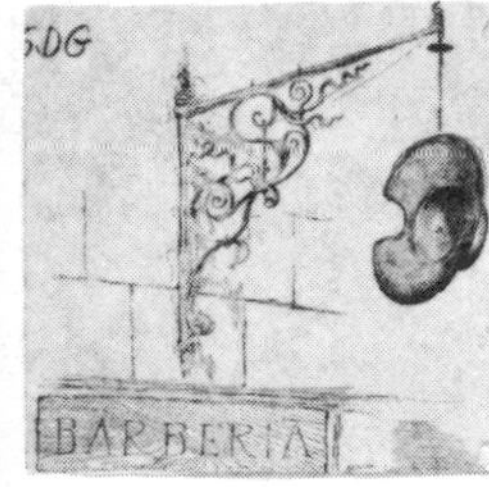

1546. Barber Trade Sign.

1547. Shampoo

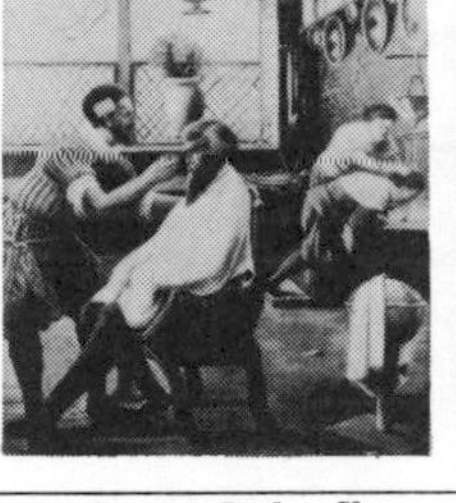

1548. German Barber Shop.

1549. Powdering Wig.

1550. Shaving Mug.

1551. Pedal-Razor.

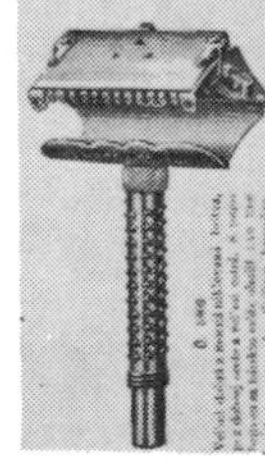

1552. Gillette.

1553. Barber Supply Catalogue.

1554. Barber Shop, Centennial Exhibit, 1876.

1555. Country Barber: Haircut, 1905.

1556. Tonsorial Bargains.

1557. Record.

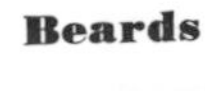

Beards

1558. Mesopotamia.

1559. Arabian Nights.

1560. Barbarossa Beard Grows after his Death.

1561. Figaro.

1562. Peter the Great has Russian beards cut.

Beard Types, 1880's.

1563. 1564. 1565. 1566.

1567.

1568. The Handle Bar Mustache.

HANDS

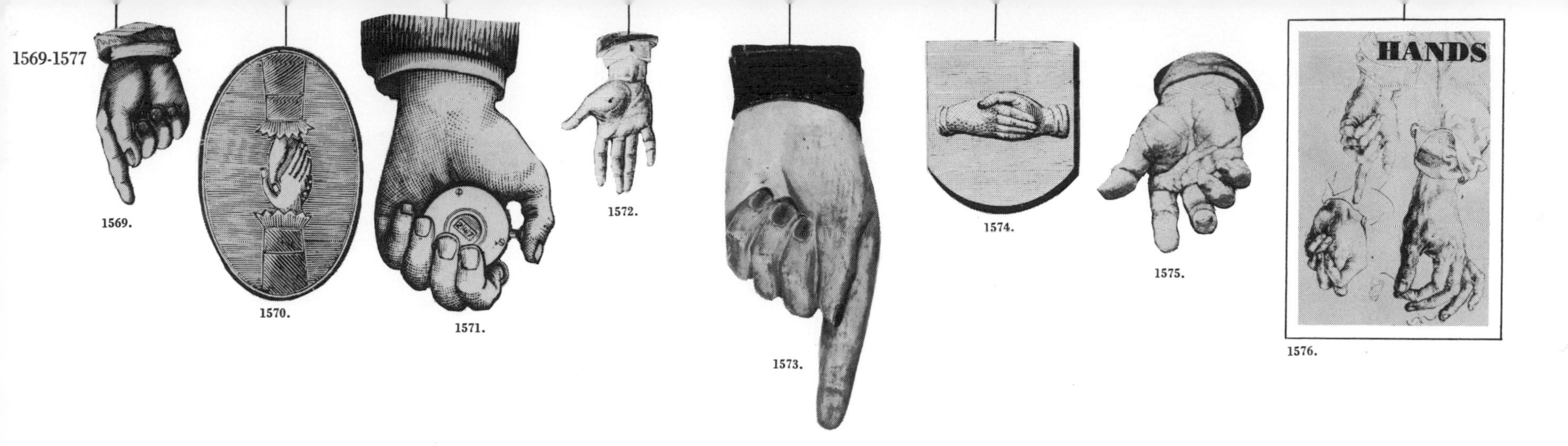

1569. 1570. 1571. 1572. 1573. 1574. 1575. 1576.

HATS

1577. The Wheel of Fashion.

HATS: WOMEN

1578. Sugar Loaf.

1579. Cashmere Turban, Empire.

1580. Male Milliner.

1581. Ostrich.

1582. Hat Serves as Rain Protector.

1583.

1584. Victorian.

1585. Privacy Hat.

Hollywood Hat Fashions

1586.

1587.

1588.

1589.

1590.

1591.

1592.

HATS: MEN

1593. Turban.

1594. Cap.

1595. Bellini.

1596. Nelsonian.

1597. Rothschild.

1598. Dude.

1599. Baron.

1600. Franz Josef.

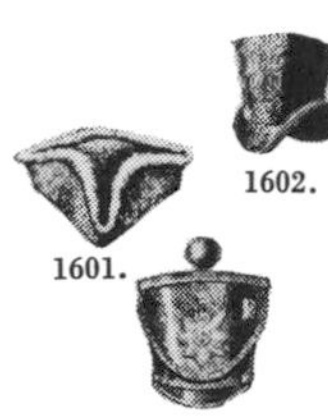

1601. 1602. 1603.

1604.

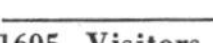

1605. Visitors.

1606. Feathered.

1607. Hat with Cigar Shelf.

1608. High Style Caller.

1609. Patent Hat.

1610. Head Measuring.

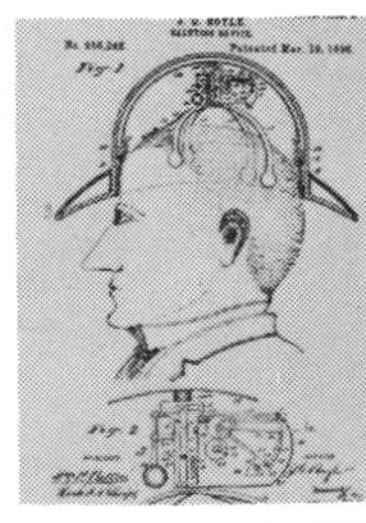

1611. Patent Drawing.

1612. Two-Wheeled London Hat Ad.

HEADACHES

1613. Hang-over.

1614. Zores.

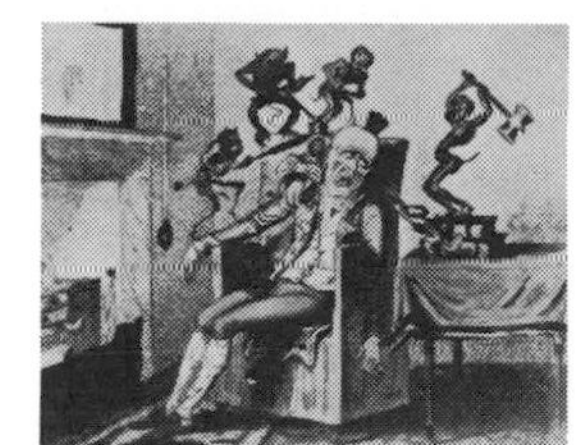
1615. Devils Splitting Skull.

1616. Sufferer.

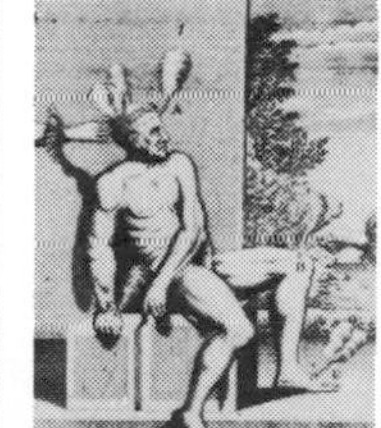
1617. Moxa Burning.

1618. Wet Compress.

1619. Worries.

1620. Migraine.

HEARTS

1621. Galen Explains Heart.

1622. Heart Solidified.

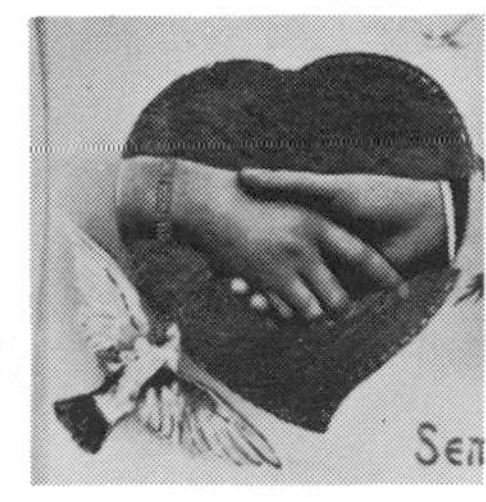
1623. Lovers' Greeting.

1624. Frilly Valentine.

1625. Queen.

1626. Dreams.

1627. Medallion.

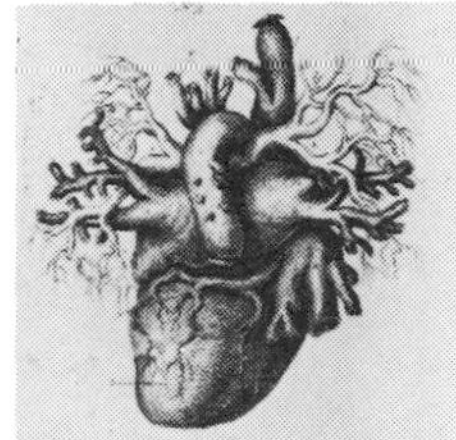
1628. Anatomical.

1629. 1630.

HEATING

1631. Victorian Fireplace.

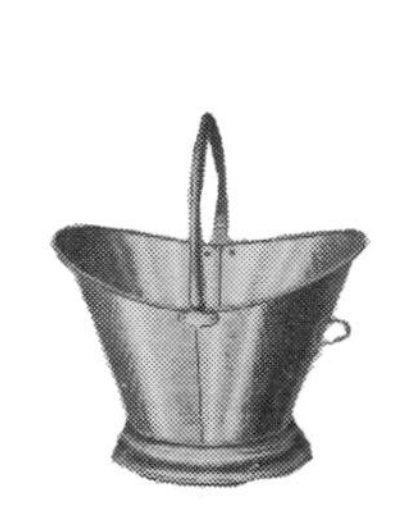
1632. Bucket.

1633. Coal Sifter.

1634. Chimney Sweep.

1635. Medieval Hot Water Kettle.

1636. Bellows.

1637. Potbellied.

1638. Open Fire, 1450.

1639. Log Fire Story Telling.

1640. Smoky Stove.

1641. New England Fireside.

1642. High Pressure—Its Dangers.

1643. Asbestos Cover for Steam Boiler.

1644. Valentine's Day. The Grand Finale.

1645. Old-New Year.

1646. Caller.

1647.

1648. Lacy Valentine.

1649. Children's Card.

1650. Cheerleader.

1651. St. Patrick's Day Parade, New York City, 1860.

1652. Easter Egg Rolling, White House.

1653. Russian Easter Eggs.

1654.

1655. Painting Easter Eggs. Colored Litho.

1656. Independence Day on the Village Green, 1840.

1657. Crowds Watching Fireworks (Winslow Homer).

1658. The Glorious Fourth: Garden Party.

1659. Village Picnic.

1660.

1661. The First Thanksgiving Feast.

1662. Turkey Shooting on the Frontier.

1663. Gift to Governor.

1664. Praying Pilgrims at Plymouth, 1621.

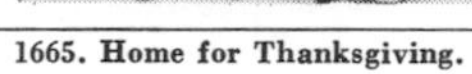

1665. Home for Thanksgiving.

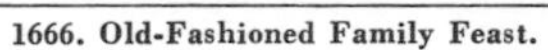

1666. Old-Fashioned Family Feast.

1667. Ducking for Apples.

1668. Pumpkin.

1669.

1670.

1671. Horse-laugh.

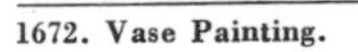

1672. Vase Painting.

1673. Assyrian.

1674. Trojan Horse.

1675. Trotter.

1676. Lucky.

1677. At the Longchamp Races.

1678. Clearing the First Hurdle.

1679. Down the Homestretch.

1680. Jockey.

1681. American Race Course, ca. 1870.

1682. Sulky Race, 1876.

1683. Indians Catching Wild Horses.

1684. New York Livery Stable.

1685. A Friend from S.P.C.A.

1686. Neck 'n Neck.

1687. Medieval Vet.

1688. Horse Gets Enema.

1689. Mazeppa Bound to Wild Horse.

1690. Military Exercise.

1691. Easy as Knowing How.

1692. Barnum Horse Act.

1693.

1694.

1695. Carrousel Horses.

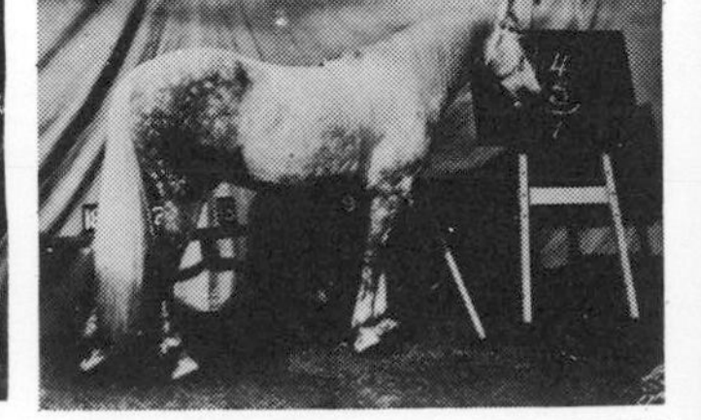

1696. Horse that Counts.

1697.

1698. First Washday.

1699.

1700. Cooperative Husband.

1701. Days of the Scrub Board.

1702. Hand-Powered Vacuum.

1703. Sweeper.

1704. Outside Vacuum.

1705. Dust Pan.

1706.

1707.

1708.

1709.

1710. Steam Washing Machine, 1872 Patent.

1711. On Hands and Knees.

1712. Hand-Washer, 1860.

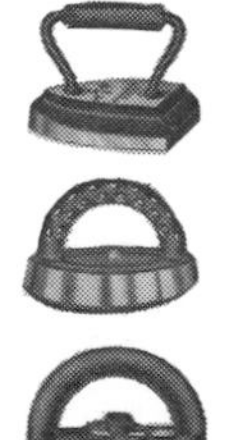

1713.

1714. 1715. 1716. 1717. 1718.

1719.

1720.

1721.

1722. Buffalo Hunt (Cave Drawing)

1723. Camouflage Hides Ostrich Hunter.

1724. Lion Hunt (Assyrian Relief).

1725. Hunter Caught.

1726. Finn Spears Bear.

1727. Hunt Club.

1728. Huntsman (Spanish Tile).

1729. Wading.

1730. Fox Hunt. England, 1840.

1731. Moose Call.

1732.

1733. Antlers with 69″ Spread.

1734. Hunter's Water Bike.

1735.

1736.

1737. Duck Hunting, England, 1820.

1738. Shooting Buffalo.

1739. Indians on Buffalo Hunt.

1740. Trophies of African Safari.

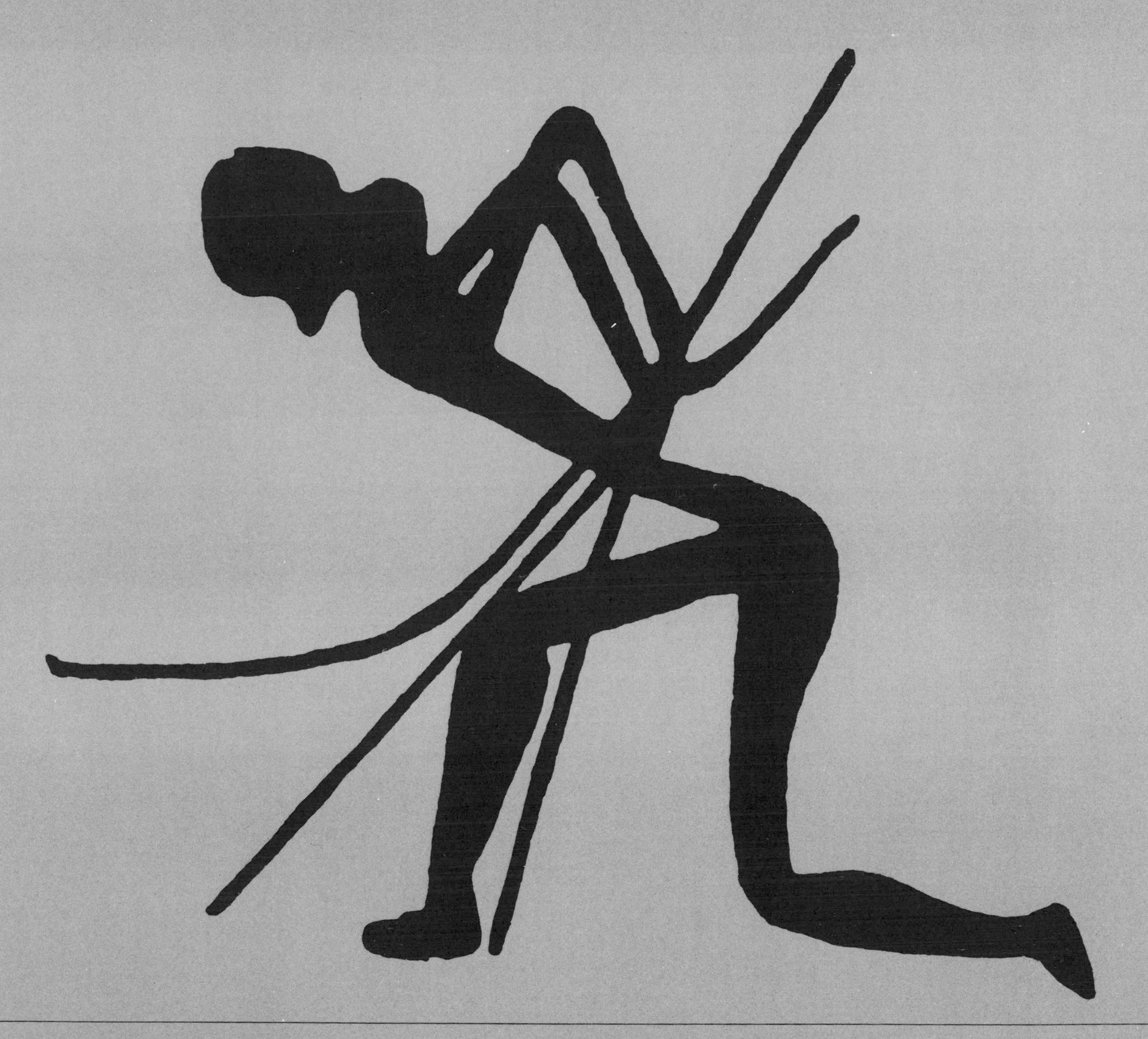

1741. Primitive Huntsman, Valltorta, Spain.

For complete, analytical subject index turn to page 221.

ICE

1742. Eskimo Building an Igloo.

1743. Ice cut from Maine lakes arrives in the West Indies.

1744. Ice Wagon.

1745. Iceman: A Freeze.

1746. Water Cooler.

1747.

1748. Ice Carriers.

1749. Ice Box.

1750. Ice Maker.

1751. Cutting Ice on the Hudson River.

INDIGESTION

1752. Gastric Pain (Cruikshank).

1753. Devils Cause Cramps.

1754. Relief.

1755. Return from Dinner.

1756. Stomach Pump.

1757. Barber Gives Enema.

1758. Excruciating.

1759. Pompeian Villa.

1760. Roman Atrium.

1761. House of a Patrician.

1762. Walpole's Study.

1763. Frontier Interior.

1764. Puritan Log Cabin.

1765. Recamier's Boudoir.

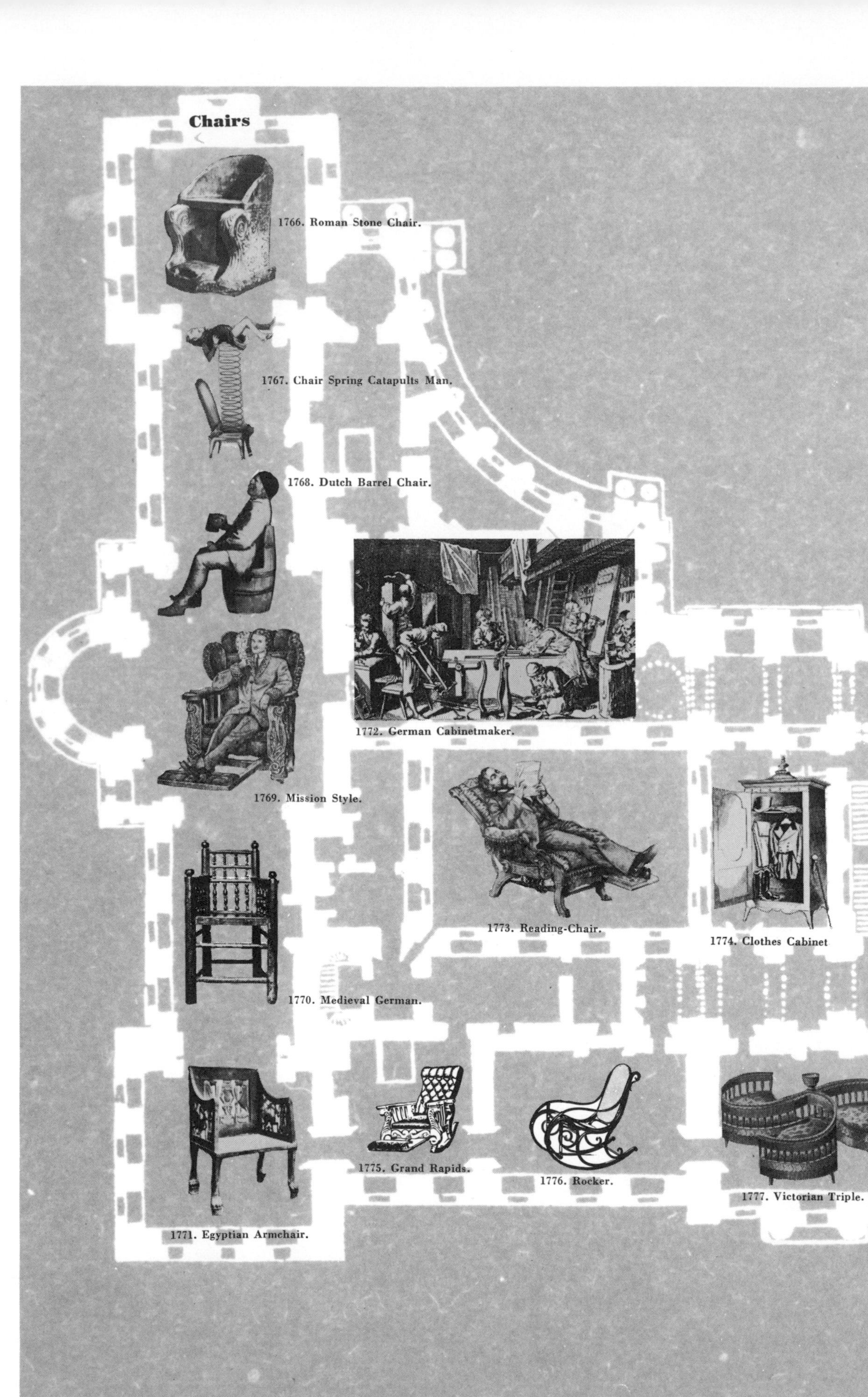

1766. Roman Stone Chair.

1767. Chair Spring Catapults Man.

1768. Dutch Barrel Chair.

1769. Mission Style.

1770. Medieval German.

1771. Egyptian Armchair.

1772. German Cabinetmaker.

1773. Reading-Chair.

1774. Clothes Cabinet

1775. Grand Rapids.

1776. Rocker.

1777. Victorian Triple.

1778. Pompeian Villa.

1779. Castle's Hall

1780. Cabinetmaker.

1799. Floor Plan of Blenheim Castle.

Beds

1787. Baldachin

1788. Louis XIV.

1789. Bed of Ware.

1790. Ad, 1905.

1791. Stands.

1792. Rack.

1781. Cabinetmaker Planes Wood.

1782. Wardrobe.

1783. Between Chairs.

4. Craftsman.

1785. Moorish Den.

1786. Biedermeier Girl's Room.

Bedrooms

1793. Sleeping Tent, Assyrian King.

1794. Gilded Age, Carved.

1795. Four-Poster.

1796. Trundle Bed.

1797. Victorian Bedroom.

1798. Hollywood Bed.

IRON

1800. Primitive Foundry, Africa.

1801. Colonial Ironmonger.

1802. Founding—Casting, 18th Century.

1803. Cannon Ball Makers, English, 1805.

1804. Mechanized Rolling Mill.

1805. Tempering.

1806. Foundryman.

1807. Man-powered Ladle.

1808. Iron Hammer, ca. 1850.

1809. Testing Steel Rods.

1810. Bessemer Process.

1811. Casting.

1812. Filling a Crucible.

1813. Chain Forge.

1814.

ITCHING

1815. Scalp Cleaning.

1816. Itch (Rowlandson)

1817. Family Cooperation.

1818. Itching Party. Napoleonic Army.

1819. God Bless the Duke....

To comfort his shepherds who were infested with vermin, the Duke of Argyll equipped his estate with "Scratching Posts." Every time a shepherd scratched himself on one of these poles, he exclaimed with relief (temporary no doubt), "God Bless the Duke of Argyll."

1821. Caesar.

1840. Roman Forum.

1839. Piazza della Porta.

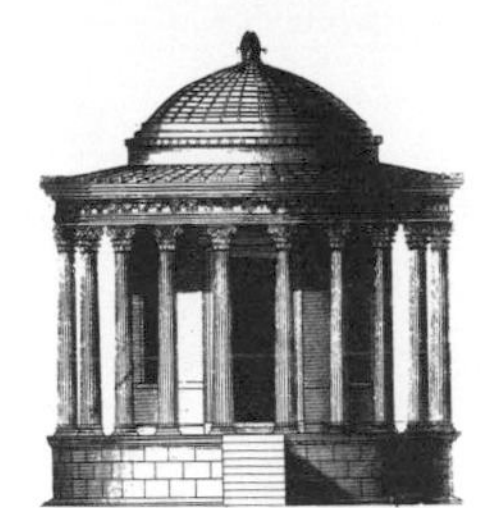

1838. Temple of Vesta.

1837. Garibaldi.

1822. Milan.

1823. Ferrara.

1824. Florence.

1825. Pisa.

1826. Medici.

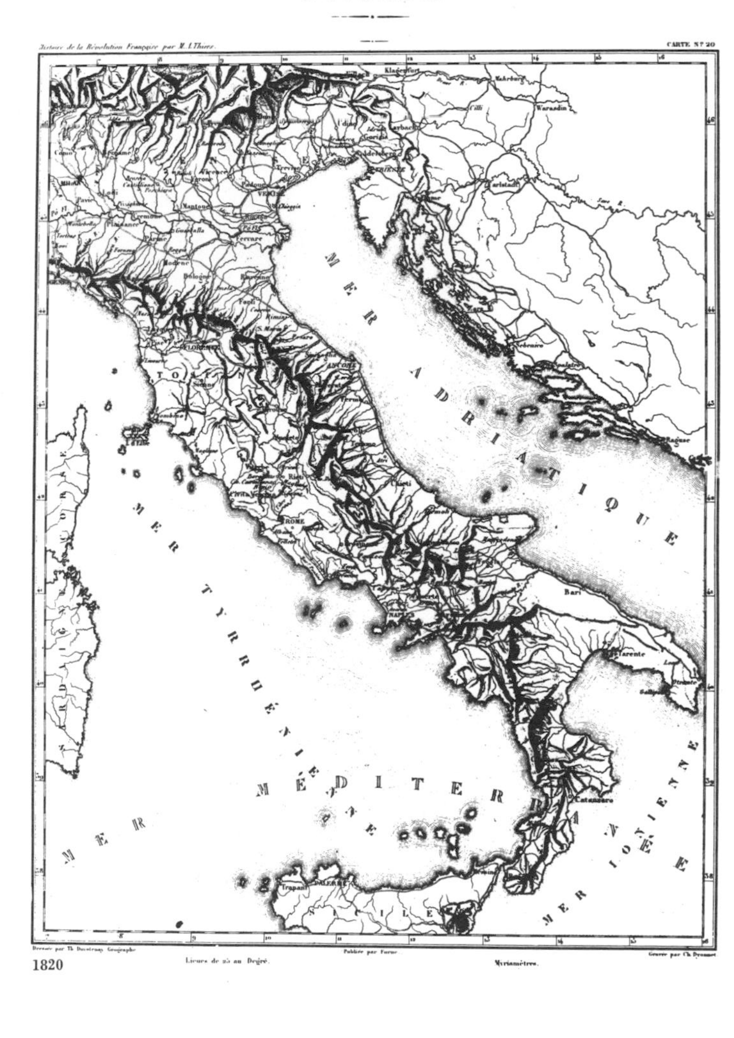

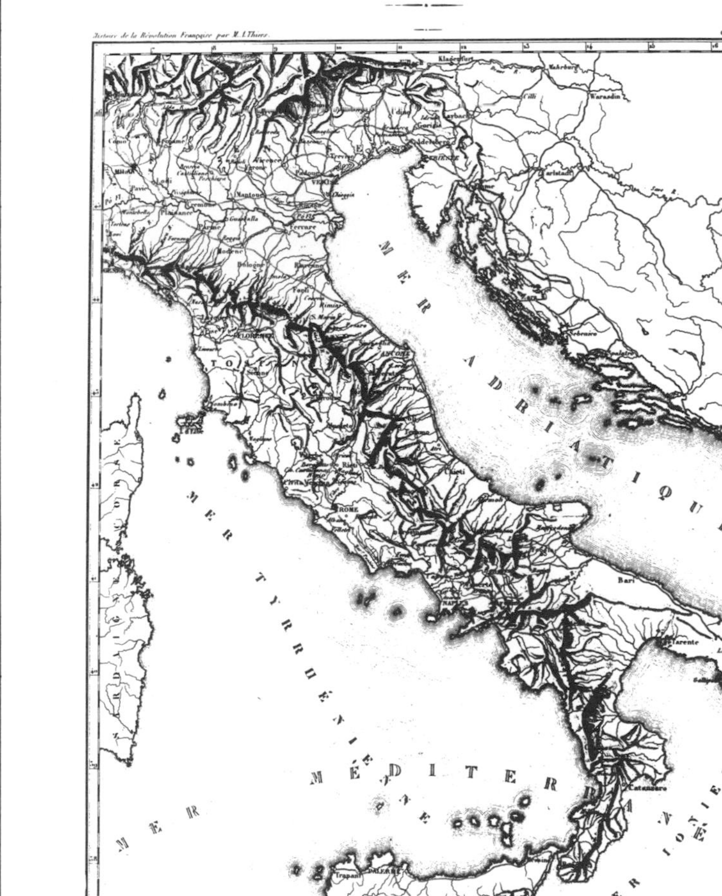

1820

1836. San Angelo.

1835. St. Peter's.

1834. Spoleto Ruins.

1833. Trevi Fountain.

1832. Pantheon.

1827. Legion Emblem.

1828. Via Appia.

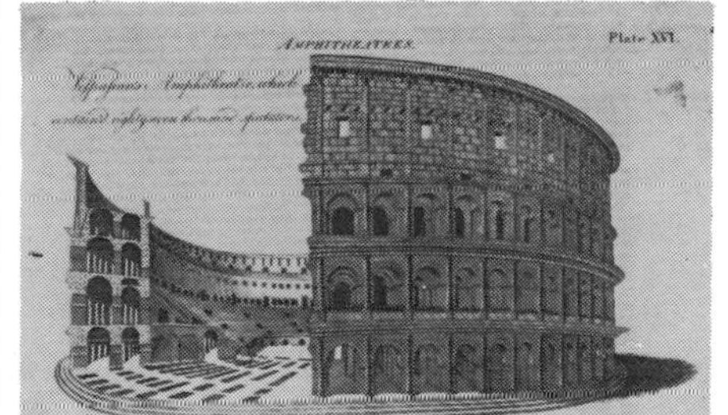

1829. Amphitheatre for 80,000 Spectators.

1830. Mosaic.

1831. Dome of St. Peter's.

1841. Japanese Sulphur Baths at Kusatsu which were reputed to cure all ailments except love.

1842. 1843. 1844. 1845. 1846. 1847. 1848. 1849. 1850. 1851. 1852. 1853. 1842.

1854. 1855. 1856. 1857. 1858. 1859. 1860. 1861. 1862. 1863. 1864. 1865.

1854. Philadelphia, 1765.

1855. Boston, 1774.

1856. Over-long Paper.

1857. Colonial Town Crier.

1858. Leading Magazines of 1900.

1859. News-Woman.

1860. News via Pictures.

1861. Extra.

1862. Newsboy.

1863. Editorial Room, N.Y. Sun.

1864. Post Cover, 1907.

JEWELRY

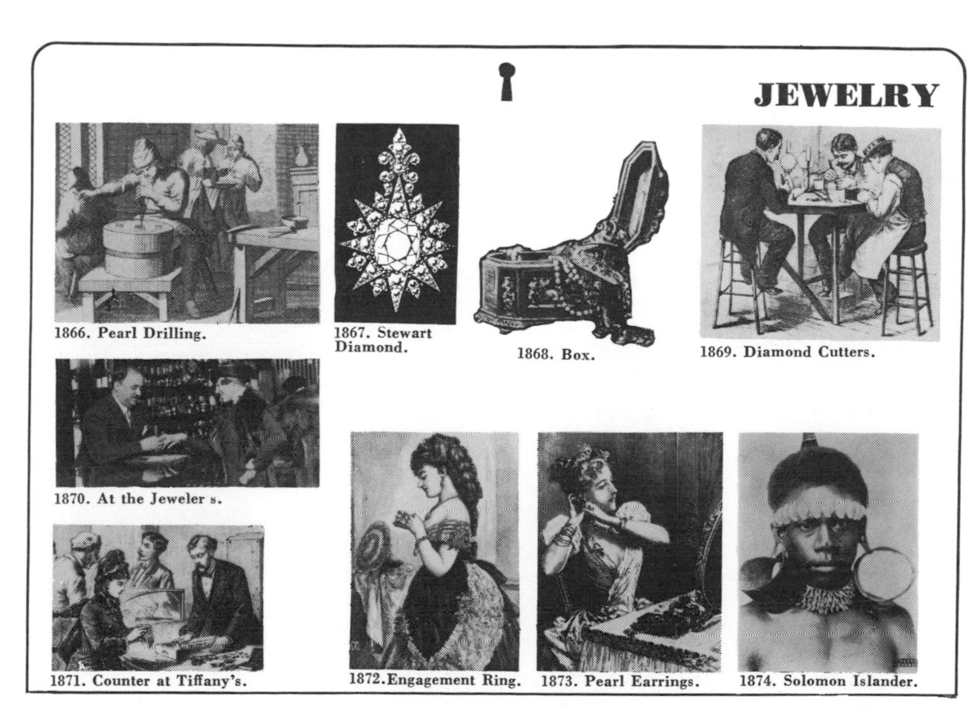

1866. Pearl Drilling.

1867. Stewart Diamond.

1868. Box.

1869. Diamond Cutters.

1870. At the Jeweler s.

1871. Counter at Tiffany's.

1872. Engagement Ring.

1873. Pearl Earrings.

1874. Solomon Islander.

KEYS

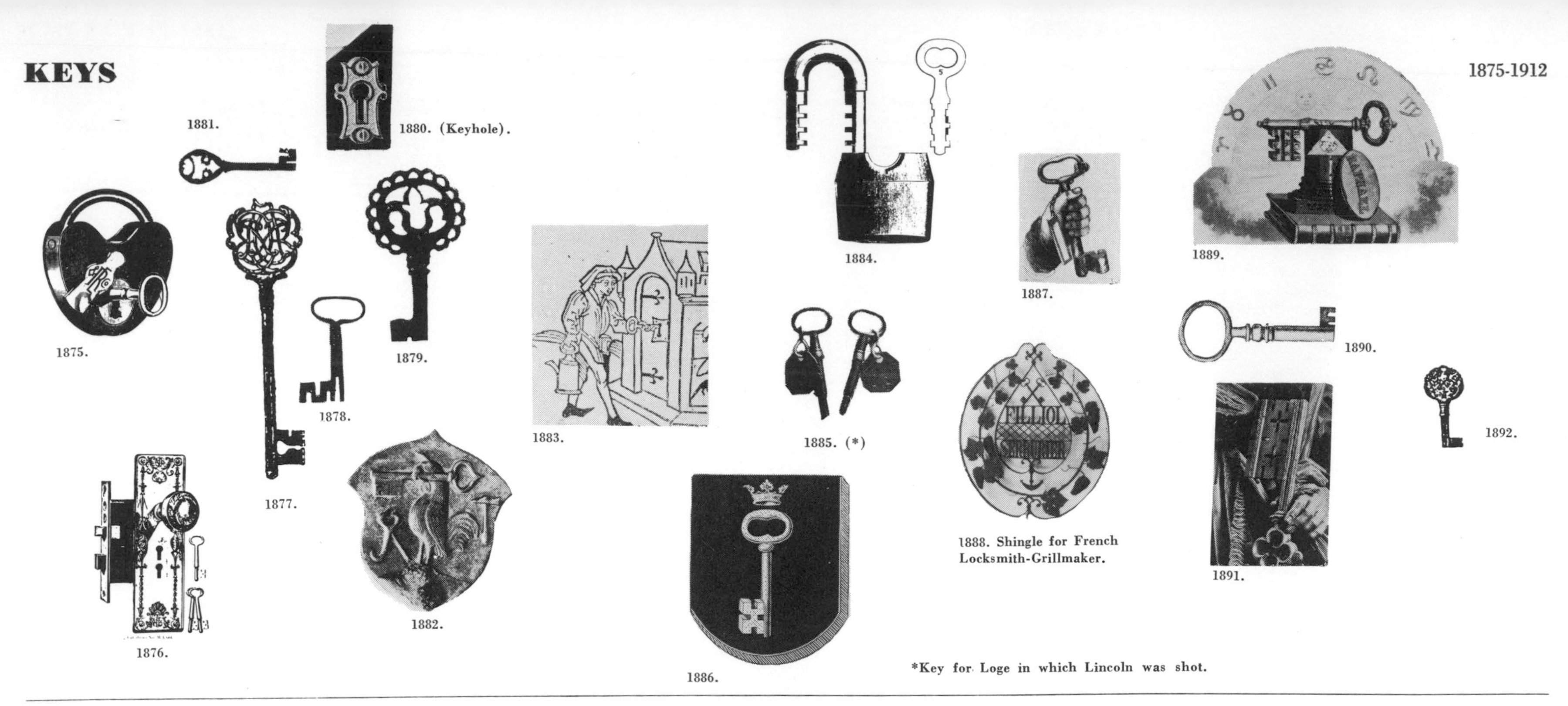

1875. 1876. 1877. 1878. 1879. 1880. (Keyhole). 1881. 1882. 1883. 1884. 1885. (*) 1886. 1887.

1888. Shingle for French Locksmith-Grillmaker.

1889. 1890. 1891. 1892.

*Key for Loge in which Lincoln was shot.

KNIGHTS

1893. 1894. 1895. 1896. 1897. 1898. 1899. 1900. 1901. 1902. 1903. 1904.

1905. Battle of Bannockburn, 1314.

1906. Medieval Tournament.

1907. 1908. 1909. 1910.

1911. Cigar Box Label.

1912.

1913. Albrecht Durer: Sketch for the famed etching, Knight, Death and Devil.

see also: Erotica p.68; Hearts p.95

For complete, analytical subject index turn to page 221.

1914.

1915. Labor Day Parade Passing Union Square, N. Y., 1905.

1916. Cruelty in English Mill.

1917. Children in Wallpaper Factory.

1918. American Machinist, 1875.

1919. Metal Punching.

1920. Recess.

1921. Child Labor.

1922. Textile Mill.

1923. Pick and Shovel.

Attention Workingmen!
MASS-MEETING
TO-NIGHT, at 7.30 o'clock,
HAYMARKET, Randolph St., Bet. Desplaines and Halsted.

Achtung, Arbeiter!
Große
Massen-Versammlung
Heute Abend, 8 Uhr, auf dem
Heumarkt,

1924. Haymarket Meeting.

1925. Before the Grievance Committee.

1926. Heading of Union Diploma.

1927. Meeting of Molly Maguires.

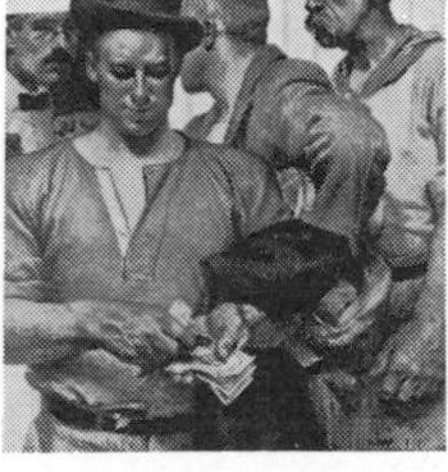

1928. Payday, 1903.

1929. Salesgirl.

1930. Pickets, 1907.

1931.

1933.

1934. Greek Oil Lamp.

1935. Candle-Dipper, 18th Century.

1936. Candlestick.

1937. Work Lamp, 1830.

1938. Street Torch.

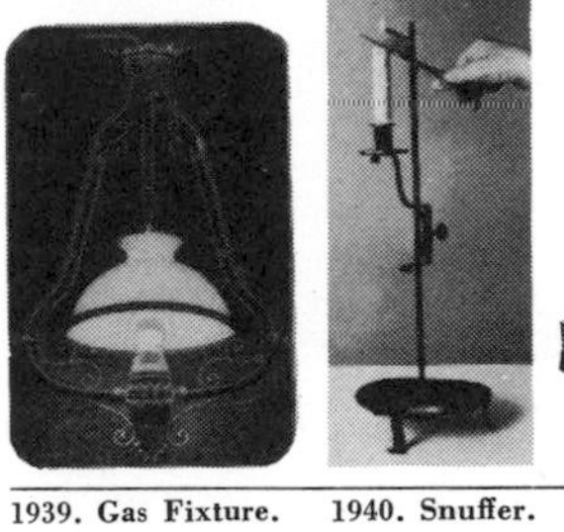

1939. Gas Fixture. 1940. Snuffer.

1941.

1942. Family Reading.

1943. Stable.

1944. Coach. 1945. 1946.

1947. Edison's Incandescent Lamp.

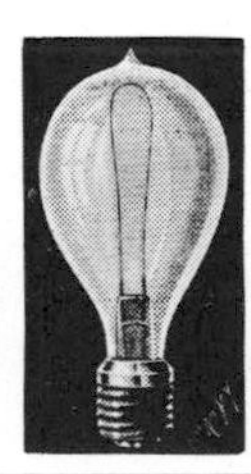

1948.

1949. Table, 1908.

1950. The New Bargain: Electricity.

Lighthouses

1951. Pharos, Egypt.

1952. Warden of the Seas.

1953. Eddystone Inundated.

1954. Beacons.

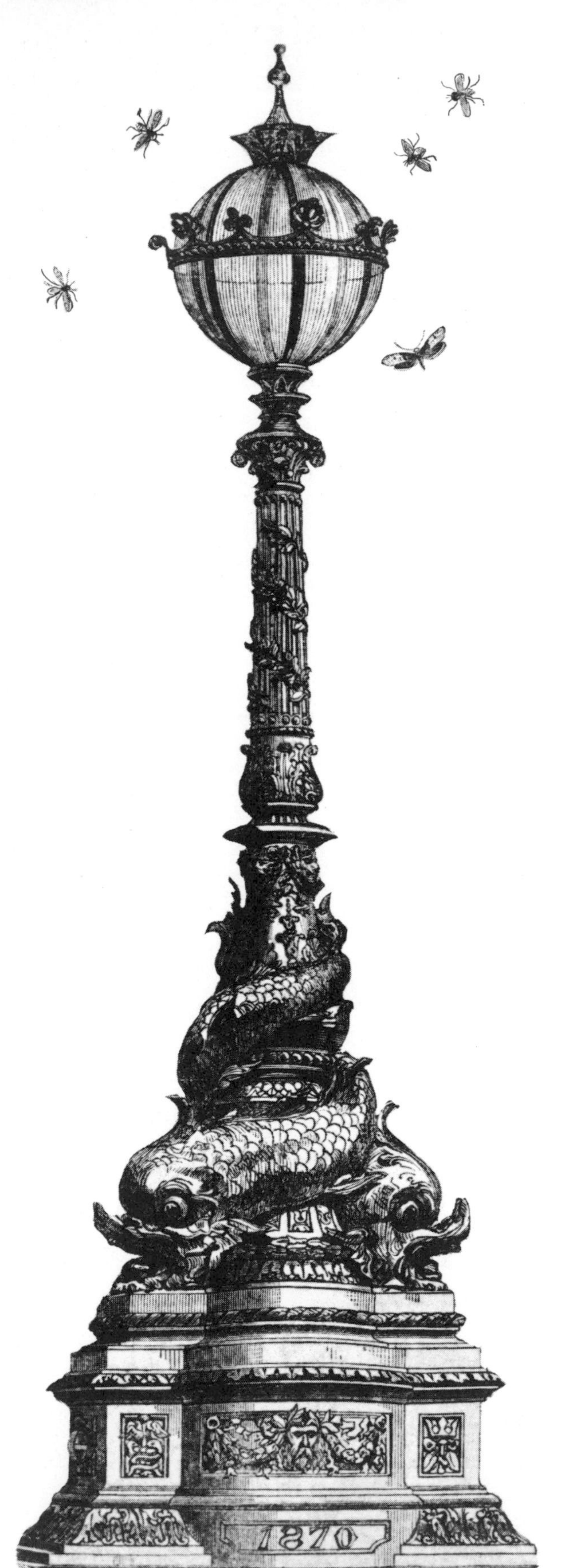

1932. Lamp on the Thames Embankment, London.

1955. Proposed Lighting for The Statue of Liberty.

With malice toward none; with charity for all; with firmness in the right as God gives us to see the right, let us strive on to finish the work we are in, to bind up the nation's wounds; to care for him who shall have borne the battle and for his widow and his orphan— to do all which may achieve and cherish a just and a lasting peace among ourselves, and with all nations.

1956. 1957. Passage from Second Inaugural Address.

1958. Log Cabin.

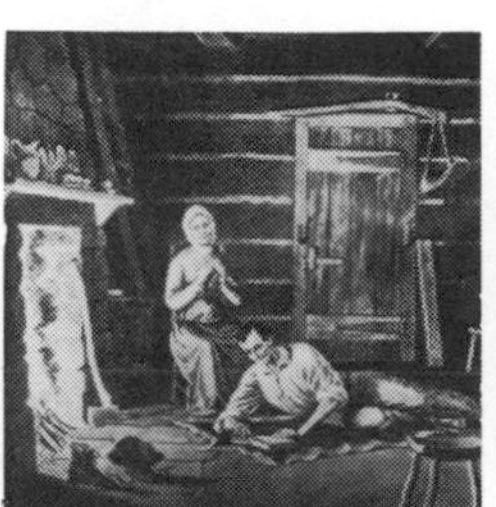

1959. Reading by Fireside.

1960. Rail Splitter.

1961. Surveyor.

1962. Home in Springfield.

1963. Douglas Debate.

1964. Farewell.

1965. First Inauguration.

A.

B.

C. D. E.

F.

G.

H.

I.

J.

1966. Civil War.

1967. Studying Military Dispatches.

1968. Emancipation Proclamation.

1969. Sketch, 1865.

1970. Gettysburg.

1971. Entry into Richmond.

1972. Assassination.

1973. Deathbed Scene. Sketch by Eyewitness.

1974. Catafalque.

Photo Biography

at left:

1978. Springfield, 1846. (A)
1979. Chicago, 1857. (B)
1980. Chicago, 1859. (C)
1981. Chicago, 1860. (D)
1982. New York, 1860. (E)
1983. August 9, 1863. (F)
1984. November 15, 1863. (G)
1985. February 9, 1864. (H)
1986. April 10, 1865. (I)
1987. April 10, 1865. (J)

1975. Memorial.

1976. Personal Articles.

1977. Family Dog.

1988.

1989.

1990. The Rail Splitter.

1991. Logger.

1992. Cutting Clapboards.

1993. Woodsman.

1994. New England Sawmill.

1999. Tree Design.

1995. American Lumber Mill.

1996. Cutting Redwood.

1997. Pedalled Rotary Saw.

1998. Load.

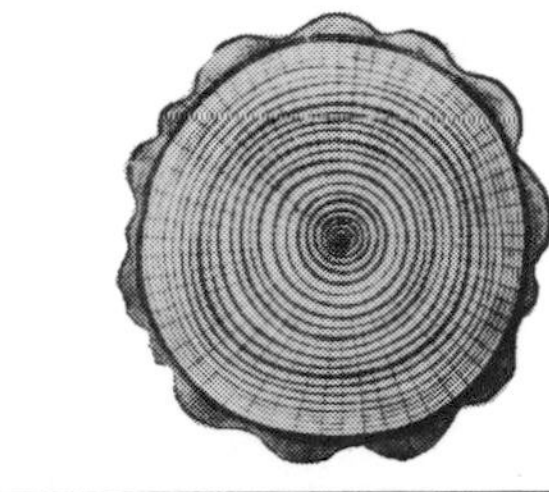

2000. Year Rings.

2001. American Lumberyard, 1820.

Log Cabins

2002.

2003. Frontier Home Repair: Boy caulking chinks in the walls of a log cabin.

2004. Blue Mountain Homestead.

2005. Pioneer Setting.

2006. Log Cabin, Mississippi.

2007. Arriving at Log Cabin, Texas, 1836.

2008.

2009.

2010. British Lion, Trafalgar Square.

2011. View of London in the 17th Century.

2012. London Bridge.

2013. Beefeater.

2014. View towards Parliament.

2015. Boswell and Johnson walking through Fleet Street, which appealed to the great lexicographer "in its very animatd appearance." So much did he see the world through the eyes of a Londoner, that he concluded: "The man who is tired of London is tired of life."

2016. Pomp and Circumstance in London: Opening of Parliament.

2017. Hyde Park, Sunday Afternoon.

2018. Traffic Stop.

2019. Whitechapel.

2020. Double-Decker.

2021. Hansom Cab.

2022. Eros, Picadilly.

2023. Royal Guards.

2024. The Baron's Proposal.

2025.

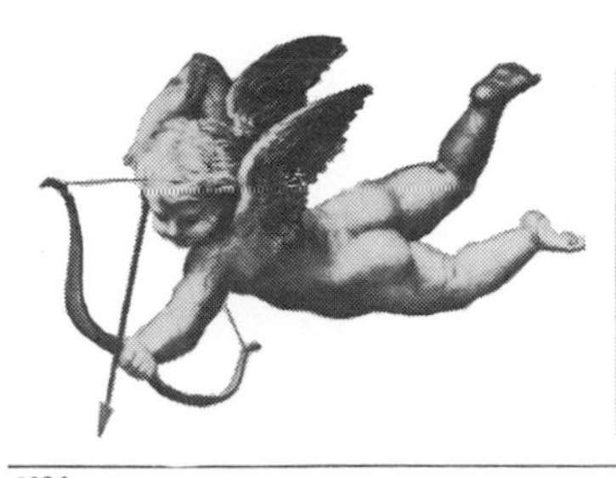
2026.

2027.

2028.

2029.

2030.

2031. Embrace (Greek Vase).

2032. Abduction (Roman Relief).

2033. Lover's Rose.

2034. Conjugal Love (Tapestry).

2035. Will You?

2036. In the Swing.

2037. He Loves Me.

2038. Newlyweds.

Love in Hollywood

2039. 2040. 2041. 2042. 2043. 2044. 2045. 2046. 2047.

The Kiss

2048. Rococo Group.

2049. Husband's Return.

2050. Park Bench.

2051.

2052.

John Held, Jr.'s flapper girl of the nineteen twenties, a flat-chested kid who rolled her stockings well above her knees and wore her skirts short enough to prove it, arrived on the scene only twenty years after the heyday of Charles Dana Gibson's delicate Gibson Girl. Her male counterpart wore bell-bottom trousers, spats, and vaselined hair parted in the middle, and played the ukelele.

For complete, analytical subject index turn to page 221.

2054. The Magician. (Rembrandt)
2055. Witches' Kitchen.
2056. Magic Medicine.
2057. Delphic.
2058. Astral Man.
2059. Ferreting out a Witch.
2060. Witch Burning.
2061. Magic Brew, 1508.
2062.
2063. Three Witches. (Fuesseli)
2064. Salem Witch Trial.
2065. Macbeth.
2066.
2067. Snake Charmer.
2068. Conjurer's Den.
2069. Faust Conjuring Devil.
2070. Palmistry.
2071. Horoscope.
2072. Optical Trick.
2073. Three-Headed Lady.
2074. Leon Harriman, Magician, 1900.
2075. Crystal Ball.
2076. Hat Trick.
2077. Master Magician.
2078. Mnemonic.
2079. Poster: Floating on Air.
2080. A Great Future.
2081. Country Fair Magician.
2082. Endless Paper.
2083. Ominous Prediction.
2084. Mind Reader, 1847.
2085. Manual of Tricks.
2086. Bottle Imp.
2087. Cabala.

MAIL

2088.

2089. U.S. Stamp, 1847.

2090. Air Mail, 1481.

2091. Mail Shoot.

2092. Medieval Lady

2093. Sorting Mail, 1770.

2094. Dropping Mailbags.

2095. Pony Express: St. Joseph to San Francisco.

2096. Poster.

2097. Chicago Mailman.

2098. Overloaded.

2099. U.S. Mail Truck.

2100. R.F.D.

2101. Cover: First Transatlantic Airmail, 1939.

2102. New York-Philadelphia Airmail, 1918.

MARKETS

2103. Phoenician Traders.

2104. Arab Market.

2105. Renaissance Italy.

2106. Crowds at a Medieval Fair.

2107. Fruit Market.

2108. New York Slums.

2109. Marketing, Washington, D.C.

2110.

2111. Cavemen Use Logs for Hauling.

2112. Egyptian Burden Carriers.

2113. Nineveh Slaves Move Monument.

2114. Stevedores, 1510.

2115. Cask Carriers, 1805.

2116. Japanese with Baskets.

2117. Unloading R. R. Car.

2118. Heavy Load, Turkey.

2119. Truck Maker's Trade Card.

2120. Freight Handlers.

2121. Stock Girl.

2122. Backbreaker.

MEAT

2123.

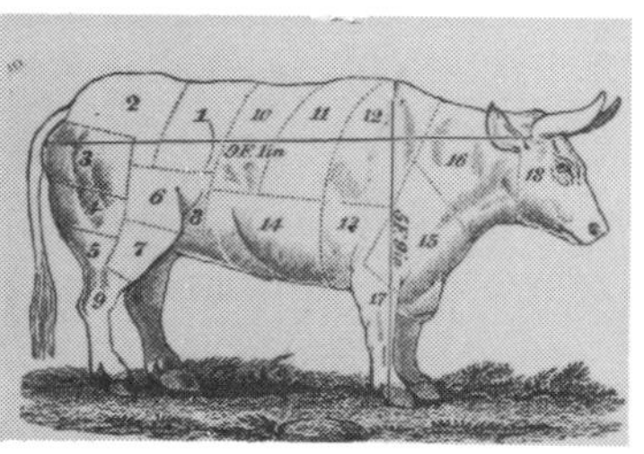

2124. Chart of Beef Cuts.

2125. Sausages*

2126. Meatman's Manual.

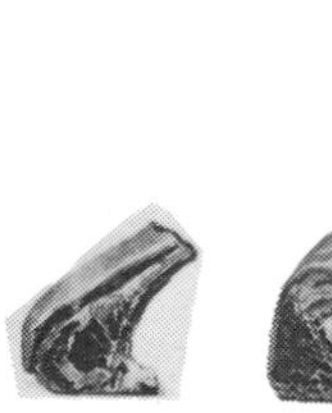

2127.

2128.

2129. Salting.

2130.

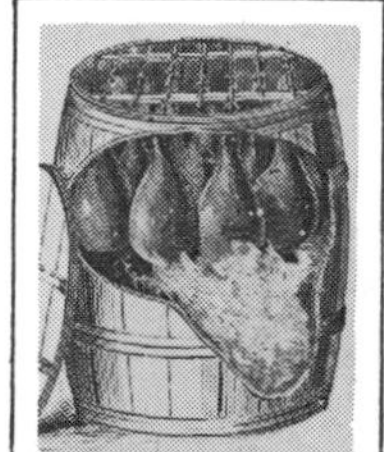

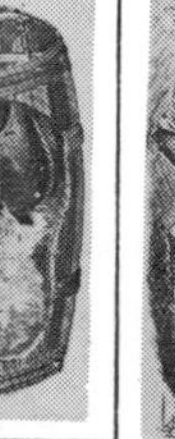

2131. Smoke Barrel.

2132. Plea for Good Cut.

2133. Bologna Butcher.

2134. Continuous Gutting.

2135. Butcher Shop (J. S. Mount).

2136. Frozen-Meat Market, Russia.

2137. Before the Days of Refrigeration.

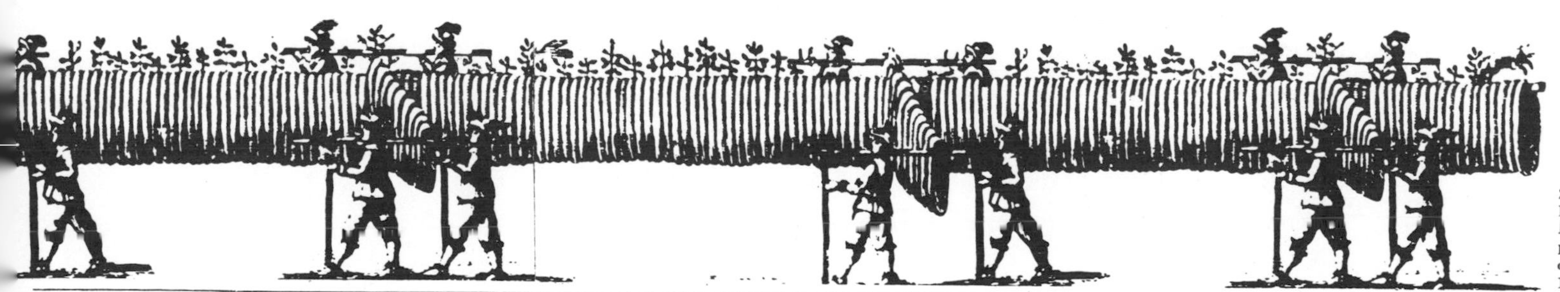

2138.
Butcher boys of Nuremberg produce largest piece of bologna, displayed in public pageant, 1683.

*First mass consumption of Frankfurters at Philadelphia Centennial, 1876.

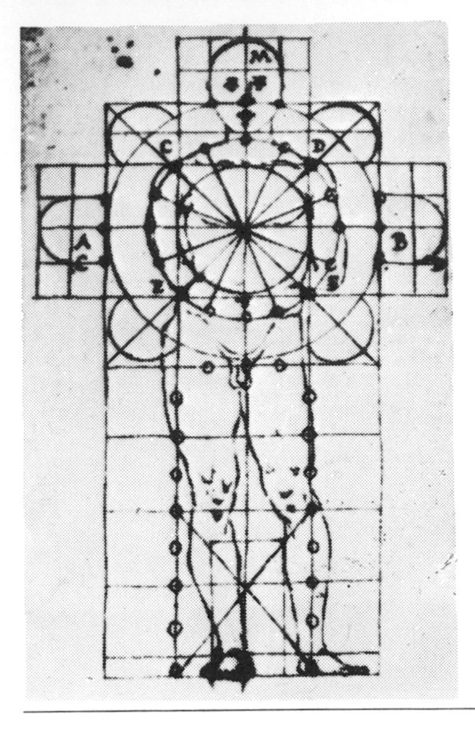

2161. Human Body Related to the Proportions of a Cathedral.

Doctor and Patient

2139. First Doctor.

2140. Egyptian Cripple.

2141. Shaman, Nigeria.

2142. Greek Doctor during Office Hours (Vase Painting).

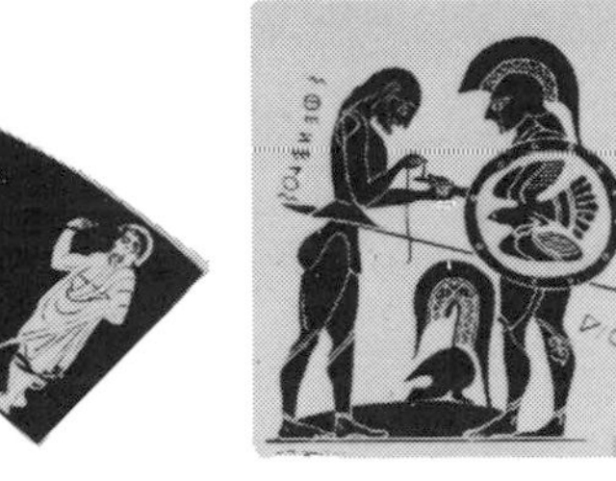

2143. Greek War Surgeon.

2144. Bonesetter, Trojan War.

2145. Urine Test.

2146. Doctor's Office, 1450.

2147. Physical, 1345.

2148. Leeches Suck Blood.

2149.

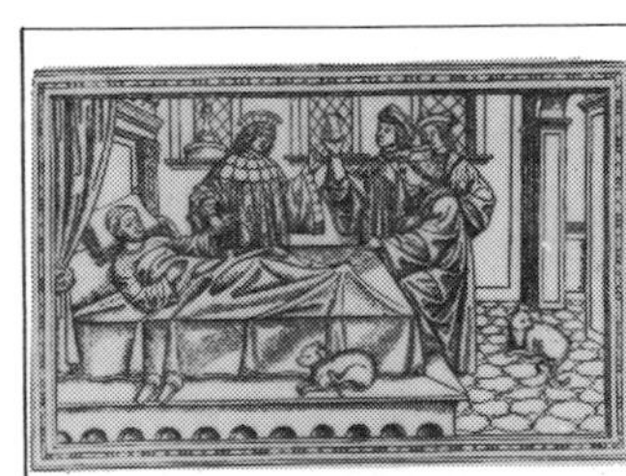

2150. Bedside Consultation, 1518.

2151. Arab Doctors Feeling Pulse of Fever-ridden.

2152. London Doctor Making House Calls.

2153. Saddle Bag Medicine.

2154. Wayside Diagnosis.

2155. Country Doc.

2156.

2157. Mountain Medico.

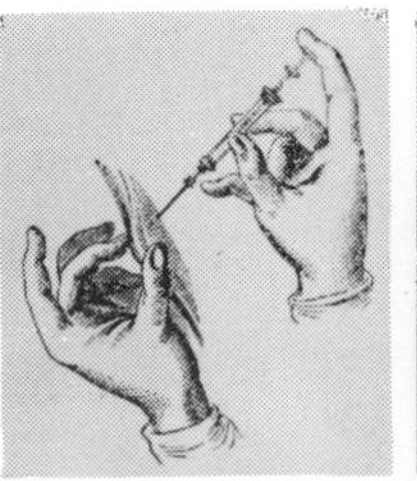

2158. Handling Syringe.

2159. Dr. Osler.

2160.

Anatomy

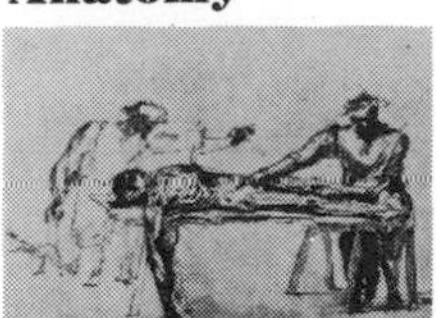

2162. Night Dissection.

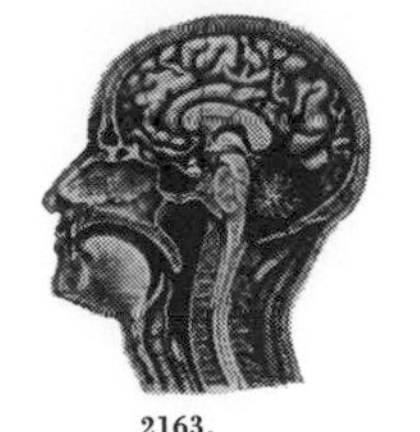

2163.

2164. Body Snatchers Robbing Grave.

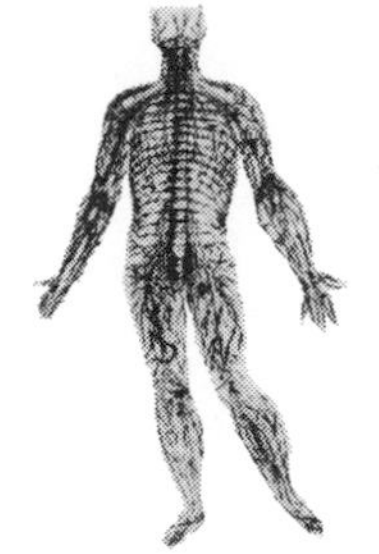

2165. Nerves.

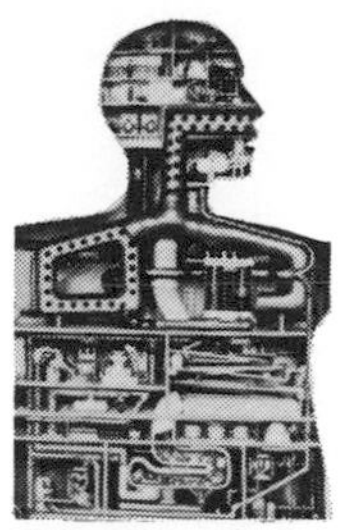

2166. Man shown as a Factory.

2167. Human Brain.

2168. Female Breast: Method of Removal.

2169. Proportions.

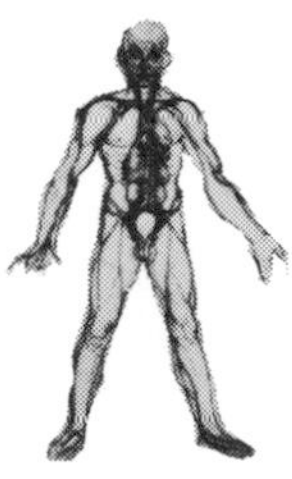

2170. Da Vinci.

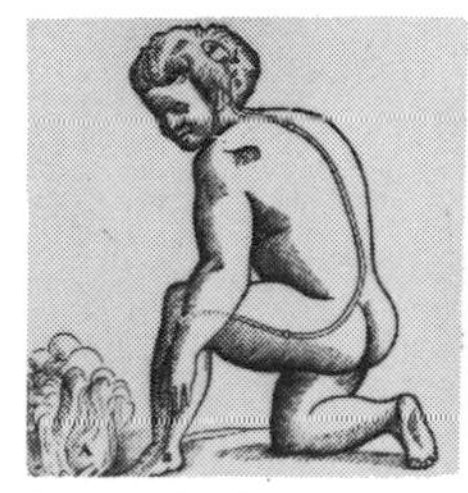

2171. Descartes: Sensation.

2172. Anatomy Lesson. (Rembrandt)

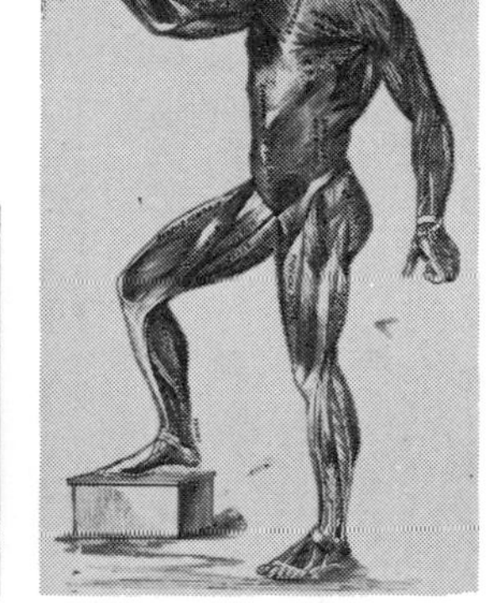

2173. Muscle Man.

Surgery

2174.

2175. Hernia Operation.

2176. Tying up Patient.

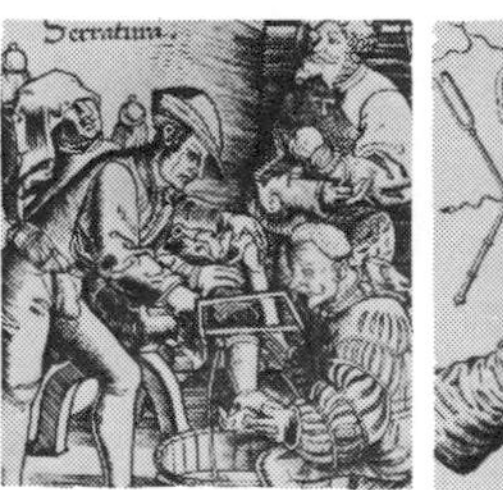

2177. Amputation.

2178. Tracheotomy, 1600.

2179. Paracentesis, 1693.

2180. Paré: Facial Sutures.

2181. Leg Amputation.

2182. Arab Doctor Cauterizing.

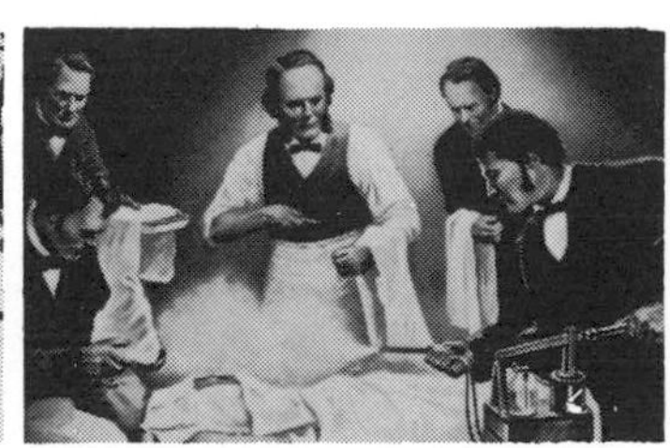

2183. Lister and Antiseptic Spray.

2184. Ward, Bellevue.

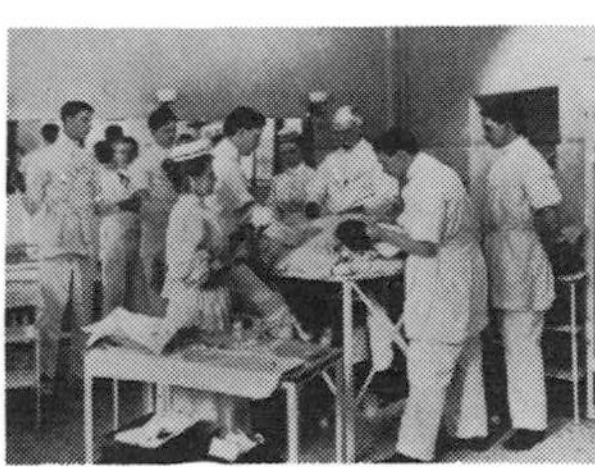

2185. McBurney Operating.

Anesthesia

2186. Demonstration.

2187. Pain-free Surgery, 1846.

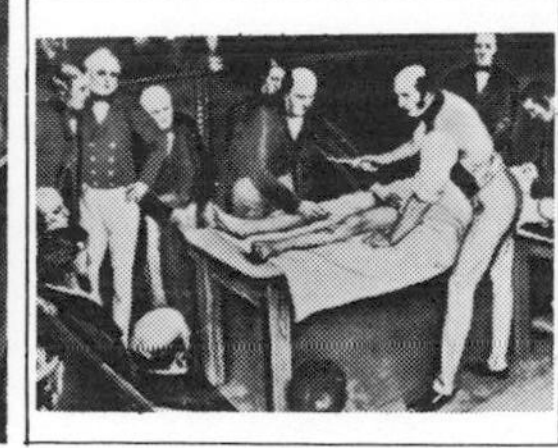

2188. First Painless Amputation.

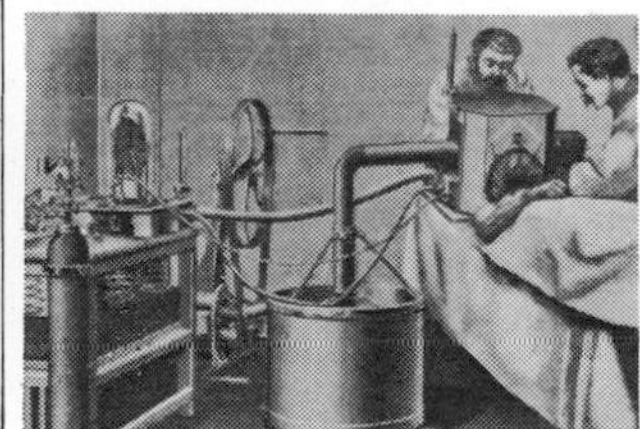

2189. Brauer-Draeger Equipment.

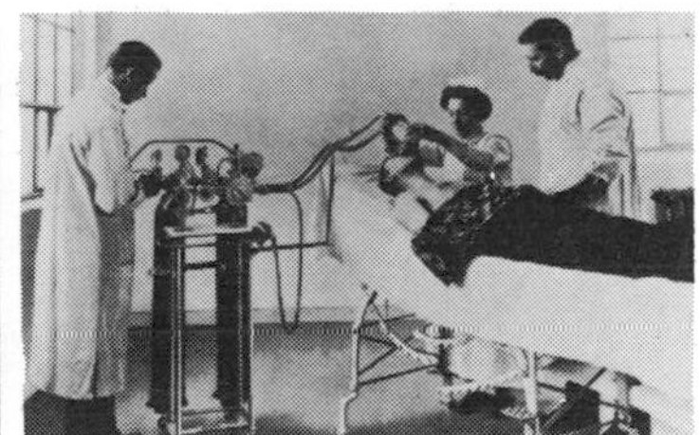

2190. Improved Draeger Method, 1905.

2191. Womb with Baby. 6th Century Illustrations.

2192. Caesarian Birth. 2193. Quadruplets.

2194. Birth Scene.

2195. Prolapsed Uterus Treated (Arabic).

2196. Vaginal Hygiene.

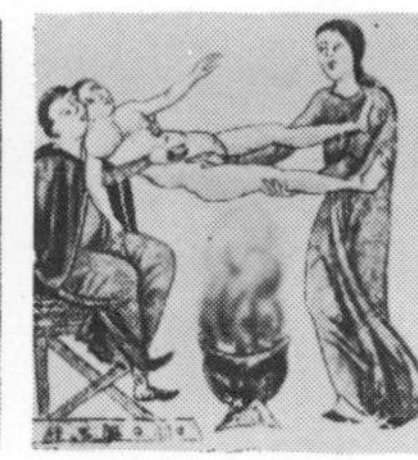

2197. Fumigating Uterus.

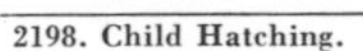

2198. Child Hatching.

2199. Caesarian Operation, 1666.

2200. Maternity Breast Pump.

2201. Strange Breasts.

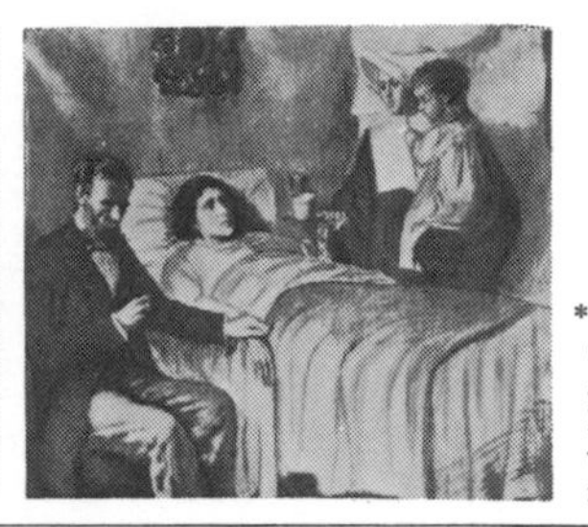

2202. Doctor and Sick Woman.*

*The name of the artist of this painting may come as a surprise: Pablo Picasso. He painted it at the age of 15, with his father serving as the model for the doctor.

Contagious Diseases

2203. Anti-Plague Costume, 1665.

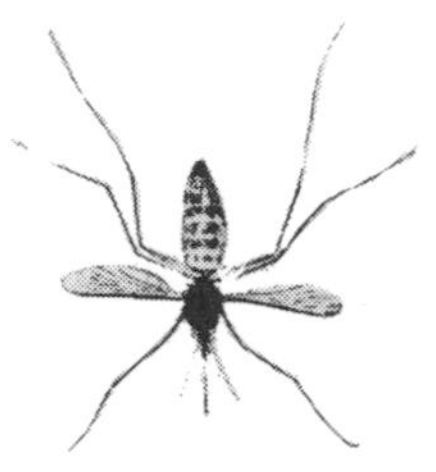

2204. Anopheles, Vector of Malaria.

2205. Gathering up the Dead, London, 1665.

2206. Plague Victims.

2207. Statistics.

2208. Anti-Cholera Garb.

2209. Epidemic, 1923.

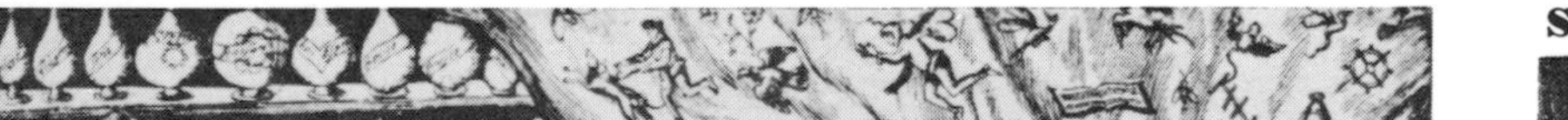

2210. Inflated ideas distilled from patient's head by way of heat-therapy, ca. 1600.

Strange Cures

2211. Blood Transfusion, 1667.

2212. Bloodletting.

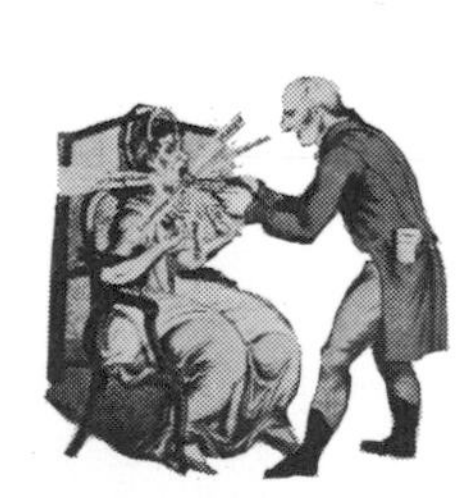

2213. Metallic Tractor.

2214. Tuberculosis Fumigator.

2215. Sweat Cure.

2216. Key to Stop Bleeding.

Scientific Medicine

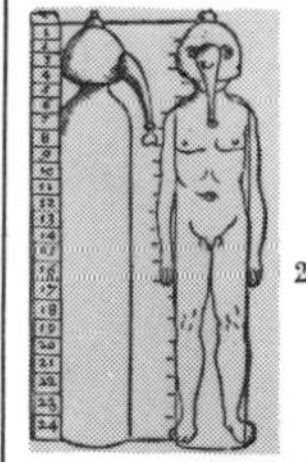
2217. Measurement.

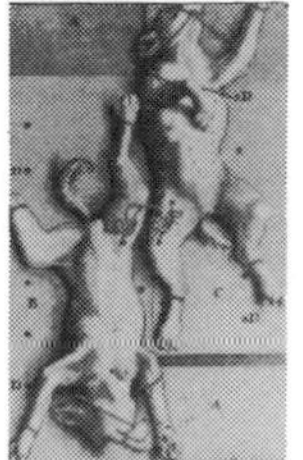
2218. Experiment.

2220. Reflex Study.

2219. Asepsis.

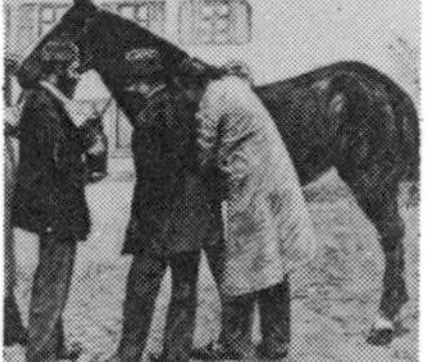
2221. Serum Plant.

2222. Research.

2223. Antibodies.

2224. Bacteria. 2225. Chemotherapy.

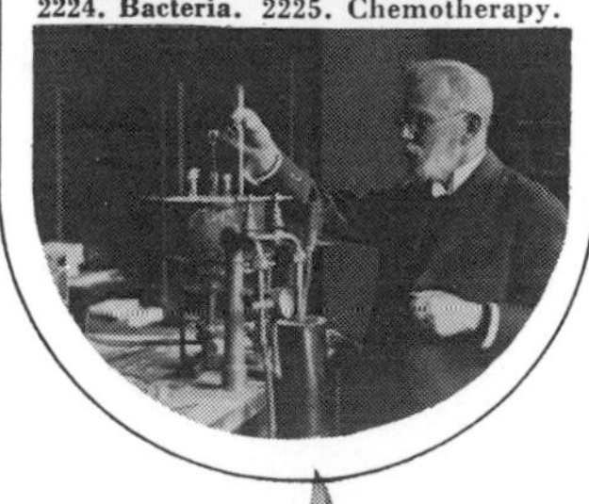

2226.

Patent Medicine

2227.

2228.

2229.

2230.

2231.

2232.

2233.

2234.

2235.

2236.

2237.

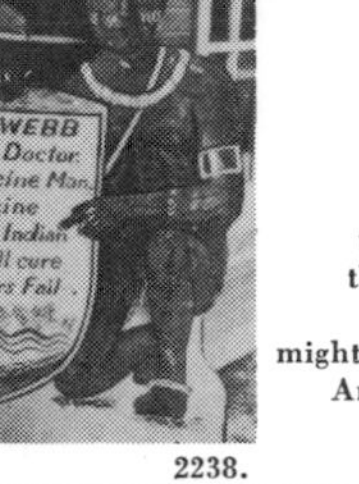

2238.

Patent Medicine: "...A tribute to the robustness of the American people... A less sturdy race might have been exterminated." Arthur Schlesinger, Sr.

2239.

Diagnosis

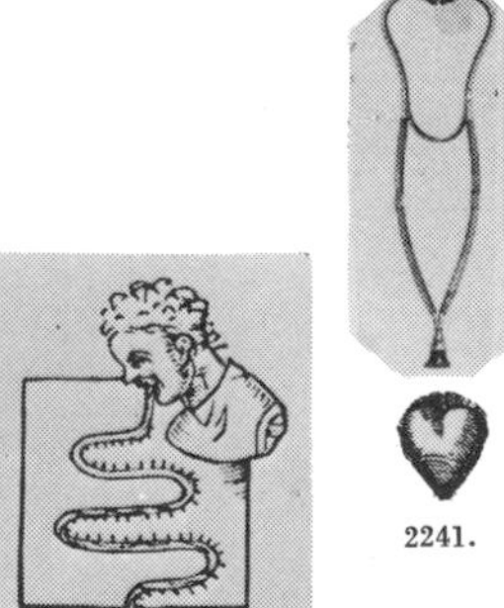
2240. Thermometer, 1614.

2241.

2242. Metabolic Scale.

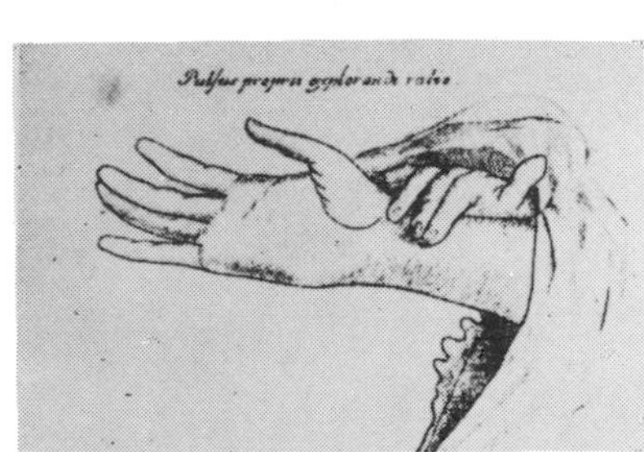
2243. Method of Pulse-Taking.

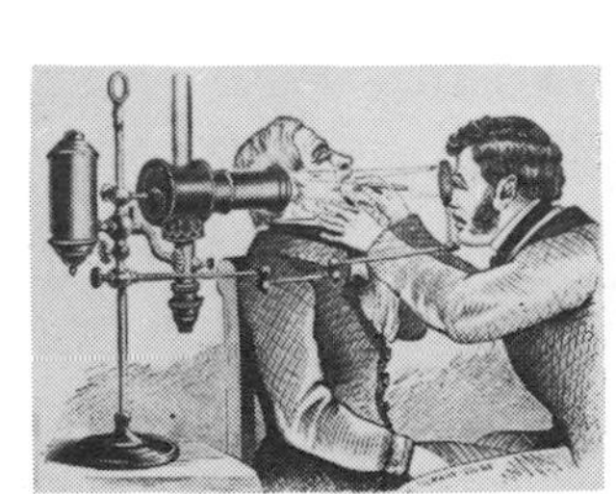
2244. Kerosene-Age Laryngoscope.

2245. "What a Marvelous Case of Hepatitis."

2246. Electro-Cardiograph, circa 1905.

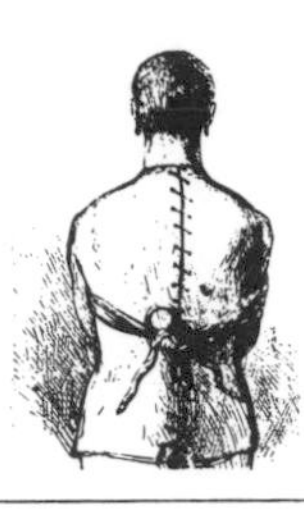

2247. Strait Jacket.

Mental Illness

2248. Exorcism.

2249. Scene in Bedlam.

2250. Hypnosis.

2251. Madness.

2252. Therapeutic Gyrator.

2253. Immobilizer.

2254. Manic Murder.

2255. Dungeon.

2256. Padded Cell.

2257. Restrained in Crib.

2258. Sound-Slide to Soothe Neurotic.

2260.

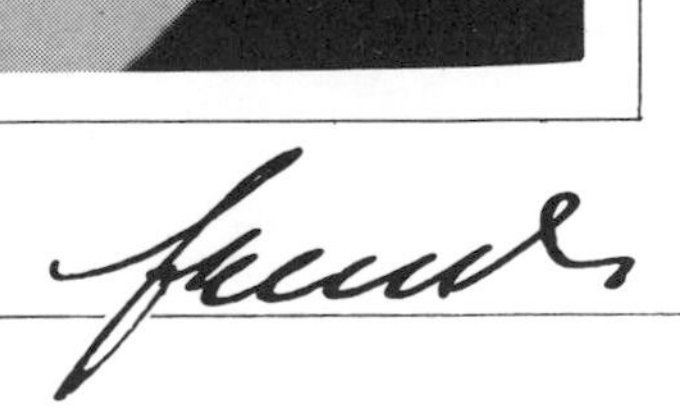

2259.

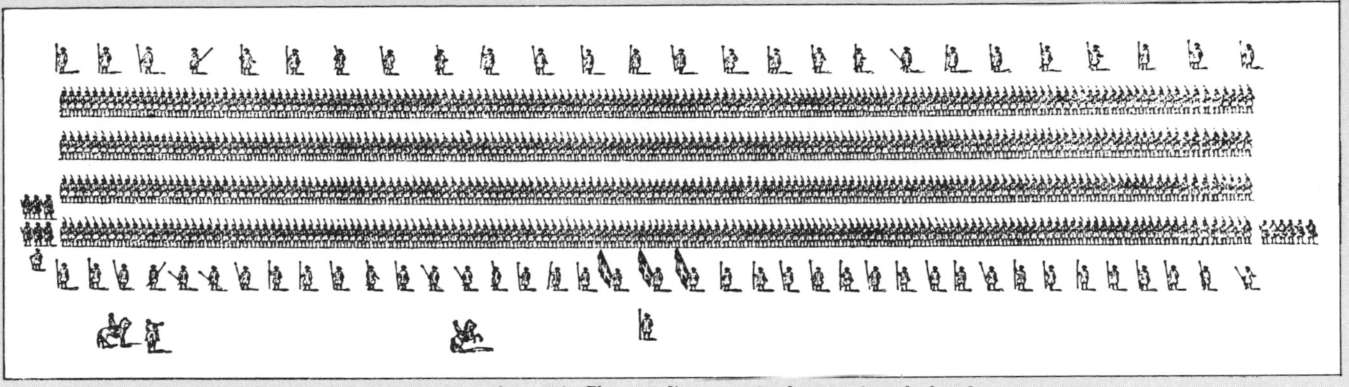

2261. Military phalanx during the war of the Spanish Succession, 1702. The grenadier companies drawn up in ranks four deep total 650 men.

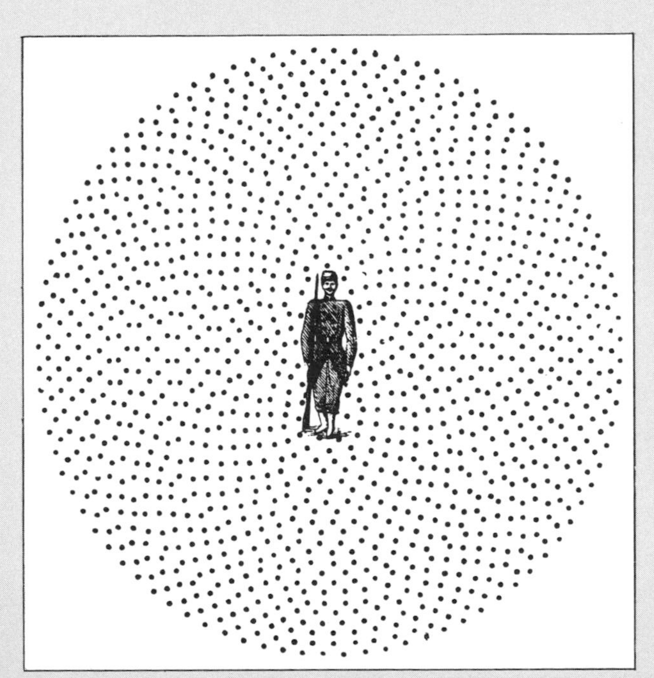

2262. Pictorial Statistic of the Franco-Prussian War. (1870-1871) - Print shows the amount of ammunition necessary in this conflict to kill one soldier. 1300 cartridges had to be fired to achieve this aim.

2263. Bugler, 1862.

2264. Macedonian Phalanx Attacking.

2265. German Warrior.

2266. Hessians.

2267. Knight's Cannon.

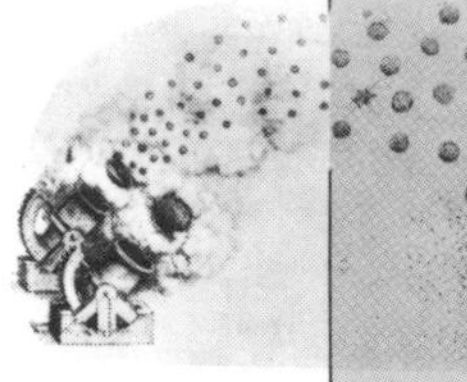
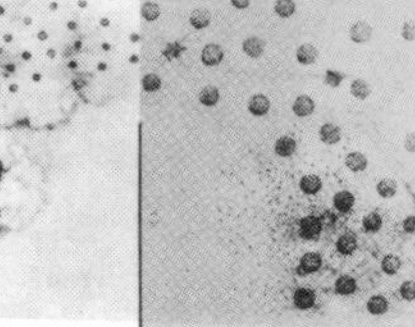

2268. India, 1858.

2269. Gunner, 1775.

2270. Crossbow.

2271. Russian Horsemen.

2272. Anglo-Saxon.

2273. Hessians.

2274. Anti-Aircraft.

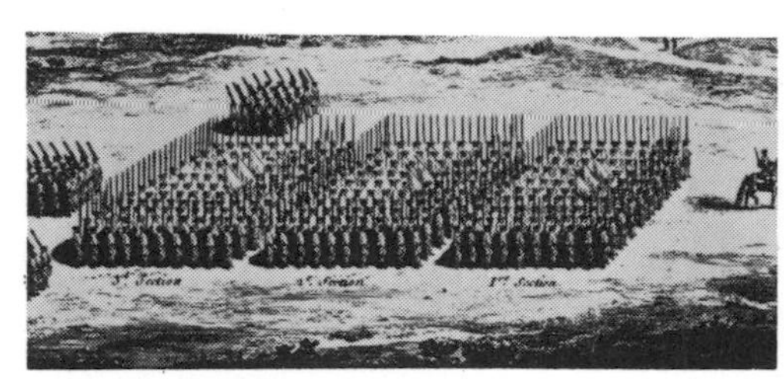
2282. Battle Formation, French.

2275. Leading the Column

2276. Prussian Horseman.

2277. Medieval Russian Warriors.

2278. Hussar, 1795.

2279. Anglo-Saxon Defense.

2280. Attack.

2281. Army Band, 1774.

2283. Soldiers of Fortune.

2284. Shell Burst.

2285. Napoleon Taking Aim.

2286. W.W.I. Howitzer.

2287. March of U.S. State Guards.

2288. Drummer.

2289. Sentry.

2290. Trumpeter.

2291. Uniform Catalogue.

2292. Fuehrer

2293.

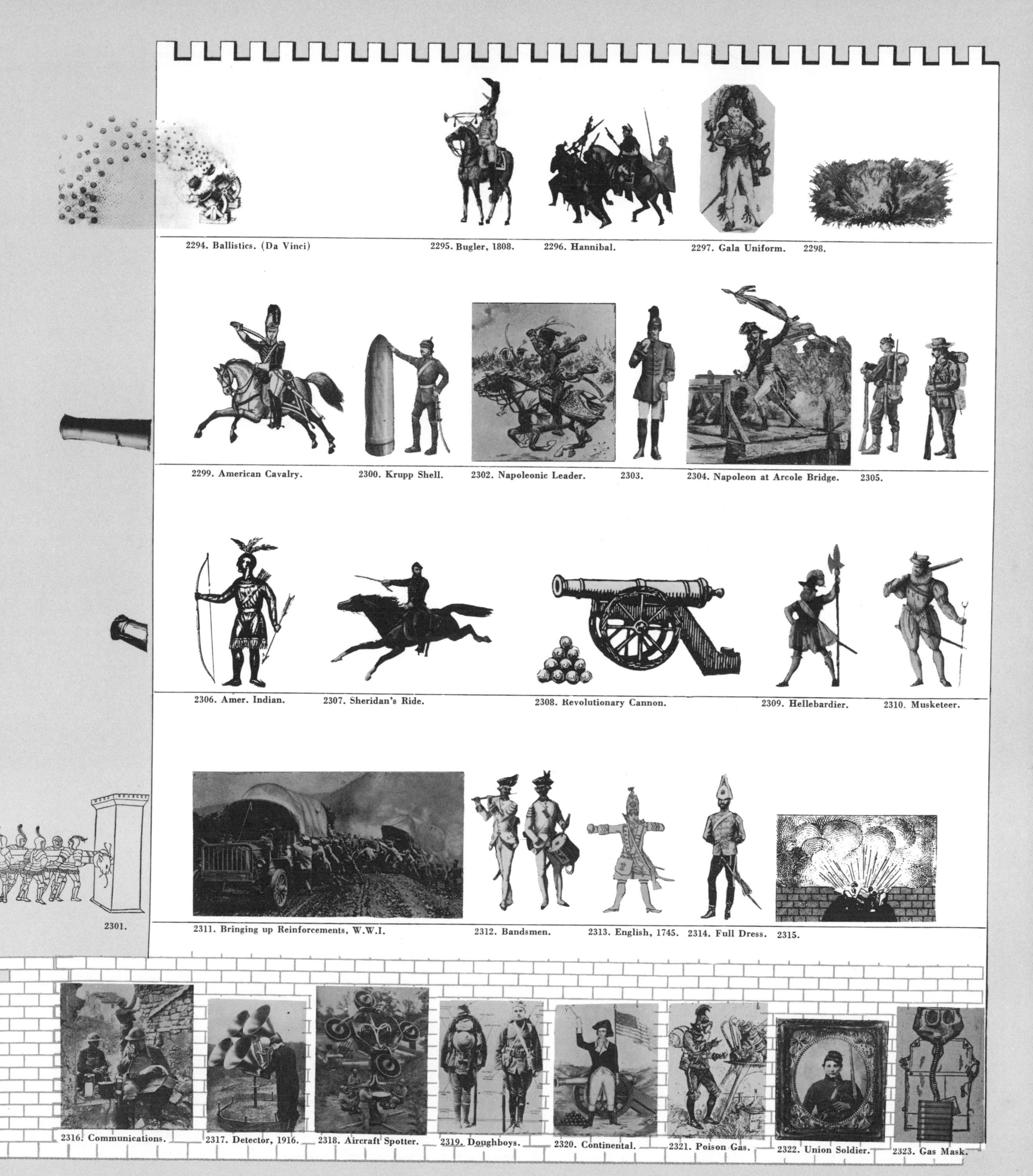

2294. Ballistics. (Da Vinci) 2295. Bugler, 1808. 2296. Hannibal. 2297. Gala Uniform. 2298.

2299. American Cavalry. 2300. Krupp Shell. 2302. Napoleonic Leader. 2303. 2304. Napoleon at Arcole Bridge. 2305.

2306. Amer. Indian. 2307. Sheridan's Ride. 2308. Revolutionary Cannon. 2309. Hellebardier. 2310. Musketeer.

2301. 2311. Bringing up Reinforcements, W.W.I. 2312. Bandsmen. 2313. English, 1745. 2314. Full Dress. 2315.

2316. Communications. 2317. Detector, 1916. 2318. Aircraft Spotter. 2319. Doughboys. 2320. Continental. 2321. Poison Gas. 2322. Union Soldier. 2323. Gas Mask.

MILK

ASPECTS OF THE COW

2324. Whole.

2325. Skeletal.

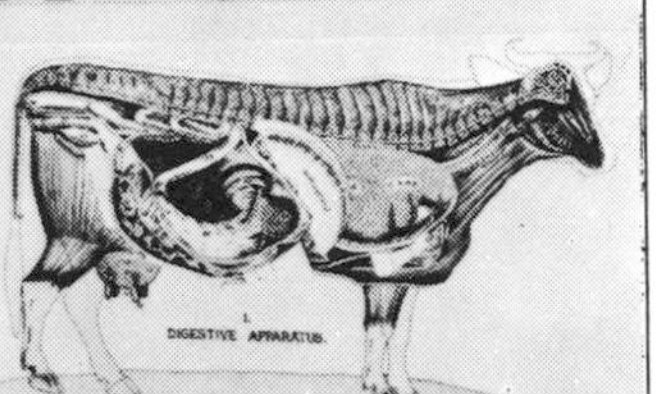

2326. Digestive.

2327. Circulatory.

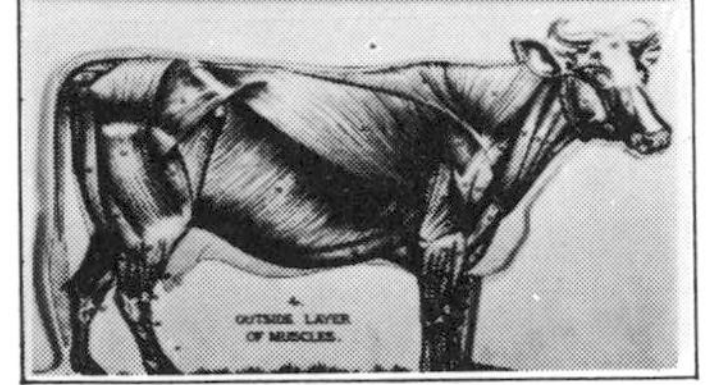

2328. Muscular.

2329. Chaldean Dairy Scene.

2330.

2331. Alpine Pastures, Switzerland.

2332. Dairy, 1700.

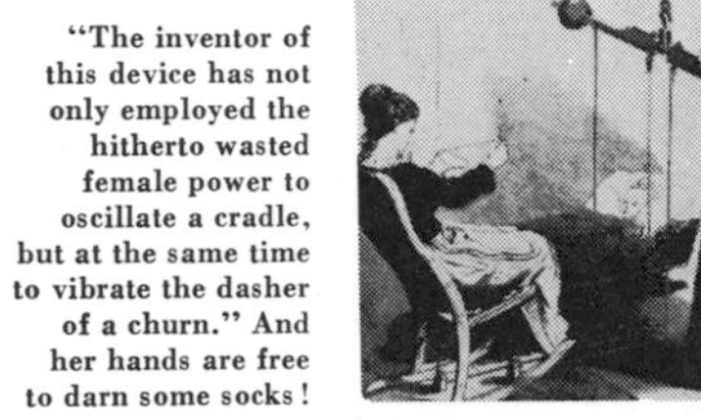

"The inventor of this device has not only employed the hitherto wasted female power to oscillate a cradle, but at the same time to vibrate the dasher of a churn." And her hands are free to darn some socks!

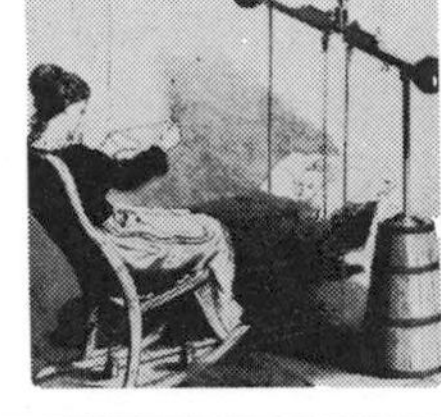

2333. Rocking Chair Churn.

2334. Milkman.

2335. Group of Churners.

2336. Direct from the Cow.

2337. Leather Churn.

2338. Milkman's Dog Cart.

2339. Perfect Aim.

2340.

2341. Patented Spout.

2342. Weighing.

MILLING

2343. Woman Corn Grinder. Egyptian Clay Figure.

2344. Wire Drawing Mill, 1540.

2345. Vinci.

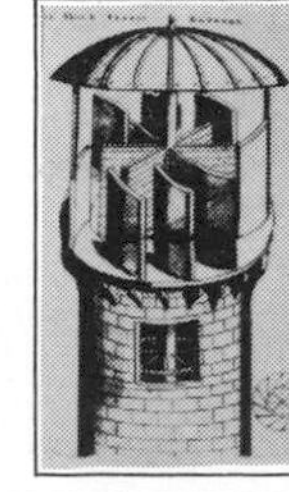

2346. Turbine.

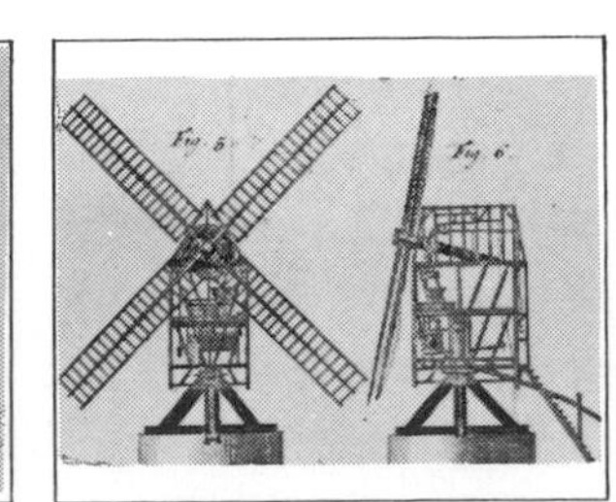

2347. Windmills. Cross Section.

2348. Western.

2349. Overshot Wheel.

2350. Dutch Mill, N.Y. Harbor.

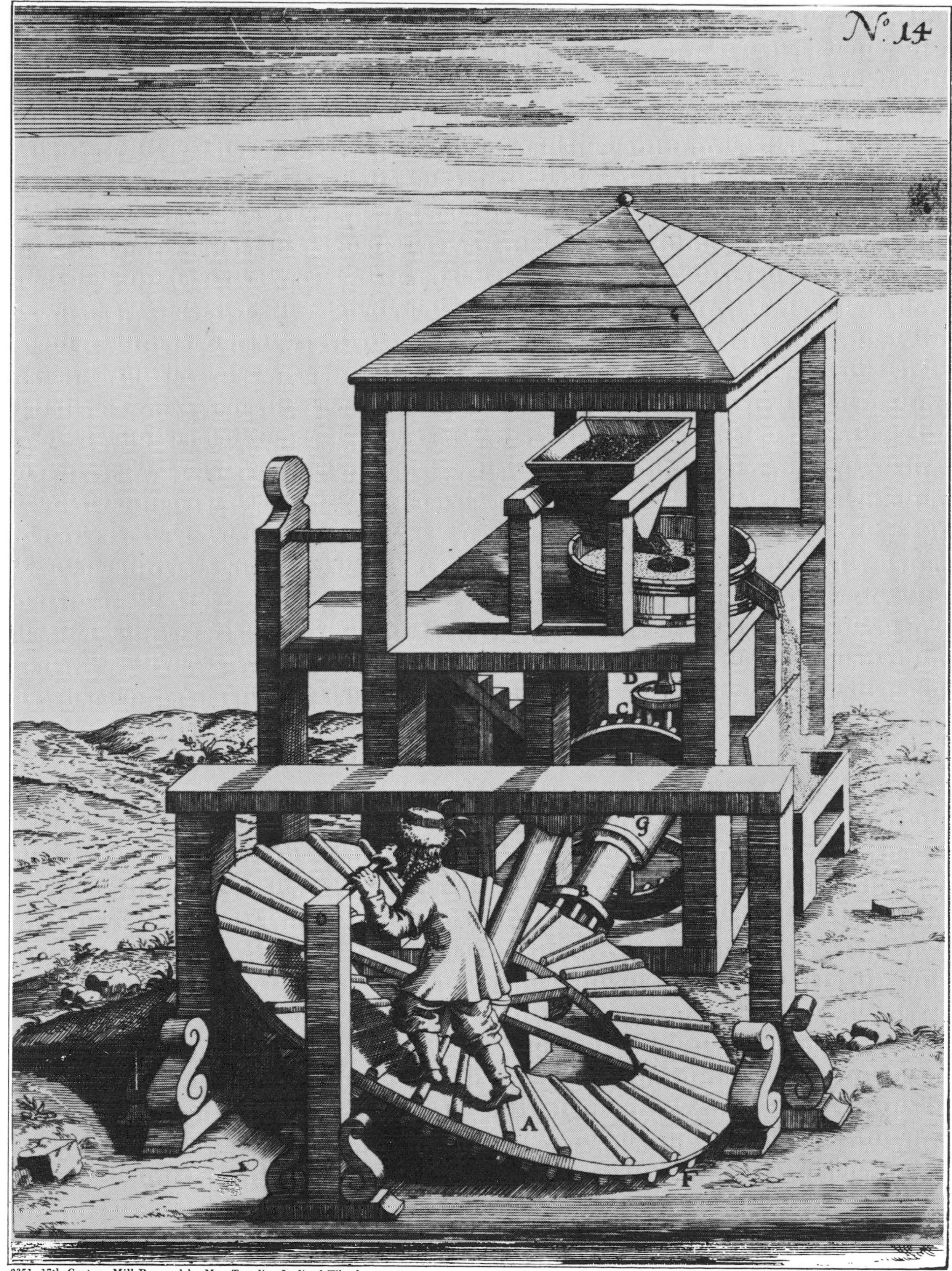

2351. 17th Century Mill Powered by Man Treading Inclined Wheel.

MOON

2352.

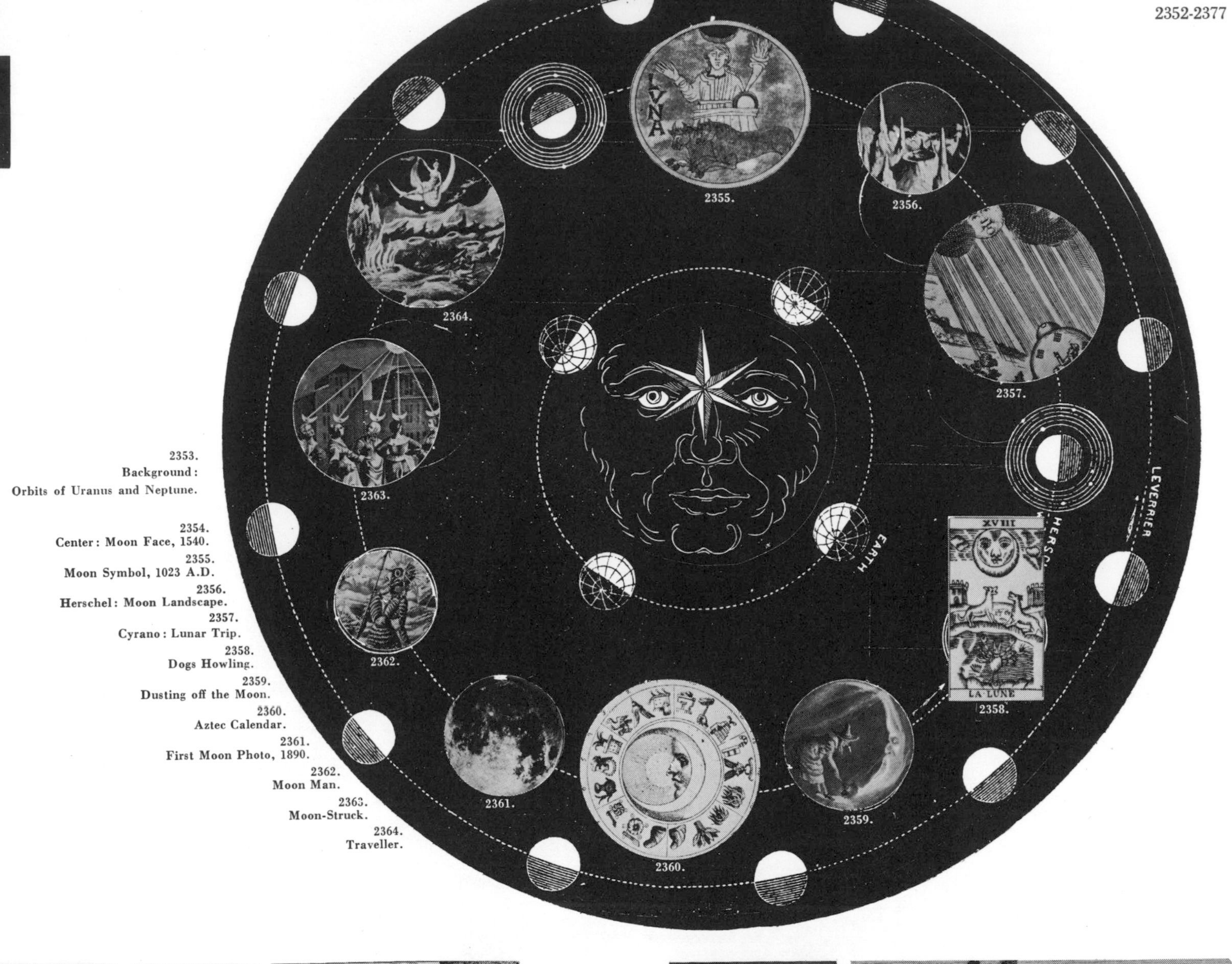

2355. 2356. 2357. 2358. 2359. 2360. 2361. 2362. 2363. 2364.

2353.
Background:
Orbits of Uranus and Neptune.

2354.
Center: Moon Face, 1540.
2355.
Moon Symbol, 1023 A.D.
2356.
Herschel: Moon Landscape.
2357.
Cyrano: Lunar Trip.
2358.
Dogs Howling.
2359.
Dusting off the Moon.
2360.
Aztec Calendar.
2361.
First Moon Photo, 1890.
2362.
Moon Man.
2363.
Moon-Struck.
2364.
Traveller.

MONSTERS

2365. Werewolf strikes at Full Moon.

2366. Hydra.

2367. Scylla and Charybdis.

2368. Dragon.

2369. Vampire.

2370. Ravenous Crocodile.

2371. Octopus.

2372. Sighted off Boston, 1819.

2373. Sea Monsters.

2374. Bathers Frightened.

2375. Friendship.

2376. Movie Monster.

2377. Arctic Monster.

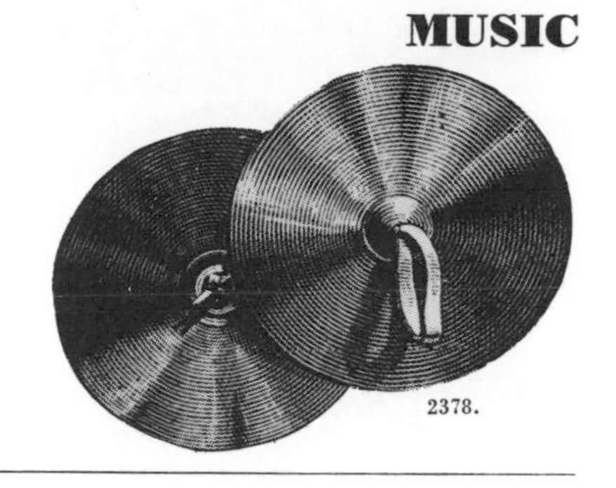

2378.

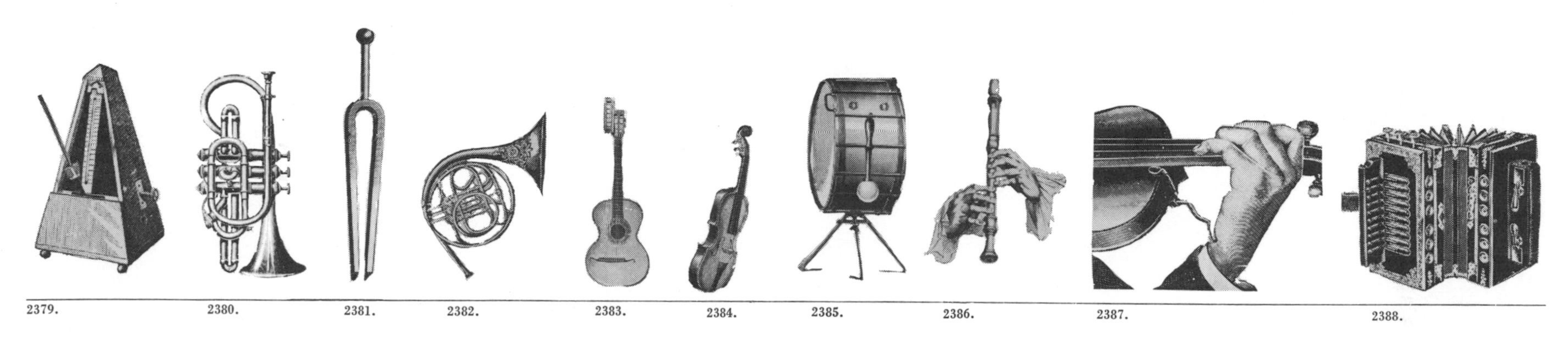

2379. 2380. 2381. 2382. 2383. 2384. 2385. 2386. 2387. 2388.

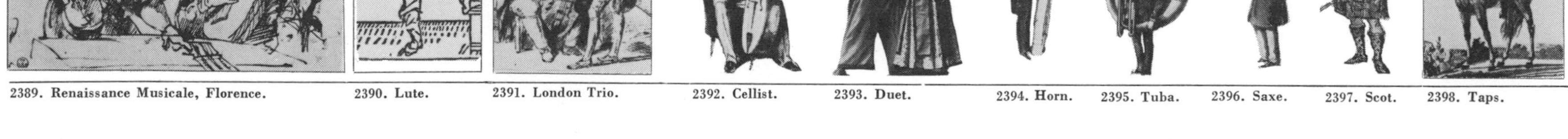

2389. Renaissance Musicale, Florence. 2390. Lute. 2391. London Trio. 2392. Cellist. 2393. Duet. 2394. Horn. 2395. Tuba. 2396. Saxe. 2397. Scot. 2398. Taps.

2399. Giant Violin Played by 17th century Soldiers.

2400. Timpanist.

2401. Kettle Drum.

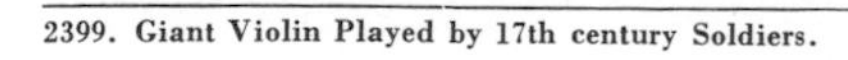

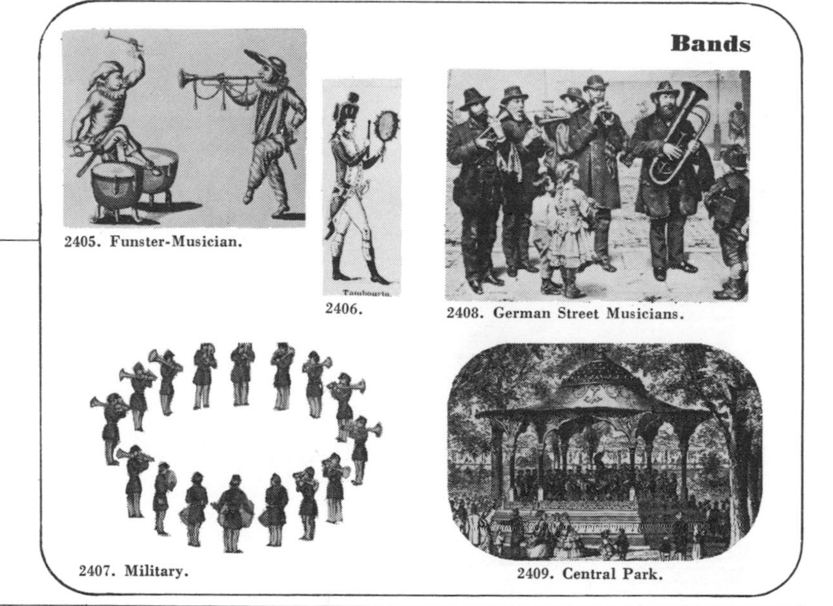

Bands

2405. Funster-Musician.

2406.

2408. German Street Musicians.

2407. Military.

2409. Central Park.

2402. Amateurs, Nebraska.

2403. Musical Family.

2404. Anvil Chorus.

2410

2410, Manuscript page from Bach's Organ Prelude in B Flat.

Composers by date of their birth.

Row 1.
2411. Schuetz, 1585.
2412. Purcell, 1659.
2413. Couperin, 1668.
2414. Rameau, 1683.
2415. Bach, 1685.
2416. Handel, 1685.
2417. Gluck, 1714.

Row 2.
2418. Haydn, 1732.
2419. Mozart, 1756.
2420. Beethoven, 1770.
2421. Weber, 1786.
2422. Rossini, 1792.
2423. Donizetti, 1797.
2424. Schubert, 1797.

Row 3.
2425. Berlioz, 1803.
2426. Strauss, 1804.
2427. Mendelssohn, 1809.
2428. Chopin, 1810.
2429. Schumann, 1810.
2430. Liszt, 1811.
2431. Verdi, 1813.

Row 4.
2432. Wagner, 1813.
2433. Gounod, 1818.
2434. Bruckner, 1824.
2435. Brahms, 1833.
2436. Saint-Saëns, 1835.
2437. Bizet, 1838.
2438. Moussorgsky, 1839.

Row 5.
2439. Tchaikovsky, 1840.
2440. Massenet, 1842.
2441. Elgar, 1857.
2442. Leoncavallo, 1858.
2443. Puccini, 1858.
2444. Mahler, 1860.
2445. Wolf, 1860.

Row 6.
2446. Debussy, 1862.
2447. Strauss, 1864.
2448. Šibelius, 1865.
2449. Scriabin, 1872.
2450. Vaughn Williams, 1872.
2451. Rachmaninoff, 1873.
2452. Schoenberg, 1874.

Row 7.
2453. Ives, 1874.
2454. Ravel, 1875.
2455. Falla, 1876.
2456. Bartok, 1881.
2457. Stravinsky, 1882.
2458. Webern, 1883.
2459. Berg, 1885.

Row 8.
2460. Prokofiev, 1891.
2461. Hindemith, 1895.
2462. Hanson, 1896.
2463. Poulenc, 1899.
2464. Copland, 1900.
2465. Barber, 1910.
2466. Britten, 1913.

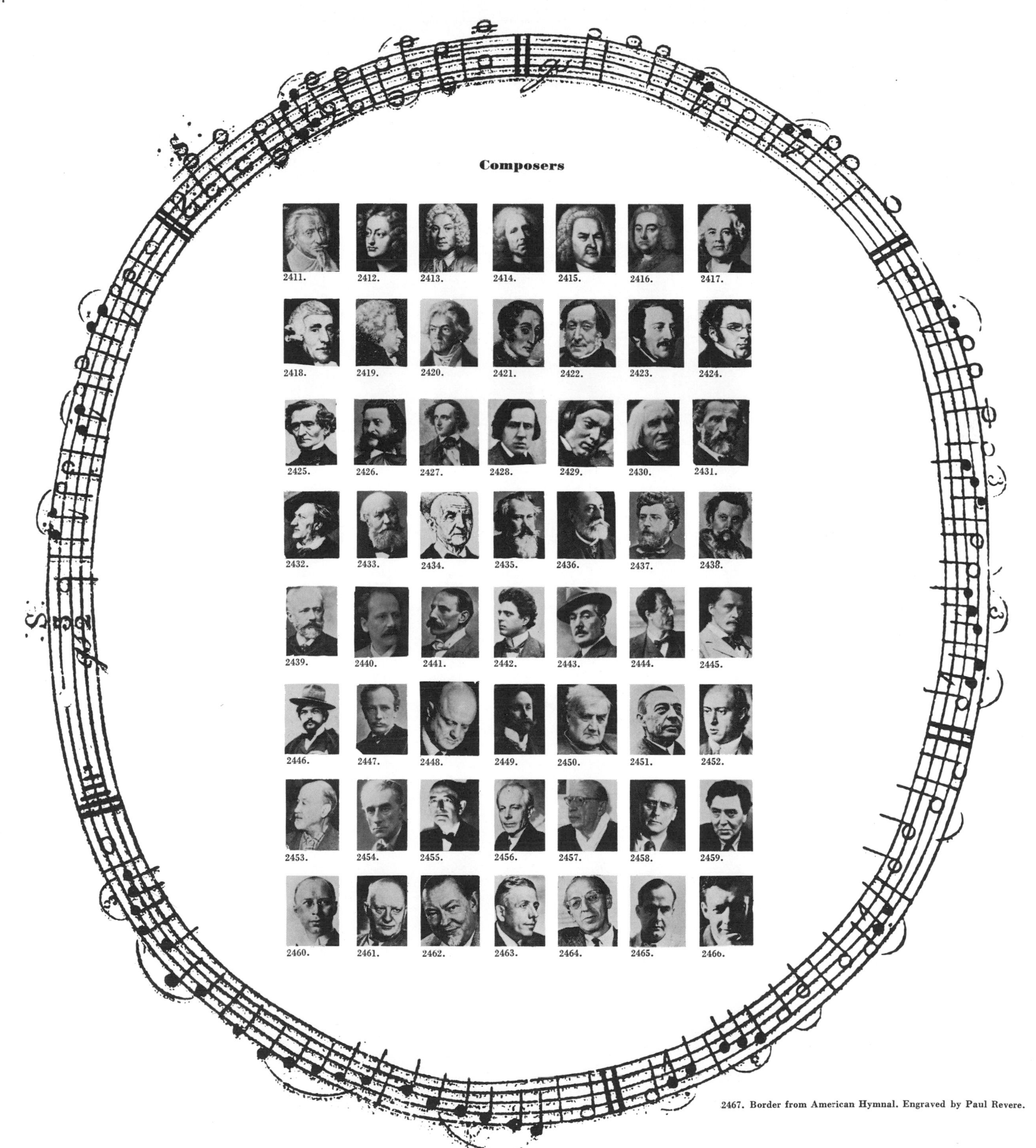

2467. Border from American Hymnal. Engraved by Paul Revere.

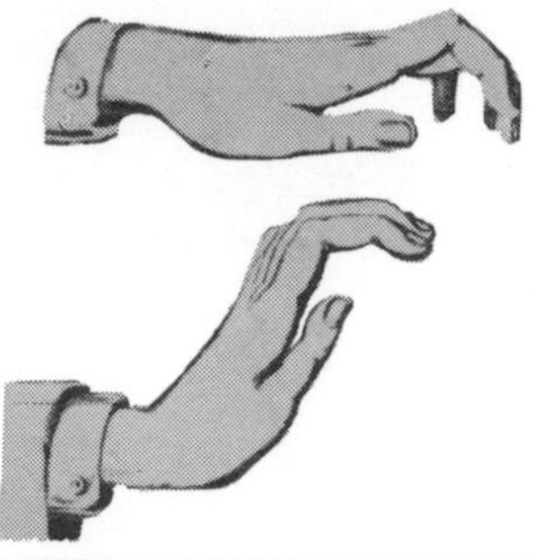

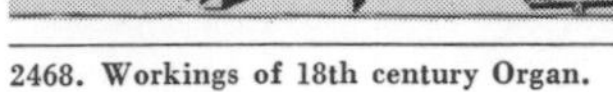

2468. Workings of 18th century Organ.

2469. Pipes.

2470. Organ Loft.

2471. Cantata.

2472. Pianistic Technique.

2473. Virtuoso with Concert Grand.

2474. Player Piano Ad.

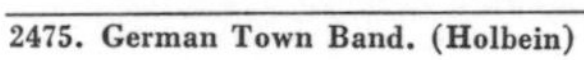

2475. German Town Band. (Holbein)

2476. Church Music.

2477. Chamber Group: Scarlatti at Piano.

2478. Frederick the Great's Flute Concert.

2479. Choir Training.

2480. The Duet.

Opera

2481. Verdi Title.

2482. Mary Garden as Salome.

2483. Caruso.

2484. In the Loge.

2485. Teatro della Scala, Milan.

2486. After Opera.

2487.

2488. Triumphal March from Verdi's "Aïda."

2489. Rudolph Kolisch, violinist, discusses with Bela Bartok his "Music for Strings, Percussion and Celeste" during rehearsals at the New School in New York, 1940.

2491. Centaur

2490. Labyrinth of Crete.

2493. Saturn. 2494. Zeus. 2492. Hercules. 2495. Prometheus. 2496. 2497. Pandora. 2498. Argus. 2499. Apollo. 2504. Nine Muses. 2500. Diana. 2502. Pegasus. 2503. Atlas.

2505. Background Clouds.

2501. Adonis born from Tree.

2506. The Sea.

2507. Mermaid. (Burne-Jones)

2508. River Nymphs.

2509. Tantalus.

2510. Andromeda.

2511. Jason finding the Golden Fleece.

2512. Neptune.

Janus.

2513. Minerva.

2514. Venus.

2515. Icarus.

2516. Helios.

2517. Pan.

2518. Mercury.

2519. Three Graces.

2520. Leda.

2521. Psyche and Cupid.

2522. Croesus.

2523. Ceres.

2524. Narcissus.

2525. Head of Medusa.

2526. Protheus.

2527. The Abduction of Helen of Troy.

2528. Mermaid.

see also: Medicine p.126

For complete, analytical subject index turn to page 221.

2534. Strategic Meeting.

2535. Retreat from Moscow.

2536. Wounded at Regensburg, 1809.

2537. On to the Pyramids.

2530.
Peace Treaty, 1807.
2531.
Typical Pose.
2532.
Popular Woodcut.
2533.
Coronation. (David).

2538.
Equestrian.
2539.
Statue.
2540.
In Russia, 1812.
2541.
Battle of Leipzig.

2542. With Son and Nephews.

2543. Candid Sketches, 1812.

2544. Crossing Alps.

2545.

2546. St. Helena.

2547. Signature.

2529. Background: Throne Room designed by Percier and Fontaine.

2548. Municipal Workers Parade on Broadway, ca. 1910.

2549. Rivoli Theater, Broadway and 49th St., 1930.

2550. Subway Entrance, 110th Street and Broadway.

2551. I.R.T. Subway Car Reserved for Women Passengers, 1903.

2552. Broadway between Grand and Howard Streets, 1840.

2553. Poster Hanger, Washington Square.

2554. Manhattan Bird's-Eye View, 1907.

2555. Canyons of New York: Mid-Town Night View.

2556. Fifth Avenue with Vanderbilt Mansions.

Streets

2557. Madison Square.

2558. Riverside Drive.

2559. Wall Street.

2560. Broadway, 1900.

2561. The Bowery with El.

People

2562. Tammany.

2563. Tweed.

2564. Jimmy Walker Speaking.

2565. La Guardia.

2566. Grover Whalen.

2567. Robert Moses.

Architecture

2568. Broadway Facade.

2569. The Old Waldorf.

2570. Cooper Union in the 1860's.

2571. Municipal Building.

2572. Madison Square.

2573. Washington Arch.

2574. Trolley with Cowcatcher.

2575. Broadway Omnibus.

2576. Jaywalker.

2577. Traffic Tower.

2578. Boy Delinquent.

2579. Crime in city streets (1865) prompted a contemporary artist to suggest that New Yorkers carry pistols, sabers, spiked umbrellas and guns. Streetcars were to be converted into vehicles resembling horse-drawn tanks.

2580. Juvenile Gang at Mulberry Bend.

2581. Tenement Life.

2582. Segars.

2583. Shoeshine Boy.

2584. Working Girl.

2585. Jump into the River.

2586. Central Park in Winter.

2587. Adults Jumping Rope.

2588. Coney Island Symbol.

2589. Police Badge.

Statue of Liberty

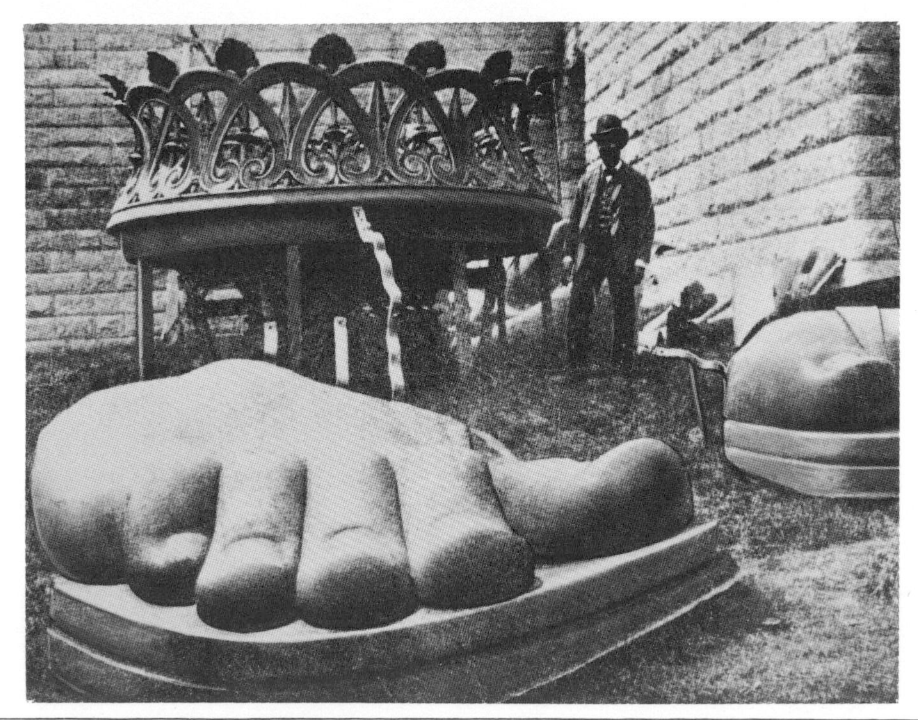
2590. Toe and Torch before Installation.

2591.

2592. Rendezvous.

2593.

2594. Cross-Section.

NURSERY RHYMES

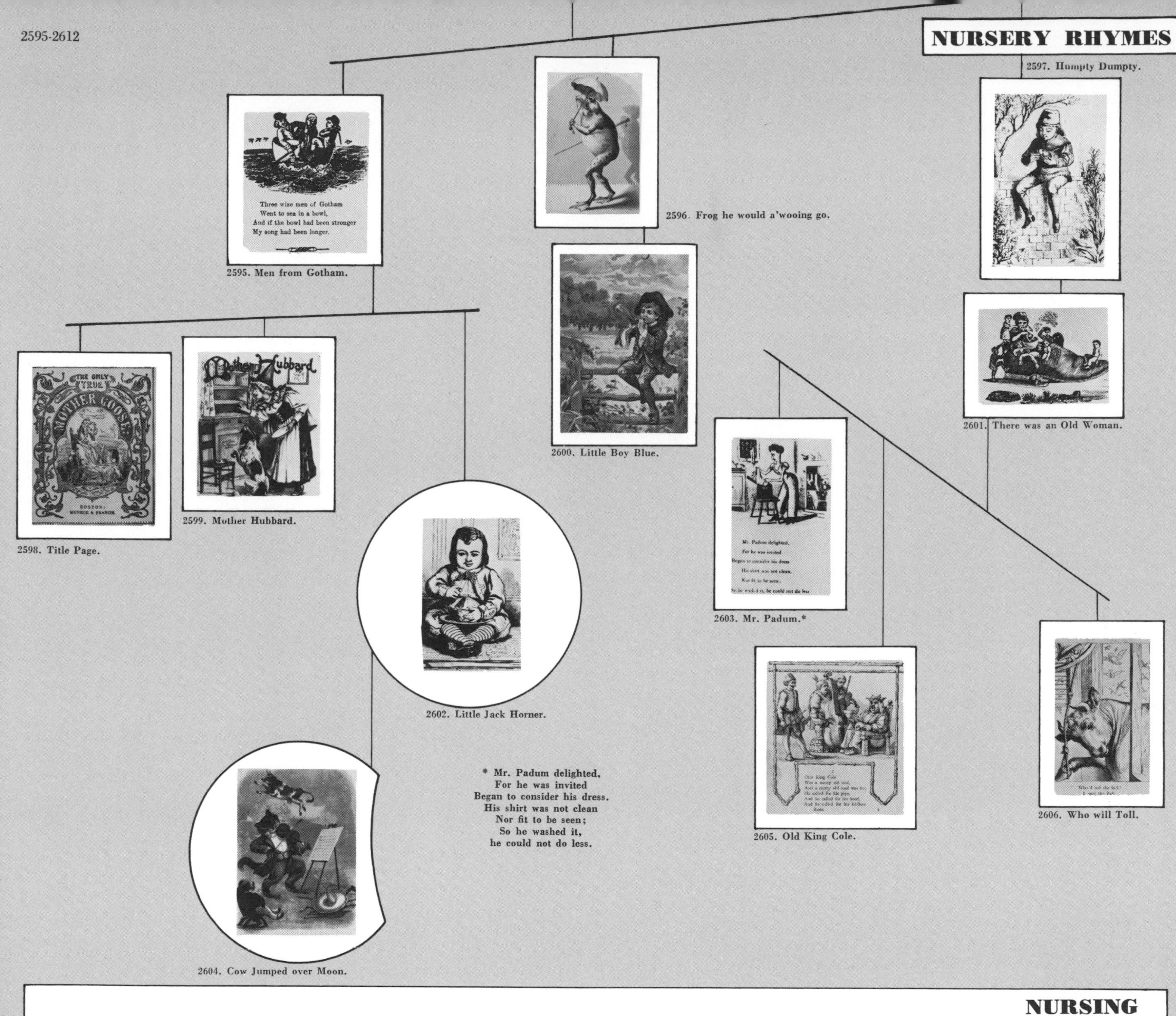

2595. Men from Gotham.

2596. Frog he would a'wooing go.

2597. Humpty Dumpty.

2598. Title Page.

2599. Mother Hubbard.

2600. Little Boy Blue.

2601. There was an Old Woman.

2602. Little Jack Horner.

2603. Mr. Padum.*

2604. Cow Jumped over Moon.

2605. Old King Cole.

2606. Who will Toll.

* Mr. Padum delighted,
For he was invited
Began to consider his dress.
His shirt was not clean
Nor fit to be seen;
So he washed it,
he could not do less.

NURSING

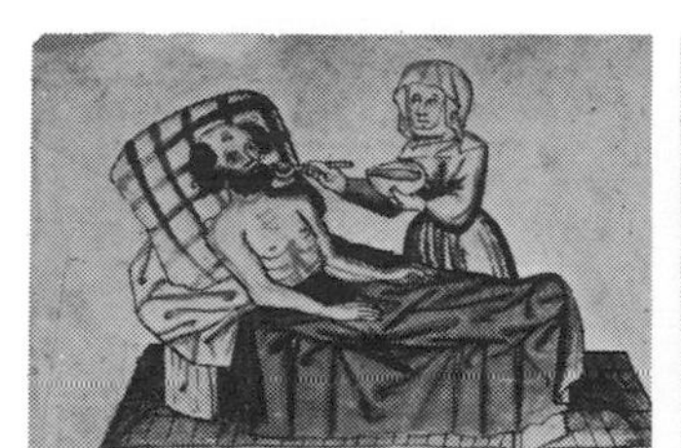

2607. Nun Feeds Sick Man. Medieval.

2608. Charity Hospital Ward.

2609. Nurse in Lab.

2610. The Lady with the Lamp.

2611. Patent Nursing Table.

2612. Nurses in Training.

For complete, analytical subject index turn to page 221.

2613.

2614. Belly Wheel.

2615. Heaviest Englishman.

2616. Public Scale, Paris.

2617. Courtier. (Van Helst)

2618. Turnstile Trouble.

2619. French Gourmet.

2620. F. J. Kellogg Diet Ad.

OFFICES

2621.

2622. Fugger's File.*

2623. Secretaries in Pants.

2624. Evasive Error.

2625. Midnight Gas.

2626. Comptometer Operator, 1896.

2627. Secretary amidst Files, 1905.

2628. Executive Meeting, 1881.

2629. File Room, 1910.

2630. Tired Clerk.

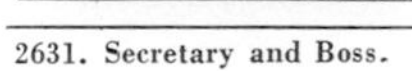

2631. Secretary and Boss.

2632. After Hours.

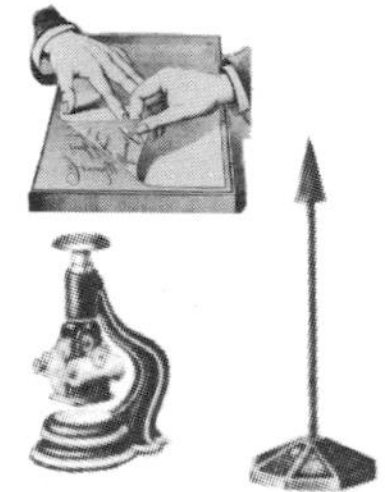

2633. 2634. 2635.

2636. 2637. 2638. 2639.

2640. Typewriter Ad.

2641. Typist, 1872.

2642. Manual Sorter. 2643. Secretary, 1901.

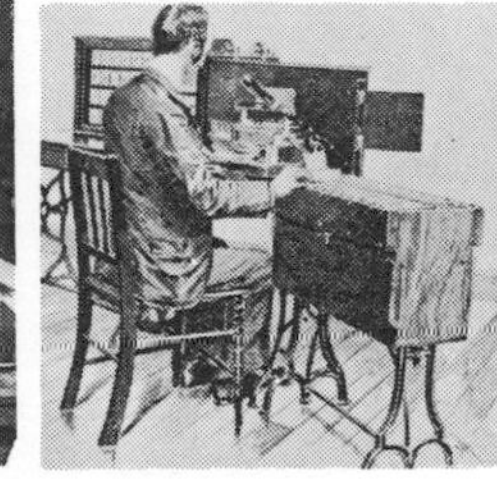

2644. Early Tabulator.

2645. Dictaphone Dictator.

*Jacob Fugger, tycoon of Augsburg, arranged his global correspondence geographically.

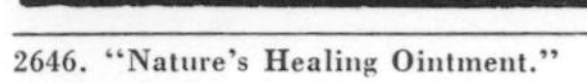

2646. "Nature's Healing Ointment."

2647. Drake, 1866.

2648. Drilling.

2649. Natural Gas.

2650. Laying Pipeline, Cairo, W. Va.

2651. Oil Train, W.W.I.

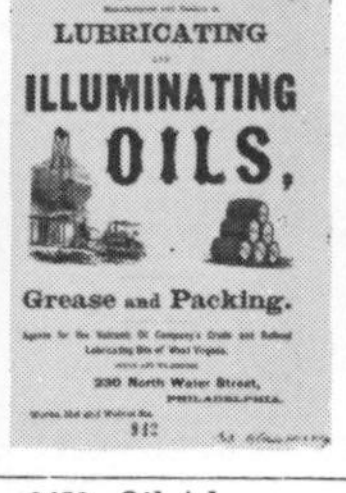

2652. Oil Ad.

2653. Making Lubricants.

£ 100
REWARD

2654. Arrest of an English Rogue.

OUTLAWS

2655.

REWARD
FOR
$10,000
A reward of
$500 EACH
VOLCANO STAGE.
MORNING OF MAY 1, 1872.
One-fourth the Amount Recovered
WELLS, FARGO & CO.

2656.

WANTED!
By U.S. Government for Robbery and Murder.
SAM STARR
and
BELLE SHIRLEY
$5000
REWARD
For Information Leading to Arrest and Conviction.
Thomas Crail,

2657.

2658. Absconding Thief.

2659. Rogues' Gallery.

2660.

2661. Train Holdup Kansas.

2662. Western Holdup.

ORATORS

2663. Concord, N.H., 1902.

2664. Table-Pounder.

2665. Exhorter.

2666. Senator.

2667. Candidate.

2668. Ward Leader.

2669. Moralist.

2670. Mouthpiece.

2671. Killed by Wyatt Earp.

2672. Catching up with Jesse James.

2673. End of a Gang, Kansas, 1892.

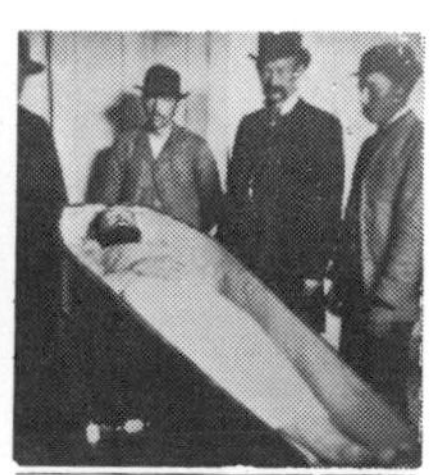
2674. Jesse James' Body.

2675. Three Sheriffs.

2676. Hanging.

2677. Gunned Down.

2678. Dime Novel Cover.

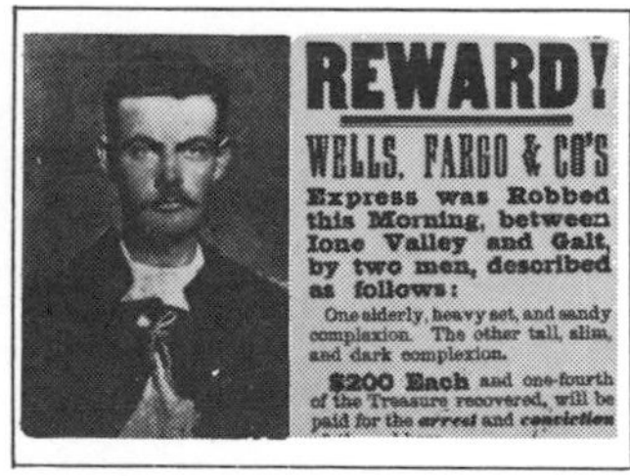

2679. Jim Younger. 2680. Reward Poster.

2681. Billy.

2682. Jane.

2683. Sheriff Black Bart.

2684. Coffin of Rube Burros.

2685. Crawford.

2686.

2687. Shooting, New York Bar.

GOOD AND BAD MEN OF HOLLYWOOD

2688.

2689.

2690.

2691.

2692.

For complete, analytical subject index turn to page 221.

PAIN

2693. Laocoön.

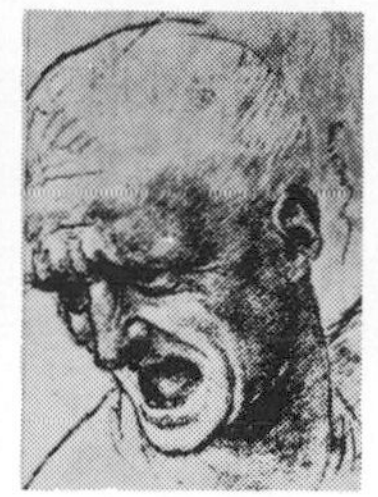

2694. DaVinci.

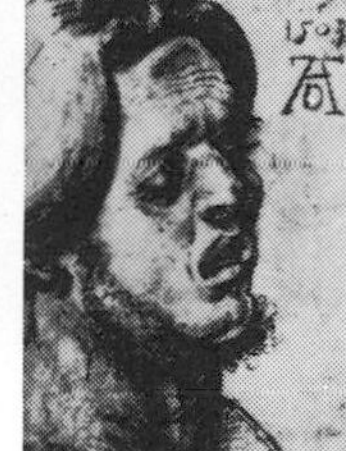

2695. Durer.

2696. Schlueter.

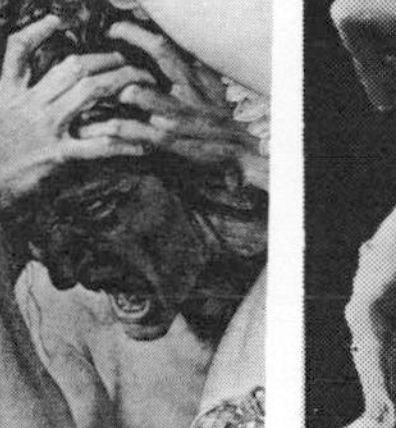

2697. Bronzino.

2698. Rodin.

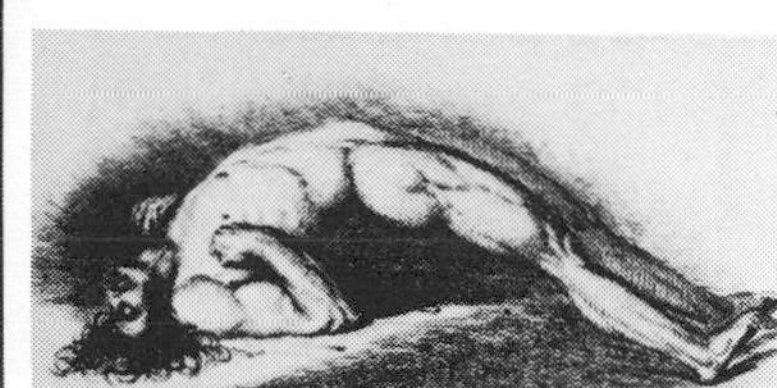

2699. Sketch by Surgeon Charles Bell.

PAPER

Titles from top center

2700.
Paper-Wetting Machine, 1882.

2701.
German Newspaper, 1813.

2702.
Lincoln Letter, 1859.

2703.
Paper Calendering.

2704.
American Papermaker, ca. 1820.

2705.
Emblem of Paper Mill.

2706.
Boston News-Letter, 1704.

2707.
Papermaker with his Tools.

2708.
Machine to Package Soap.

2709.
18th century Papermaker.

2710.
First Paper Mill in New England, 1717.

2711.
An Overload of Cartons, 1810.

2712.
Children Making Paper Boxes.

2713.
Machine to Make Paper Bags.

2714.
Gluing Boxes, 1850's.

2715.
Wrapping Chemical Bottles.

2716.
Still Life, 17th century. (W. Vaillant)

2717. Second Empire.

2718. Sign.

2719. Gargoyle.

2720. Sacre Coeur.

2721. Trocadero.

2722. Arc de Triomphe.

2723.

2724. Outing, Champs-Elysées.

2725. Poster, 1890.

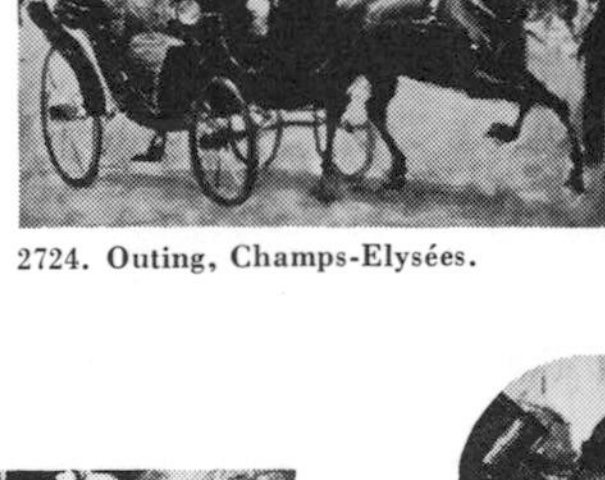

2726. Admirer.

2727. At the Café. (Manet)

2728. Café Dansant.

2729.

2730. Mealtime.

2731. Apotheosis.

2732. The Seine and its Bridges.

2733. Varieté. (Seurat)

2734. Montparnasse Artists.

2735. Cocottes. (Steinlen)

2736. Glaces.

2737. Street, 1865.

2738. Maurice.

2739. Cakewalk.

2740. Josephine.

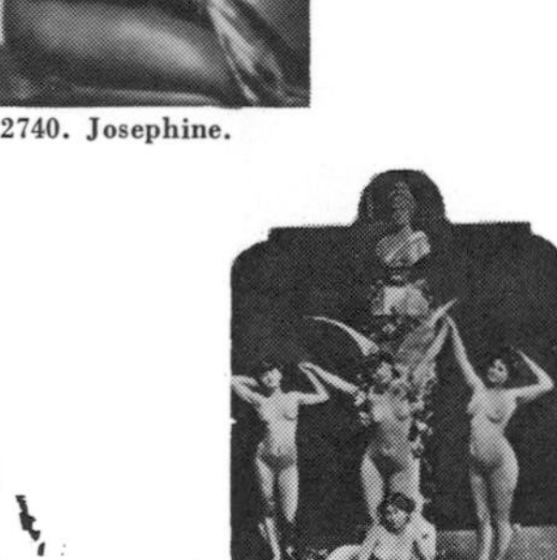

2741. Vive la Républic.

2742. Ice Crusher.

2743. Moustache Guard.

2744. Horse Medication.

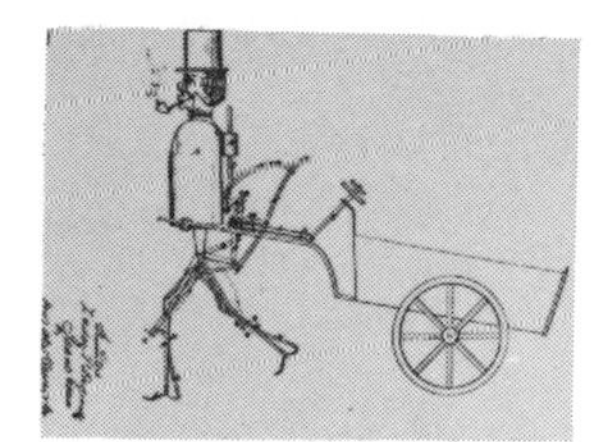

2754. Steam Carriage, 1868.

2746. Flying Machine, 1889.

2748.*

2750. Insect Guard.

2753. Inflated Life-Saving Collar.

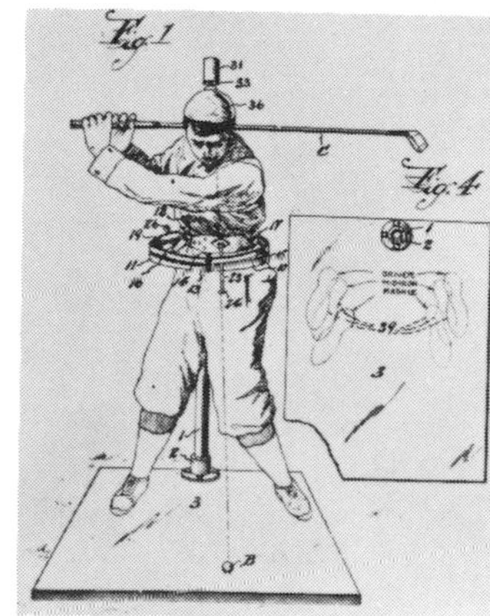

2749. Golf Instructor.

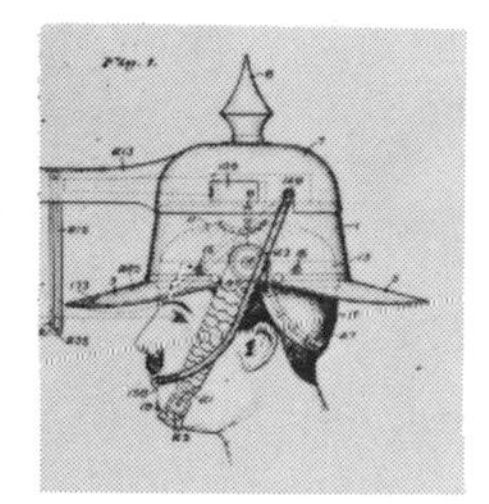

2752. Helmet with Built-in Gun.

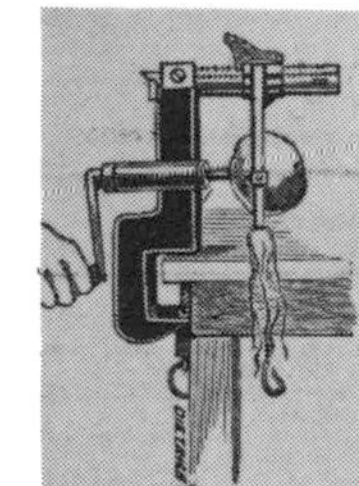

2747. Fruit Peeler.

2745.

2751. Swim Suit.

2757. Camouflaged Streetcar.

2755. Cherry Stoner.

2756. Apple Parer.

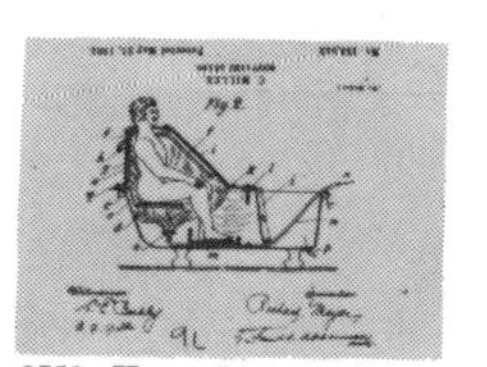

2758. Home Steam-Bath.

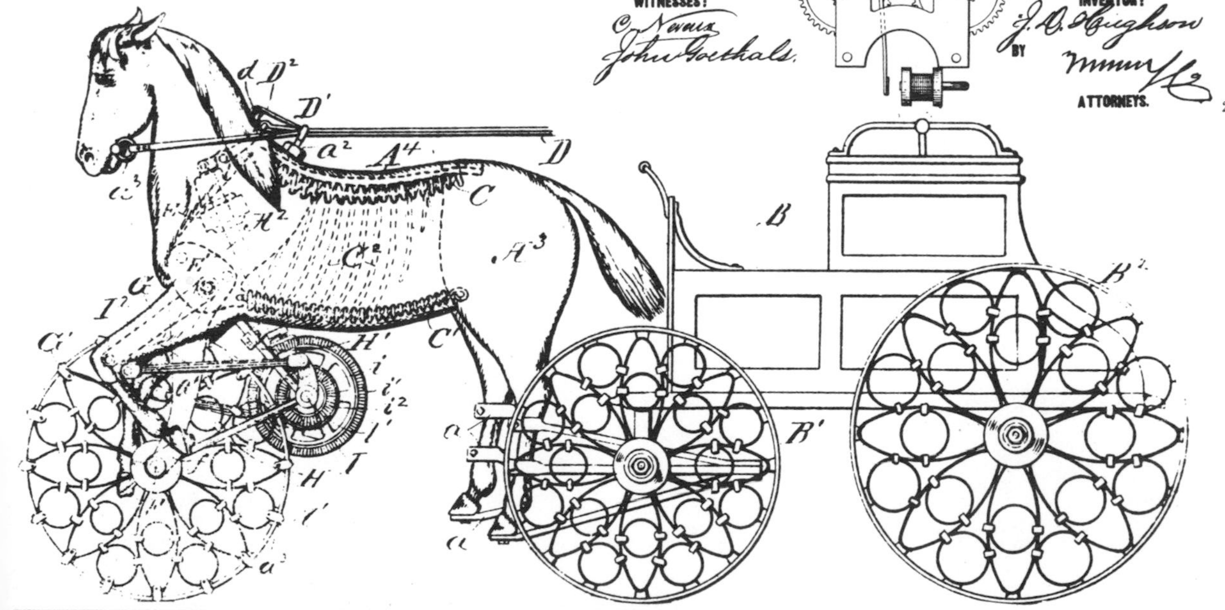

2759. Self-Propelled Vehicle Invented by Thomas J. Thorp. Patented, April 18, 1893.

*Burglar repelled by spreading pepper.

PEDDLERS

2760. Closing a Deal.

2761. French Itinerants, 16th century.

2762. Portugese.

2763. Forceful Sales Appeal.

2764. New York Tradesman.

2765. Soft Sell.

2766. Sieves.

2767. Tin-Pan Pushcart, N.Y.

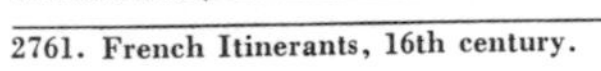

PERFUMERY

2768.

2769. Egypt. Sweet Herbs.

2770.*

2771. Medieval Lady Perfumer.

2772. Open-Air Sales Stand, 18th cent.

2773. Making Rosewater, Bulgaria.

2774. Testing Laboratory, 1910.

2775.

2776.

2777.

Make-up

2778. Egypt, 800 B.C.

2779. Rococo.

2780. Fragrant Flowers.

2781. Powder.

2782. Teenager, 1890.

2783. Beauty Spot.

* Egyptian Ointment Spoons

PHARMACY

2784. Monastic.

2785. Arabian Herbal.

2786. Jar, 16th cent.

2787. Renaissance Lab.

2788. English Apothecary.

2789. Prescription Filled.

2790. Corner Drugstore, 1878.

2791. Government Laboratory.

2792. Apprentice.

2793.

2794.

2795.

2796.

2797.

2798.

2799. German Drugstore, 1750.

2800. Drugstore, Broadway, N.Y. 1910.

2801.

PHONOGRAPH

2802. Talking Tree Stand.

2803. Edison Poster.

2804. Recording Session.

2805. Record Sales Booth.

2806. Trade Ad.

2807. Entertainer, 1895.

2808. 2809. Hand-Cranked. 2810.

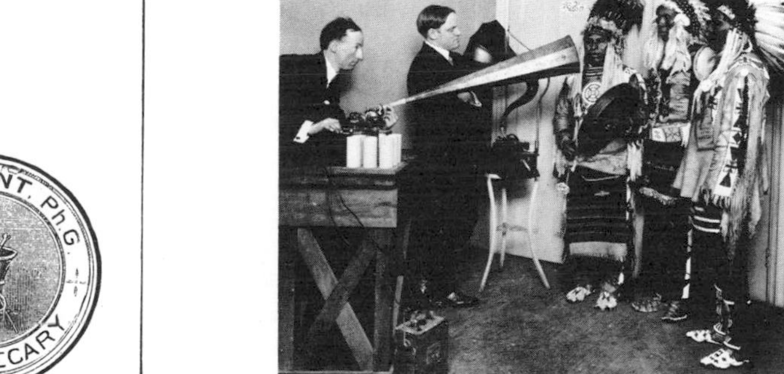
2811. Recording Indian War Songs, 1913.

2812. Advertising in Window of Midwestern Small Town Portrait Studio, 1932.

PHOTOGRAPHY

2813.
Rooftop Photoprinting Establishment in Edinburgh, 1880. "At that period, all photographs were printed by daylight. The tables covered with frames ran on rails. They were wheeled under the glass roof in wet weather. At its height, this establishment employed close to one hundred women copyists."

2814. Developing.

2815. Plate Package.

2816. Daguerre.

2817. Daguerre's First Camera.

2818. Central Park.

2819. Black-Cloth Man.

2820. Close Focus.

2821. Stereopticon.

2822. Studio Camera.

2823. Time Exposure: Man Immobilized.

2824. Tintype Man in Hyde Park, London.

2825. Baby Charmer.

2826. Photographic Chemicals.

2827. Kodak.

2828. Professional

2829.

2830.

2831. "You Push the Button."

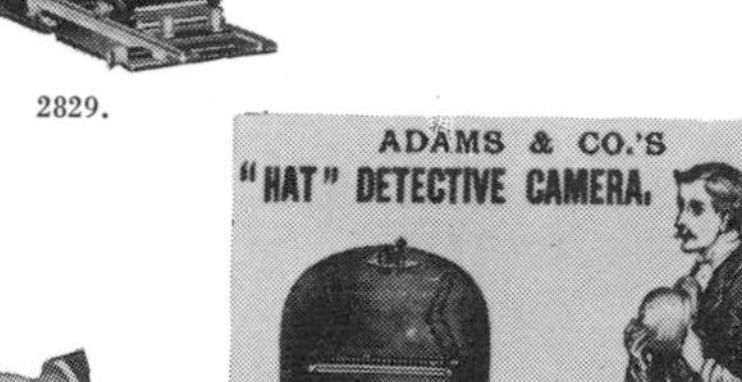

2832. Candid Camera.

2833. Carrier Pigeon with Aerial Camera.

2834. Aerial Photographer.

2835. Harding and White House Lensman.

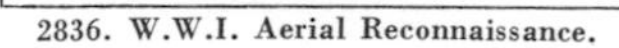

2836. W.W.I. Aerial Reconnaissance.

2837.

2838. Early Photo. (Talbot)

2839. News for Besieged Paris, Franco Prussian War Reports Projected, 1871.

2840. Family Sees itself in Magic Mirror.

PHYSICS

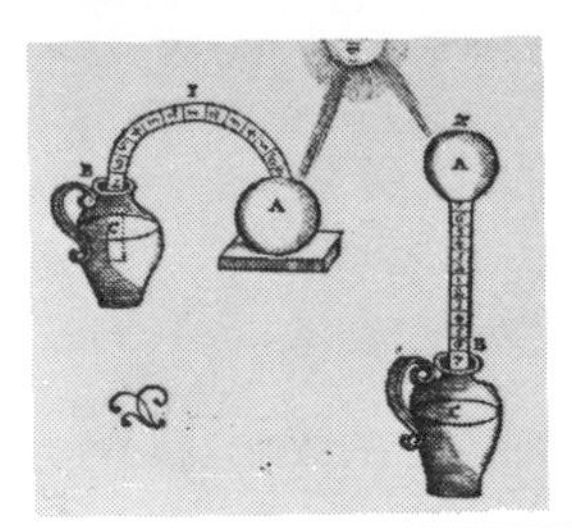

2841. Air Thermometer, ca. 1610.

2842. Galileo: Gravity.

2843. Torricelli: Air Pressure.

2844. Reaumur: Temperature.

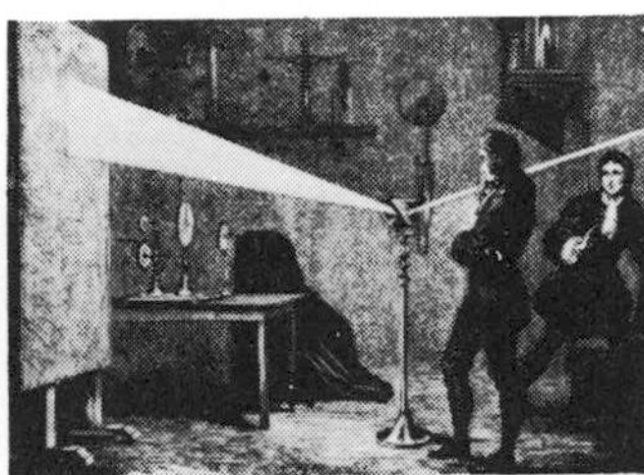

2845. Newton: Analysis of Sunlight.

2846. Guericke's Vacuum Pump Experiment. Magdeburg, 1654.

2847. Foucault Proves Earth's Rotation.

2848. Title Page.

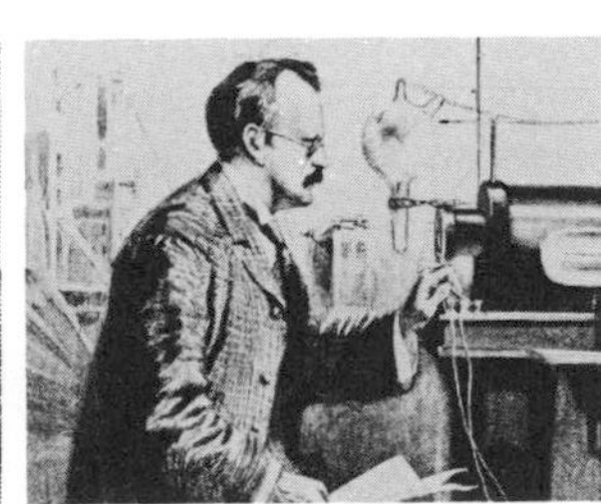

2849. J. J. Thomson: Cathode Rays.

2850. 2851. 2852. 2853. 2854. 2855. 2856.

2850. A. A. Michelson.
2851. Max Planck.
2852. Walter Nernst.
2853. Albert Einstein.
2854. V. F. Hess.
2855. Niels Bohr.
2856. Enrico Fermi.

PICNICS

2857. Outing in the Days of the Crinoline.

2858. Romantic Outing.

2859. Basket Lunch.

2860. Highland Party.

2861. Pre-W.W.I. Picnickers.

2862.

2863. Auto Picnic.

2864. Tristan entertained by Isolde. Note Portable Stove. Medieval Miniature.

PIONEERS

2865. Pioneer Statue. Saint-Gaudens.

2866. Plymouth Rock.

2867. Pioneer Couple.

2868. Westward Trek.

2869. Wagon Train Crossing the Prairie.

2870. In Search of Trail.

2871. Starting a Homestead.

2872. Settled on Nebraska Plains.

PIRATES

2873.

2874. Treasure.

2875. Drake's Treasure Ship with Loot.

2876. Boarding.

2877. Torture.

2878. Loading.

2879. Land Attack.

2880. Blackbeard.

2881. Captain Kidd Highstrung.

POSTCARDS

2893. Mail Truck, 1910.

POTTERY

2894.

2895. Pottery Making, Greece.

2896. Clay Figure, Peru.

2897. Potter's Wheel, 1530.

2898. Firing Kiln. 1890.

2899. Pottery Market, Mexico.

2900. 16th Century Printer with Inking Balls.

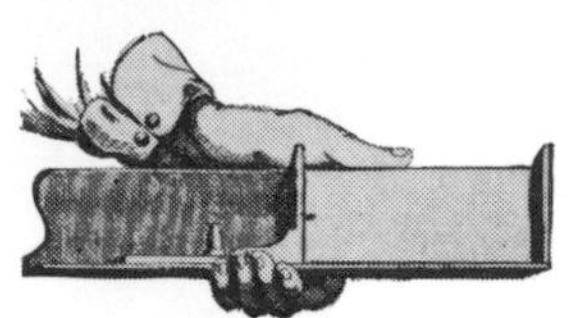

2901. Composing Stick.

2902. Chinese Block Printing.
2903. Gutenberg Inspects Proofs.
2904. 16th cent. Print Shop.
2905. Estienne, Master-Printer.
2906. Hand Press.
2907. Printer Inks Forms.
2908. Walking Print Shop.
2909.
2910. Frontier Printers, 1880.
2911. Inspecting Proofs.
2912. Press Run by Solar Energy, 1889.
2913. Rotary Press, 1840.
2914. Typsetting Machine.
2915. Advertisement, ca. 1860.
2916. Job Printer with Pedal Press.
2917. Stereotyper at Work.

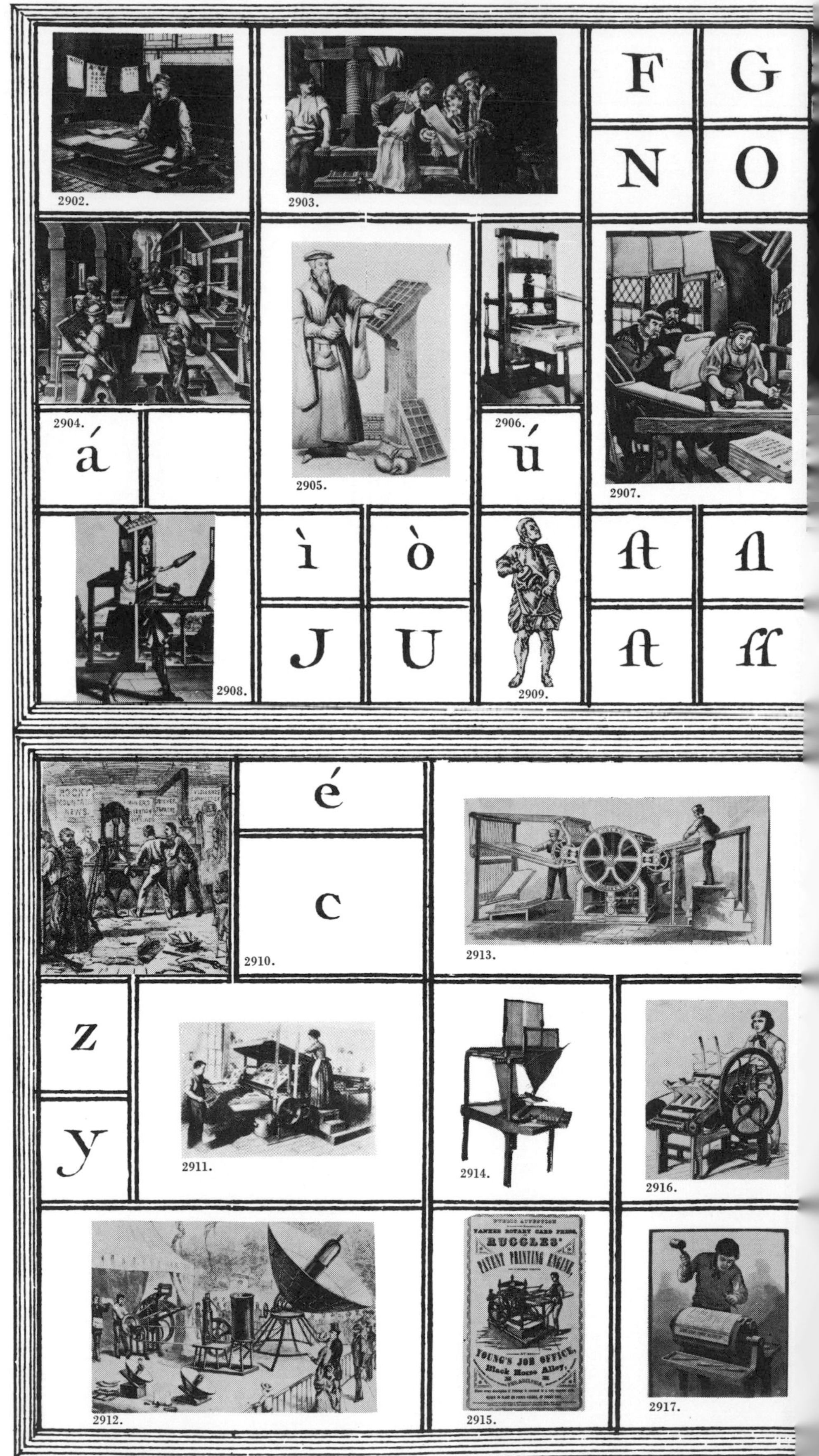

2935. Background: Type Case.

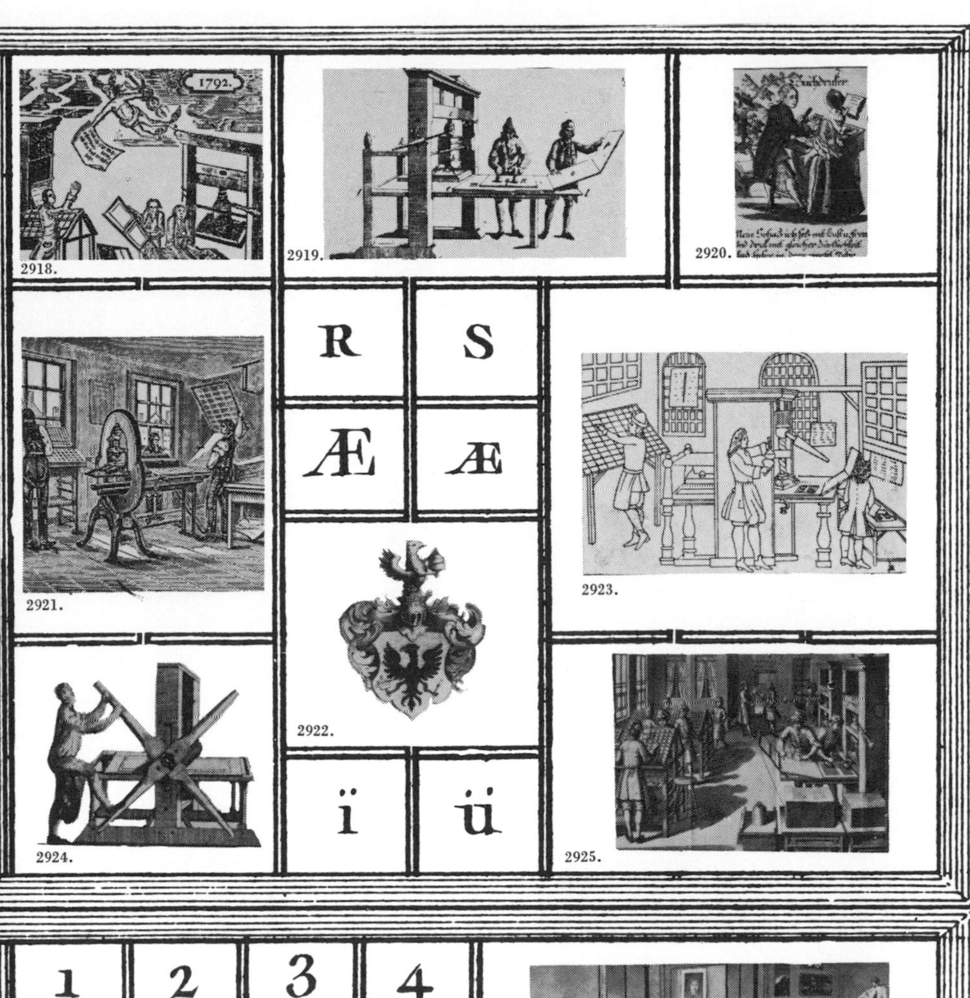

2918.
American Press.
2919.
Hand Press, 1770.
2920.
German Typesetter.
2921.
Press Shop, 1810.
2922.
Printers' Coat of Arms.
2923.
English Print House.
2924.
Copper Engraver's Press.
2925.
German Print Shop, 1740.
2926.
Roller Frame.
2927.
2928.
Inking Stand.
2929.
Currier Ad.
2930.
Women Typesetters, 1910.
2931.
Lithographer's Art Department.
2932.
Inking Lithographic Stone.
2933.
Master Printer Inspects Proofs.

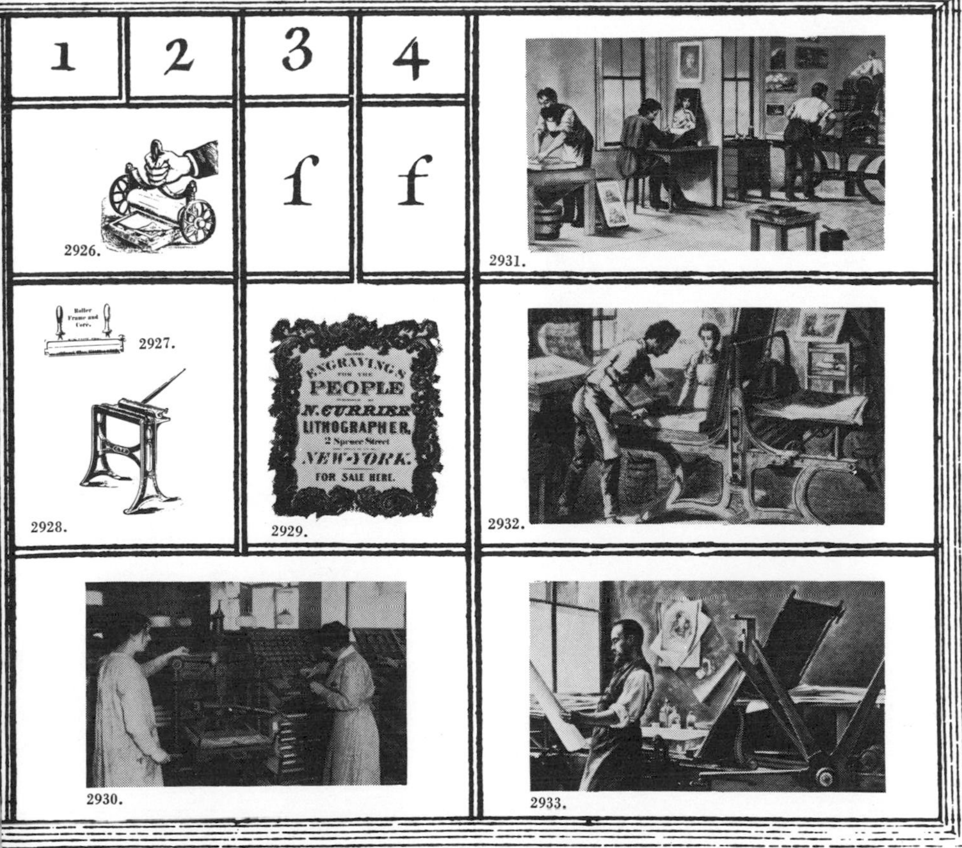

2934.
"It just can't be done."
Spoof ridiculing the idea of setting type by machine, 1880.

2936.

The eye of the Master does more than his hands.

2937.

Borrowed garments never fit well.

2938.

Much meat, much malady.

2939.

Make hay while the sun shines.

2940.

Too many cooks spoil the broth.

2941.

Caution is the parent of safety.

2942.

Good books create happiness.

2943.

Much coin, much care.

2944.

Haste makes waste.

2945.

If you want a thing done, go; if not, send.

2946.

Man things himself wise, till God shows him his folly.

2947.

Prove all things, hold fast that which is good.

2948.

A stitch in time, saves nine.

2949.

He that is warm, thinks all are so.

2950.

He who catches fish, gets wet.

2951.

Having too many things is worse than having none.

2952.

Let sleeping dogs lie.

2953.

Injuries are harder to revenge than to bear.

2954.

Strike while the iron is hot.

2955.

Goods well bought, are half sold.

Man thinks himself wise, till God shows him his folly.

A man was wondering why the acorn small,
Should grow on oaks so mighty, and so tall,
While on the slender pumpkin vine abound
Much larger fruits than on great oaks are found
But soon an acorn chanced to rattle down,
Which hit the foolish fellow on the crown:
Had pumpkins grown upon the oak instead,
He, doubtless, would have got a broken head.

READ THE BIBLE BY SYMBOLS.

And the angel said unto them, "Fear [symbol] for behold,

2957.

2958.

2959. Quaffers.

2960. Quadriga.

2961. Quadrille.

2962. Quadruplets.

2963. Quaker.

2964. Quarantine.

2965. Quarry.

2966. Quartet.

2967. Queen.

2968. Quill.

2969. Quintuplets, 1719.*

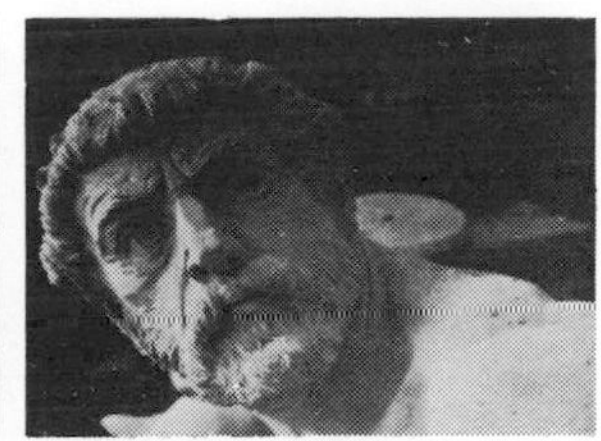

2970. Quiz

2970. For what building was this head of Hermes made? For answer see next page.

* Drawing by Dutch artist shows father gently guided by midwife for first glance at his progeny.

For complete, analytical subject index turn to page 221.

Answer to puzzle from previous page: Head of Hermes.
Detail on facade of Grand Central Station, New York.

2971. Wood Burner, 1869.

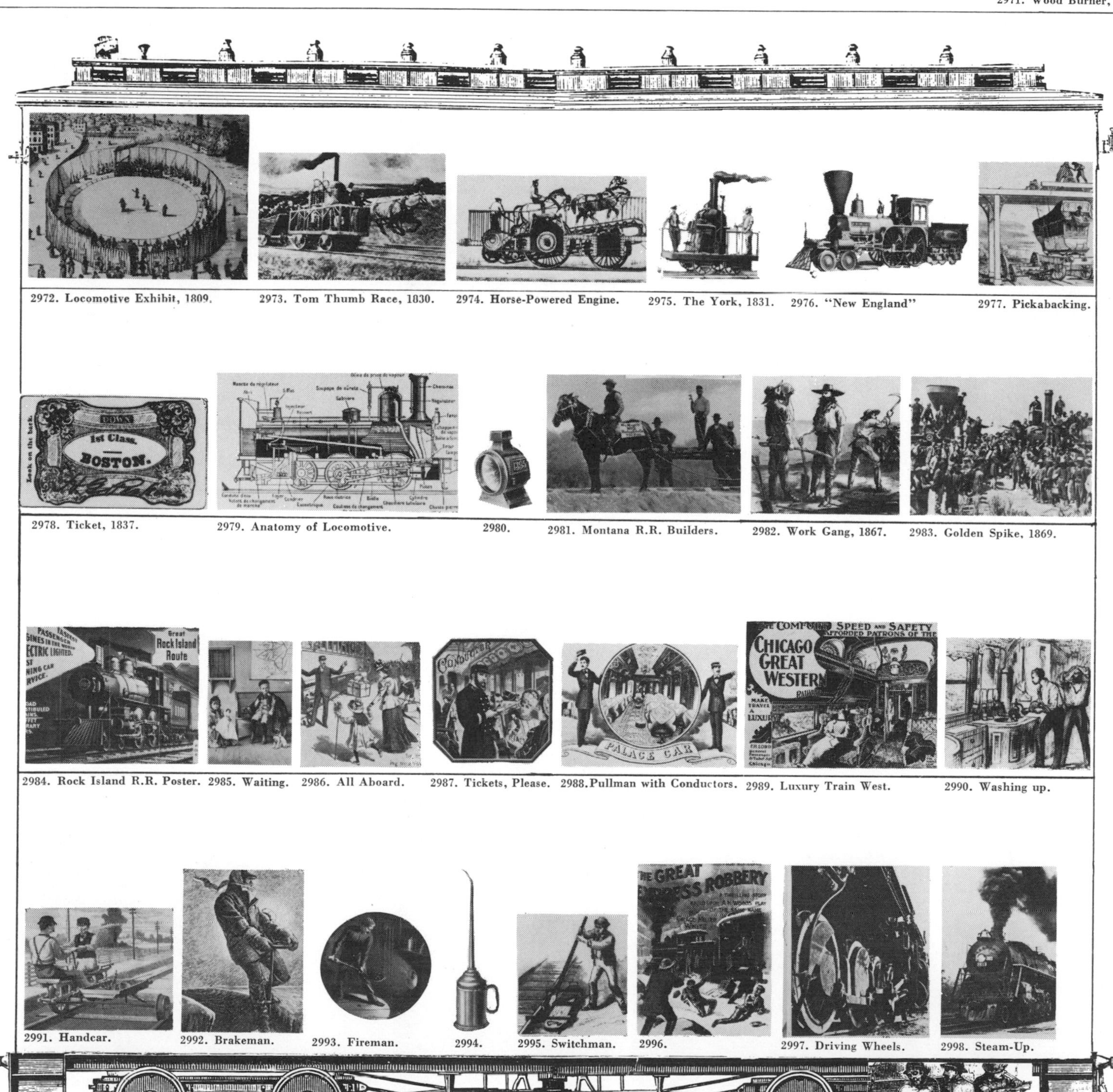

2972. Locomotive Exhibit, 1809. 2973. Tom Thumb Race, 1830. 2974. Horse-Powered Engine. 2975. The York, 1831. 2976. "New England" 2977. Pickabacking.

2978. Ticket, 1837. 2979. Anatomy of Locomotive. 2980. 2981. Montana R.R. Builders. 2982. Work Gang, 1867. 2983. Golden Spike, 1869.

2984. Rock Island R.R. Poster. 2985. Waiting. 2986. All Aboard. 2987. Tickets, Please. 2988. Pullman with Conductors. 2989. Luxury Train West. 2990. Washing up.

2991. Handcar. 2992. Brakeman. 2993. Fireman. 2994. 2995. Switchman. 2996. 2997. Driving Wheels. 2998. Steam-Up.

2999.

3000. Riding the Rods.

ROADS

3001. Via Appia near Rome.

3002. Medieval Road Building.

3003. Uphill.

3004. Road Scraping.

3005. Plank Road.

RUSH

3006.

3007.

3008.

3009.

ROCKETS

Scenes from Melié's "A Trip to the Moon"

3010.

3011.

3012.

3014. Bull's-eye!

3013. Blast Off.

3020. Homemade, 1882.

3019. Floating across Craters.

3018. Rocket Trip Prediction, 1880.

3017. Before Impact.

3016. Launching Pad.

3015. Chinese Rocket-Chair.

3022.
Clutching Rocket.

3021. Man Floating in Space. Illustration from 18th century Novel.

For complete, analytical subject index turn to page 221.

SALT

3023.

3024. Verona Salt Shop.

3025. Cellini Saltcellar.

3026. Evaporation.

3027. Saltworks, 1774.

3028. Salt Mining, Wieliczka, Poland.

3029. Selling Bulk Salt, Morocco.

SCALES

3030. Gold Weigher, Egypt.

3031.

3032. Justice.

3033. Medieval Scales, 1023.

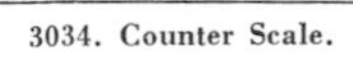

3034. Counter Scale.

3035. Cattle Scale.

3036. The Critical Moment.

3037.

3038.

3039.

3040.

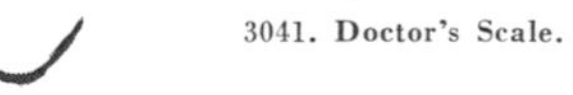

3041. Doctor's Scale.

3042. Medieval Merchants.

3043. Household.

SCHOOLS

3044. From a Student Notebook, 1836.

3045. Plato.

3046. Class, Bologna University.

3047. Brueghel.

3048. Rector, Padua.

3049. Boys' School, 17th cent.

3050. Froebel's First Kindergarten.

3051. Caught Napping.

3052.

3053. French System of Mutual Education, 1811.

3054. Frontier School.

3055. Dunce.

3056. School Desk, 1862.

3057. N. Y. School, 1890.

3058. American Country School.

SEASONS

3059. The Four Seasons.

3060. Spring.

3061. Summer.

3062. Fall.

3063. Winter.

3064. Boy Shooting.

SEWING

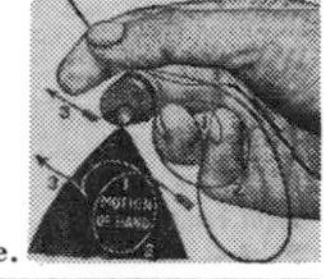
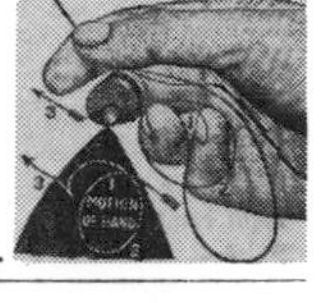

3065. Thread Cutting Thimble.

3066. Colonial Seamstress.

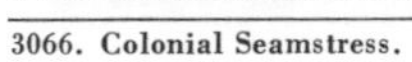

3067. Sewing Room, Stewart Store.

3068. New Family Sewing Machine.

3069. Pincushion.

3070. Motor-driven.

3071. Ad, 1860.

3072. Singer, 1851.

3073. Machine, 1870's.

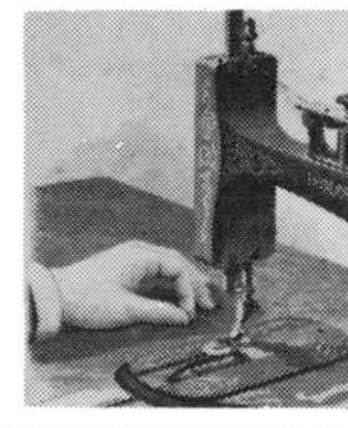

3074. Threading.

3075.

3076.

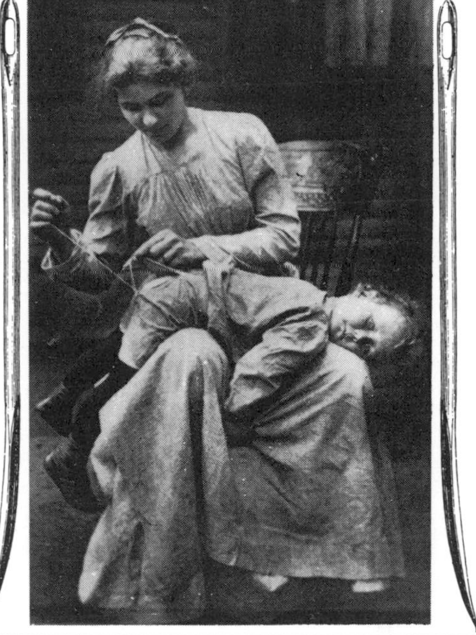

3077. A Stitch in Time. Photograph, 1895.

SHAKESPEARE

3078.

3079.

3080. "My Kingdom for a horse."

3081. Performance.

3082. Falstaff.

3083. Portia.

3084. Midsummer Night's Dream.

3085. Romeo and Juliet.

3086. Macbeth and Lady.

3087. Edition, 1623.

3088. Hamlet: Sarah Bernhardt.

3089. Hamlet: Lawrence Olivier, 1948.

3090. Fulton's Clermont.

3091. First Atlantic Steamer: Savannah.

3092. Signalling Ashore.

3093.

3094. S. S. Mauretania.

3095. Pilot.

3096. Leaving for Europe.

3097. Captain, 1857.

3098. Ship and Anchor.

3099. Rough Seas.

3100. Heroes (for detail see p. 182).

3101. Capstan.

3102. Indian Great Lakes Raft.

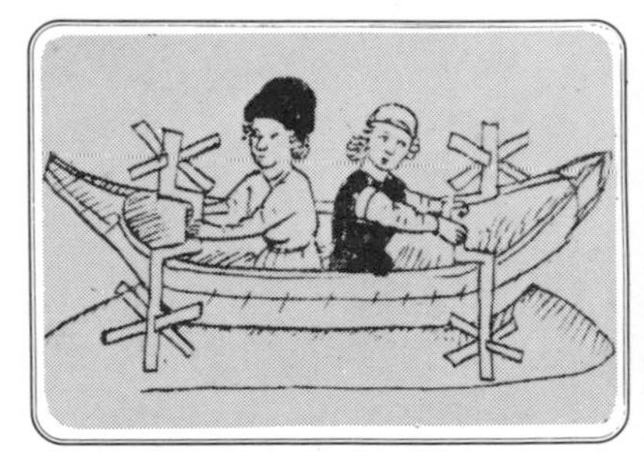

3103. Mechanized Paddle Boat, 1450.

3104. Egyptian Rowboat.

3105. Canoe Race with Blankets as Sails.

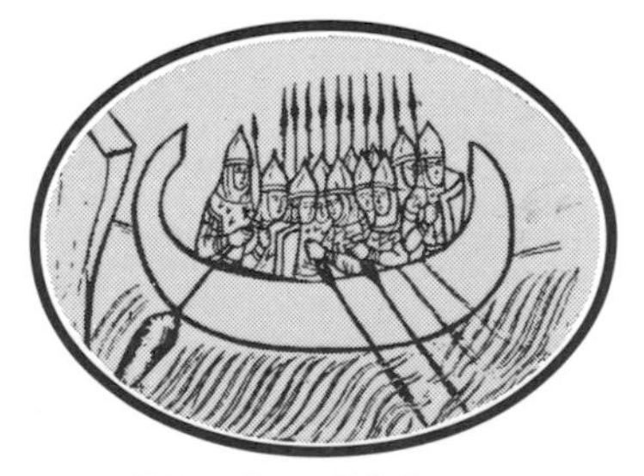

3106. Military Barge, 10th Cent.

3107. Columbu

3108. Pilot at the Wheel.

3109. Mississippi Side-Wheeler.

3110. Pilot's Manual.

3111. Mississippi Ferry.

3112. Explosion of the Natchez.

3113. Pilot's Wheel.

3114. Binnacle.

3115. The Ships of Columbus.

3116. Tobacco Wharf.

3117. Shooting a Life Line.

3118. Tea Clipper.

3119. Loading a Mississippi Steamer.

3120. Detail from Old Map.

Maria.

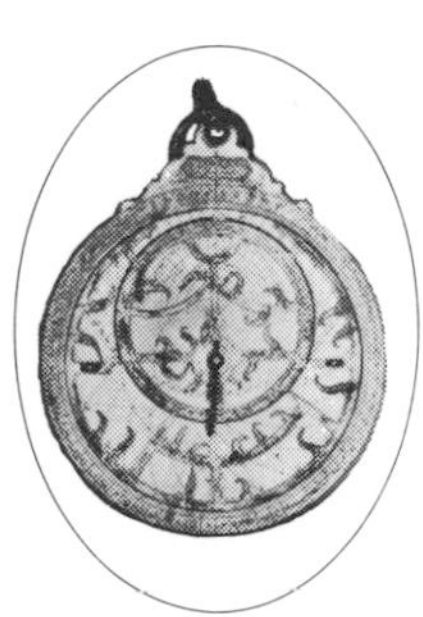

3121. Astrolabe.

3122. Italian, ca. 1580.

3123. Crow's Nest.

3124. Clipper Ship Poster.

3125. Gay Excursion.

3100. Heroes of the Goodwin Sands: 710 lives were saved by these men.

3126. Florentine Shoe Shop, 1492.

3127. Elevated Shoes. Venice.

3128.

3129. German Shoe Market.

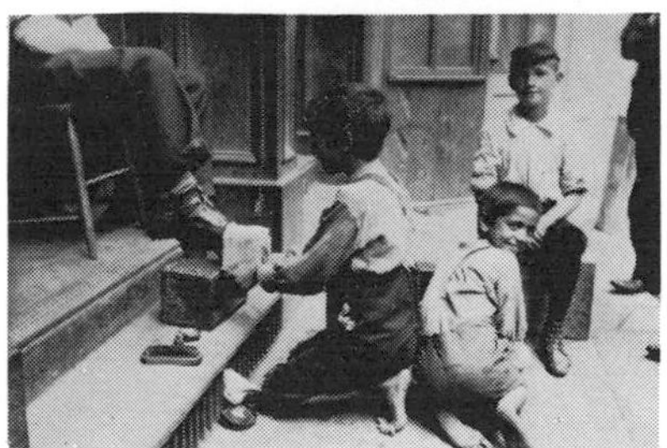

3130. New York Shoeshine Boys, 1900.

3131. Fin de Siècle Styles.

3132. Trade Sign.

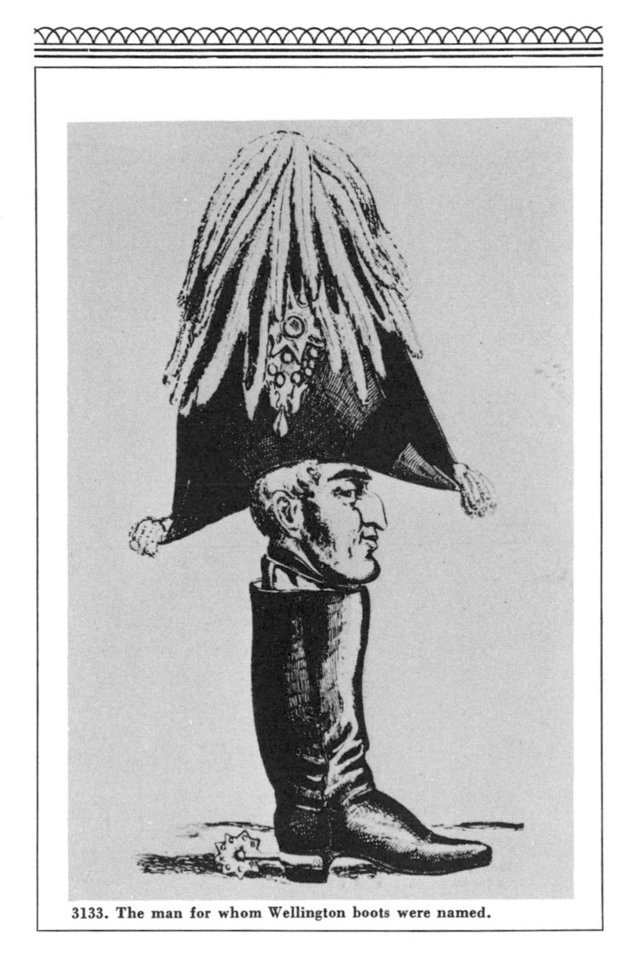

3133. The man for whom Wellington boots were named.

3134. Cobbler's Bench.

3135. Haines Shoemobile.

3136.

3137.

3138.

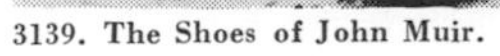

3139. The Shoes of John Muir.

3140. Craftsman.

3141.

3142. 18th Century Clog.

3143. Hand-sewing.

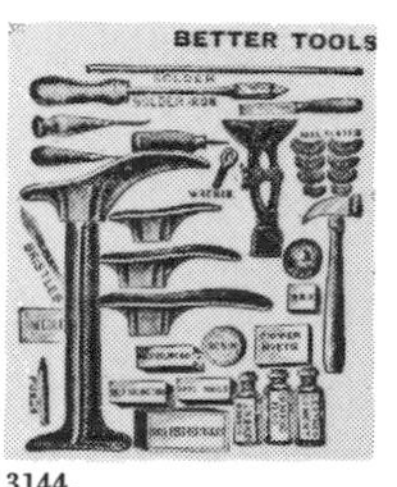

3144.

3145. Display, 1852.

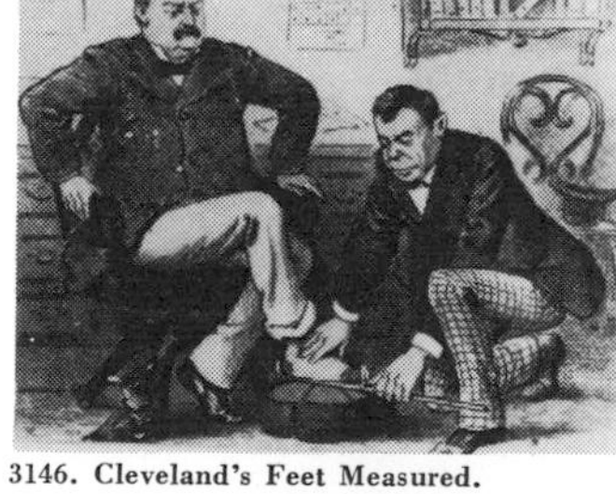

3146. Cleveland's Feet Measured.

3147.

3148.

3149. Head of Hypnos.

3150. Sleeping Beauty.

3151. Fiddling to Sleep.

3152. Santa Barbara. (Carpaccio)

3153. Drowsy Head Song.

3154. Sound Country Sleep.

SOUND

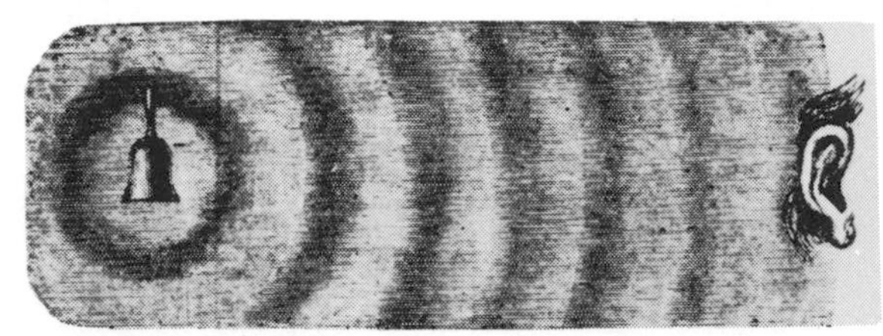

3155. Sound Waves.

3156. Echo Personified.

3157. Whispering Rod.*

3158. Acoustic Experiment, 1673.

3159. Greek Command Horn.

3160. First Megaphone.

Radio

3161. Radio Studio, 1923.

3162. Early Ham.

3163. Battery Set, 1923.

3164. Boys Listening to New Set.

3165. Strange Antenna.

3166. Ben Turpin and Friend.

3167. Electric Amplifier.

3168. Best Foot Forward.

Vision of Television

3169. Opera and ballet at home.
3170. Employer supervising office

3171. Police TV predicted in 1900
3172. Televised Education, 1882.

* Hollow pipe used in Colonial Period by lovers to exchange private confidences in crowded family parlor.

SLEEP

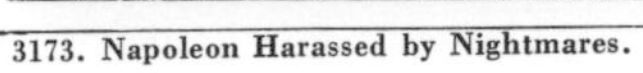

3173. Napoleon Harassed by Nightmares.

3174. Post Prandial Nap.

3175. Mechanized Alarm.

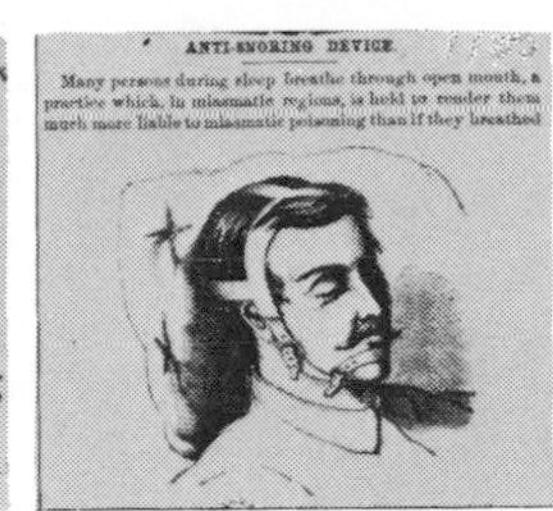

3176. Anti-Snoring Mask.

3177. Romantic Vignette.

SOUND

3178. Nautical Pickup.

3179. Sound System suggested by the German Jesuit Scholar, Athanasius Kircher (1601-1680): Sound channel (G) modelled after ear's cochlea transmits conversations from courtyard to supervisor's curtain-insulated studio. Here sound emanates from sculptured loud speaker (E).

3180. 3181. 3182. 3183. 3184. 3185. 3186. 3187. 3188. 3189.

Baseball

3190. Brooklyn Diamond, 1866.

3191. Pitcher.

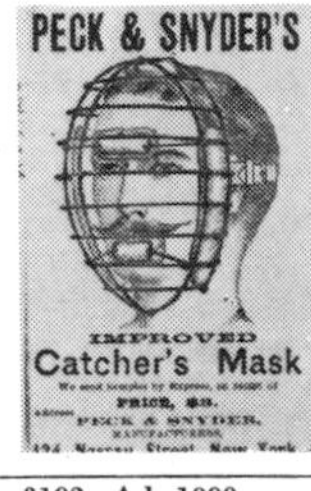

3192. Ad, 1890.

3193. Baseball Delivery Gun.

3194. Tagged out at Second Base.

3195. Ty Cobb.

Football

3196. First Intercollegiate Game, 1869.

3197. Match between Yale and Princeton, 1879.

3198.

3199.

3200. Flying Wedge.

Tennis

3201.

3202. Aftermatch.

3203. Davis Cup Donor.

3204. First Tournament, Staten Island, 1880.

3205. 3206.

Golf

3207.

3208.

3209. Babe Ruth.

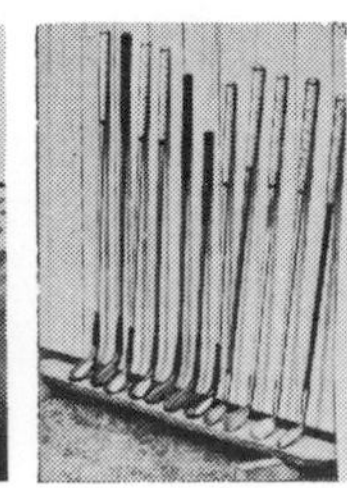

3210.

3211. Putting: Tense Moment.

3212. Bobby Jones.

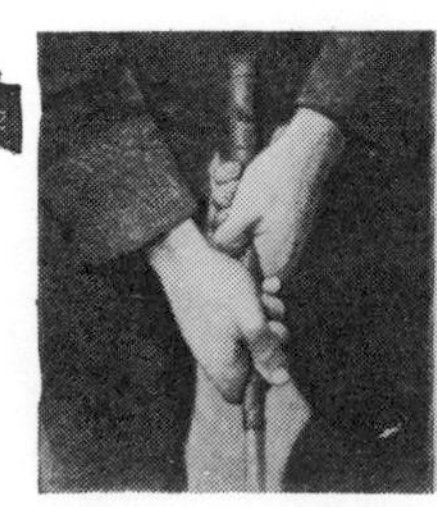

3213.

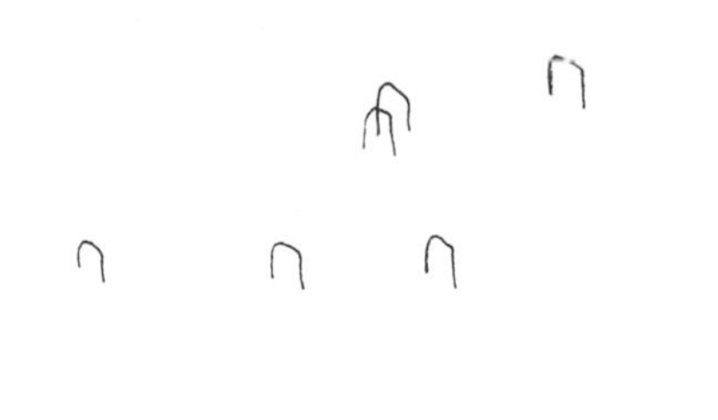

3214.

Bowling

3215. Medieval.

3216. Colonists on Bowling Green.

3217. Ladies' League.

Croquet

3218. Garden Party, ca. 1870.

3219. Cricketers in Top Hats.

Boxing

3220. Heenan-Sayers Fight.

3221. Punch.

3222. Amazon Prize Fighters.

3223. Clinch.

3224. Disputed Knockout, Johnson-Willard, 1915.

3225. Slugging it Out.

3226. The Finishing Punch, 1886.

3227. Stance.

Basketball

3228. Girls' Basketball Team, ca. 1900.

3229. First Use of Peach Basket, 1902.

POLISHED MAPLE TEN PINS.

3230.

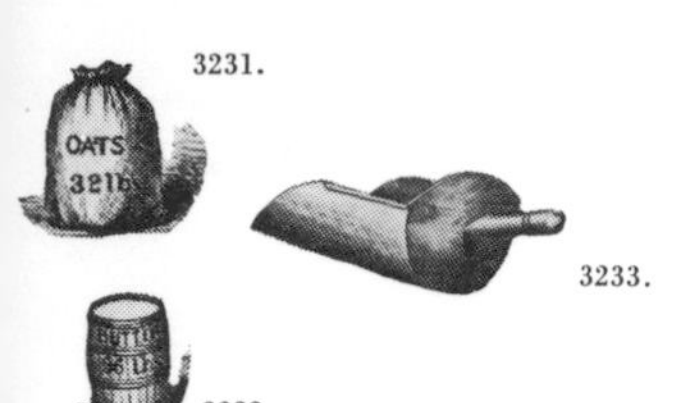

3231.

3232.

3233.

3234.

3235. Haberdashery and Bookshop, 1820.

3236. Roman Dry Goods Store.

3237. Merchant.

3238. Outdoor Display.

3239. Jewelry.

3240. Grab a Bargain.

3241. Fashion Store, 1903.

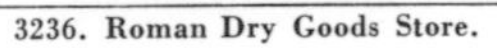

3242. Early 5 and 10.

3243. Notions.

3244. French Department Store: Fabrics.

3245. Regency Store Front.

3246. Catalogue Cover.

3247. Harry Truman in his Store.

3248. Potbellied Buddies.

3249. American Grocery, 1830.

3250. Grocer, 1880.

3251. Inventory.

3252. Store Front with Prices. Ben Shahn Photograph, 1933.

3253. General Store, Nebraska.

3254. The Corner Grocer Ready to Serve.

3255. Interior of Grocery, 1895.

3256. Frontier Store.

SUNS

3257.

3258.

3259.

3260.

3261.

3262

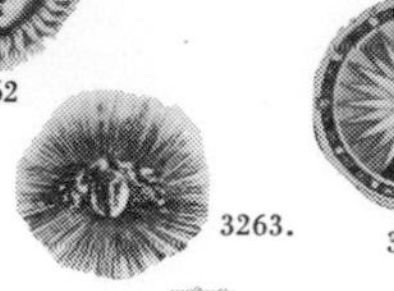

3263.

3264.

3265.

3266.

3267.

3268.

3269.

SURVEYING

3270. England, 1598.

3271. German Geometer.

3272. Surveying in Warfare.

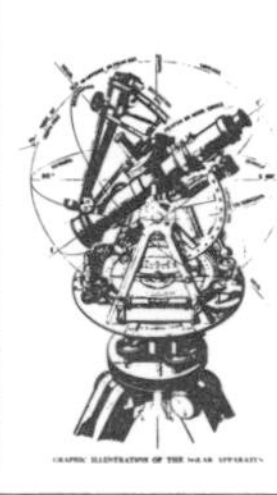

3273. Level.

3274. George Washington, Surveyor.

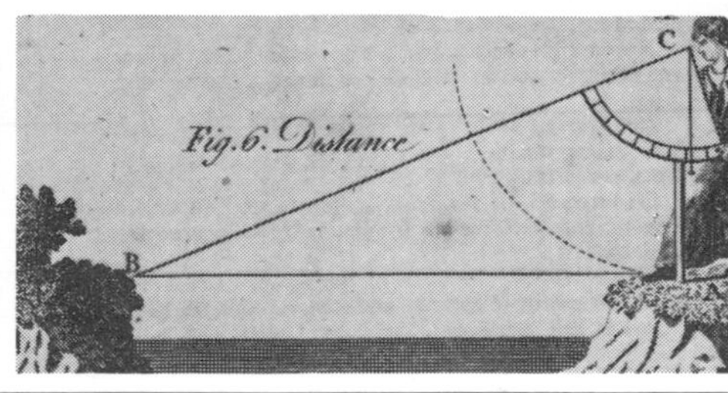

3275. Measuring Width of a River.

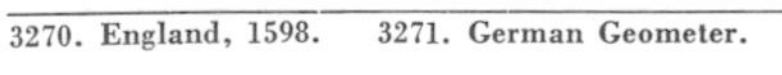

3276. Team of Egyptian Surveyors measuring Nile delta. River's ebb and flow necessitated frequent surveys. This spurred rise of mathematics in ancient Egypt.

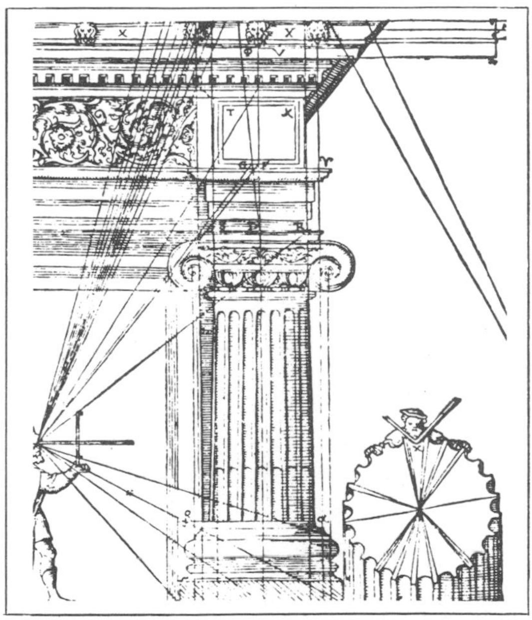

3277. Surveying a Renaissance Building.

For complete, analytical subject index turn to page 221.

TAXES

3278.

3279. Greeks Pay Taxes with Grain.

3280. Roman Tax Collector Counts Coins.

3281. Peasant Pays with Eggs, ca. 1530.

3282. Paying Tax in 18th century France.

3283. Shooing Collector.

3284. Tax Paid.

TEAMS

3285.

3290.

3291.

3292.

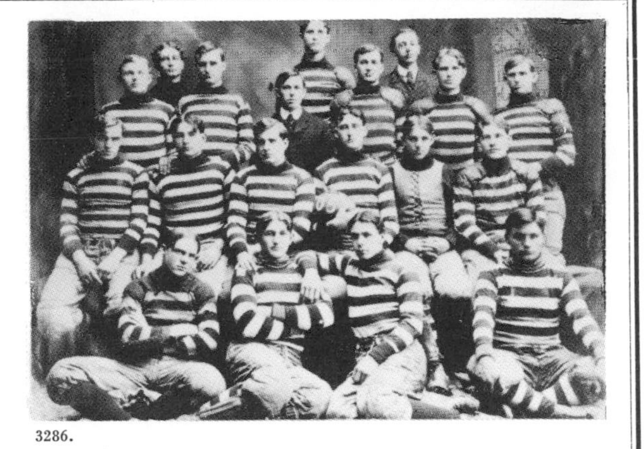

3286.

3293.

3294.

3296.

3295.

3287.

3297.

3299.

3298.

3300.

3301.

3288.

3302.

3289.

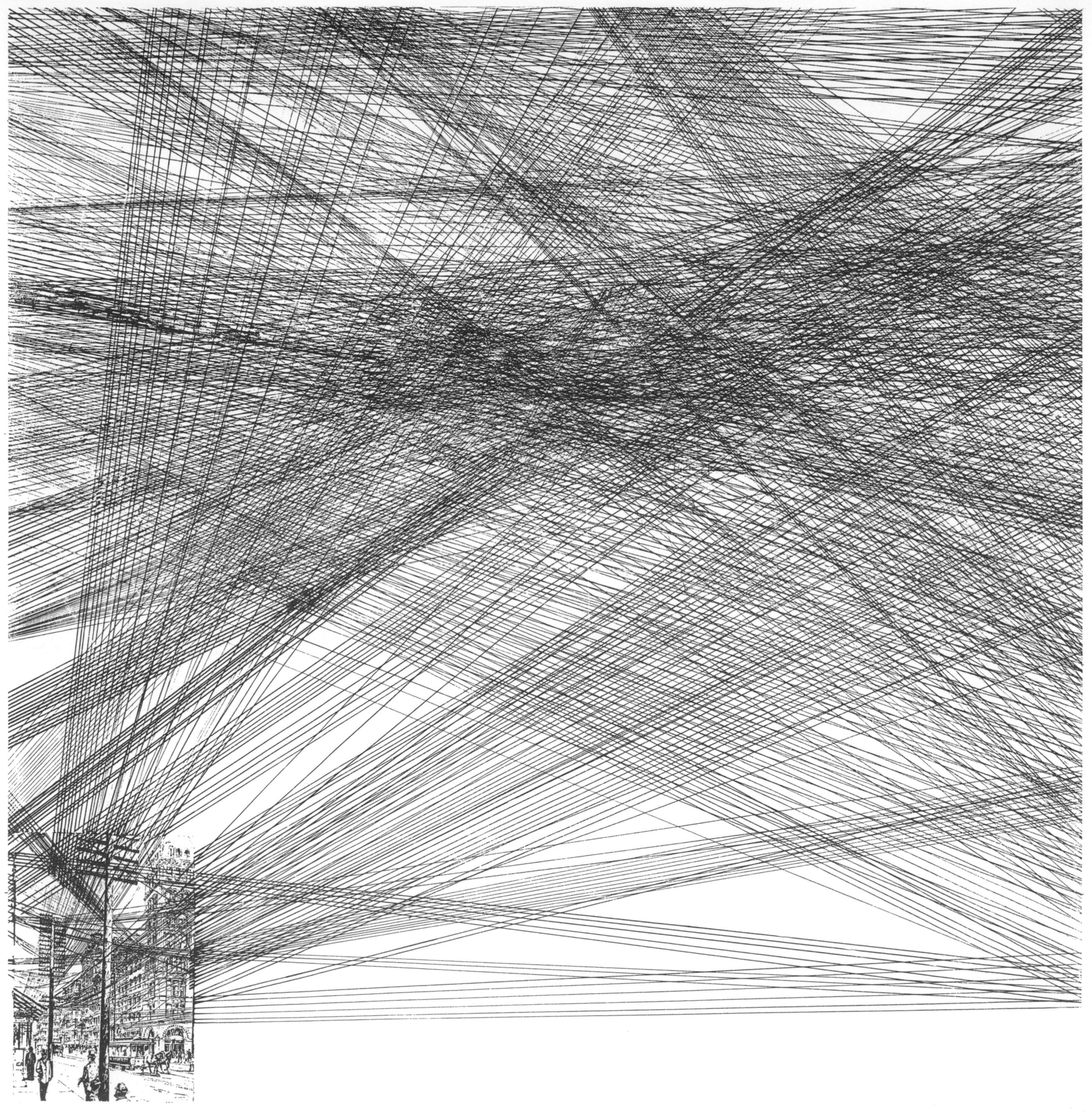

3303. Disorderly Wires on lower Broadway, New York City, 1889.

TELEGRAPH

3304. Morse Demonstration.

3305. Telegraph Key.

3306. Transmitting a Message.

3307. Pretty Operator.

3308. Marconi and Wireless.

3309. Transatlantic Cable, 1866.

TELEPHONE

3310. Ear of Dionysius. *

3311. Bell Experiment.

3312.

3313.

3314.

3315.

3316.

3317.

3322.

3323.

3324.

3318.

3319.

3325.

3326.

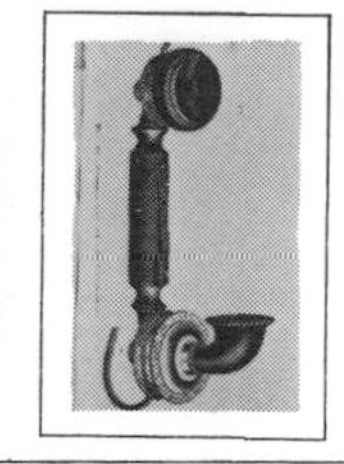

3320.

3321.

*Ear of Dionysius: This Tyrant of Syracuse supervised prisoners in mountain dungeon by way of secret sound channels—an early case of "bugging".

3327. Golden Fleece.

Spinning

3328. Egypt.

3329. Colonial Wheel.

3330. Priscilla.

3331. Spinning Equipment.

3332. Hargreaves' Spinning Jenny.

3333. Wrecking Power Looms.

3334. Yarn-Spinning Plant, ca. 1830.

Weaving

3335. Exhibiting the Old and New Ways.

3336. Yarn Mass-Produced.

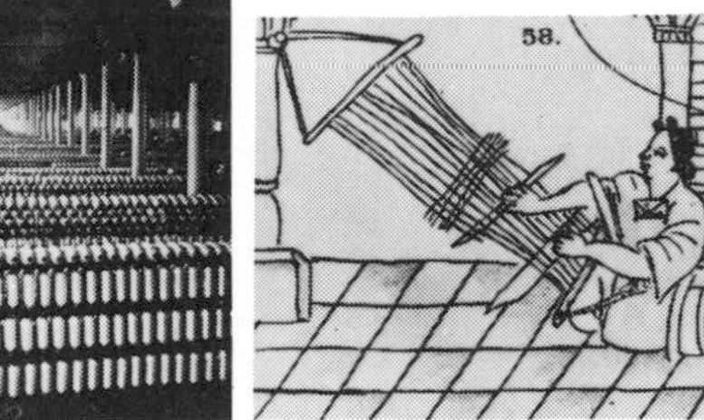

3337. Aztec Woman Weaving.

3338. Cross-Section, 1760.

3339. Loom.

3340. Housewife Weaves on Attic Loom.

3341. Inspection.

3342. English textile factory (1835) showing steam-driven calico printing machines.

3343. Woollen Press, England, 18th Century.

Finishing

3344. Manufacture of Dyestuffs.

3345. Bleachery, 1853.

3346. Dyer, 1568.

3347. Shearing Cloth.

3348. Cloth Smoothed with Thistles.

3349. Silk-Screen Printing.

3350. Final Inspection.

Silk

3351. Silkworm in Cocoon.

3352. Chinese Empress. * 3353. Weaving.

3354. Unwinding Cocoons.

Cotton

3355.

3356. Introducing Cotton Gin.

3357. Whitney Model.

3358. Southern Ruler.

3359. Cotton Hand Truck.

3360.

3361. Cotton Wharf, New Orleans.

3362. Mississippi Plantation.

3363. Calico Ball staged to promote cotton goods, Manchester.

3364.

* Hsi-ling Shih, purported originator of silk culture, 3rd Millenium B.C.

3365.

THEATER

3366. Amphitheater, Verona.

3367. Theater of Dionysus, Athens.

3368. Mask. Pompeii.

3369. Proscenium, 1810.

3370. "Emile, let's go already."

3371. 3372. 3373. 3374. 3375.

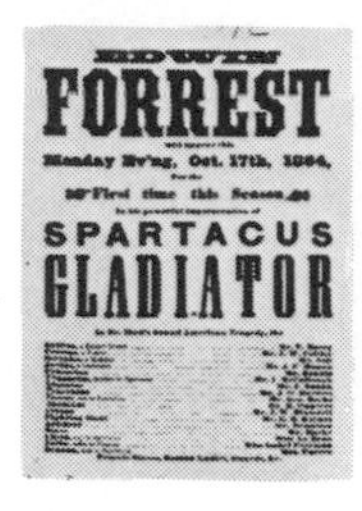

3376. Poster.

3377. Booth.

3378. Ziegfield's.

3379. Fin de Siècle Melodrama.

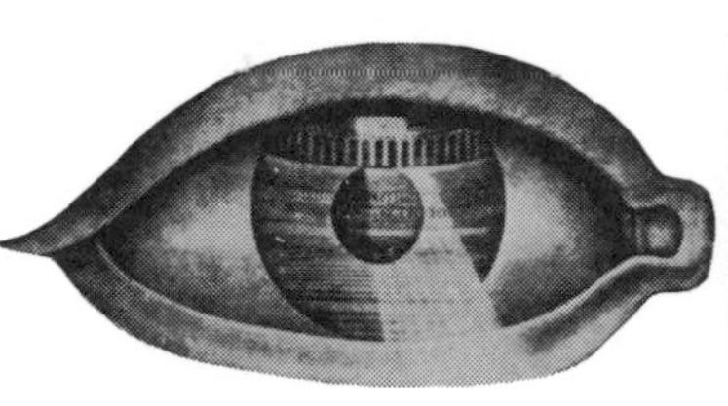

3380.

3381. Anna Held.

3382. Bernhardt.

3383. Adams.

3384. At the Theater. Wash drawing by Constantin Guys.

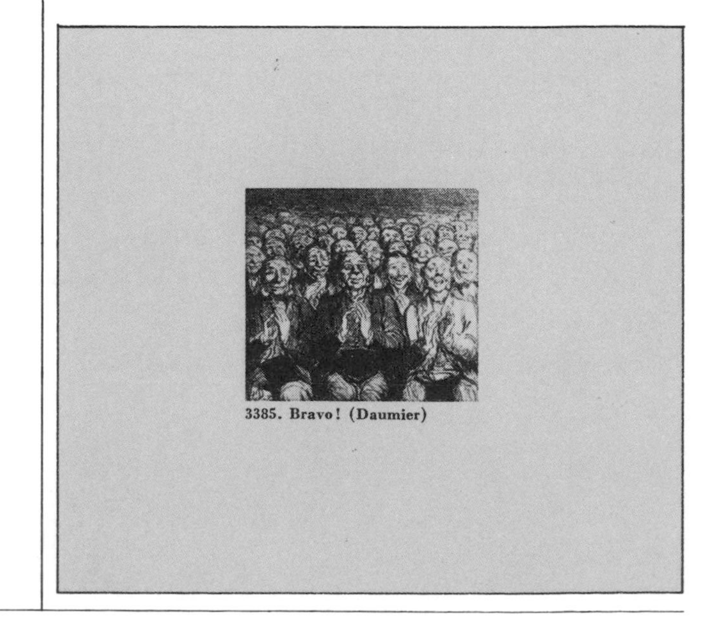

3385. Bravo! (Daumier)

3386.
Park Theater, New York,
November 7, 1822
Charles Matthews and Miss Johnson
in Montcrieff's Farce,
"Monsieur Tonson."
Water color by John Searle.
(N.Y. Hist. Soc.)

Cigar Box Labels of the 19th century, a form of graphics impressive in its flowery inventiveness and close in technique to Pop Art and Camp.

3387.

3388.

3389.

3390.

3391.

3392. Rolling Tobacco Leaves, ca. 1700.

3393. Pipe for 36 Men, Vienna, 1789.

3394.

3395. New Guinea Pipe.

3396. Peace Pipe.

3397.

3398. Collegium of Pipe Smokers.

3399. Britain's Favorite.

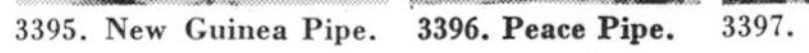

3400. Lighter.

3401. Insufficient Reach.

3402. All-Day Smoke.

3403. Pinch of Snuff.

3404.

3405. Lapp Woman.

3406. Burmese Smoker.

3407. Pipe.

3408. Daring Females.

3409. Demimonde of the 1920's.

3411. Lady Smoker.

3410. Cigar Box, ca. 1880.

3412. Label.

For complete, analytical subject index turn to page 221.

UNICORNS

3413. 3414.

3415

3416. 3417. 3418.

UMBRELLAS

3423. Lifted.

3420.

3419.

3421. Pocket-Umbrella Ad, 1770.

3422. Sea of Umbrellas, Hyde Park, London.

3424. Greek.

3425. Umbrella-shaped Tree.

3426. The Leaking Roof.

3427. Protection.

UNDERWEAR

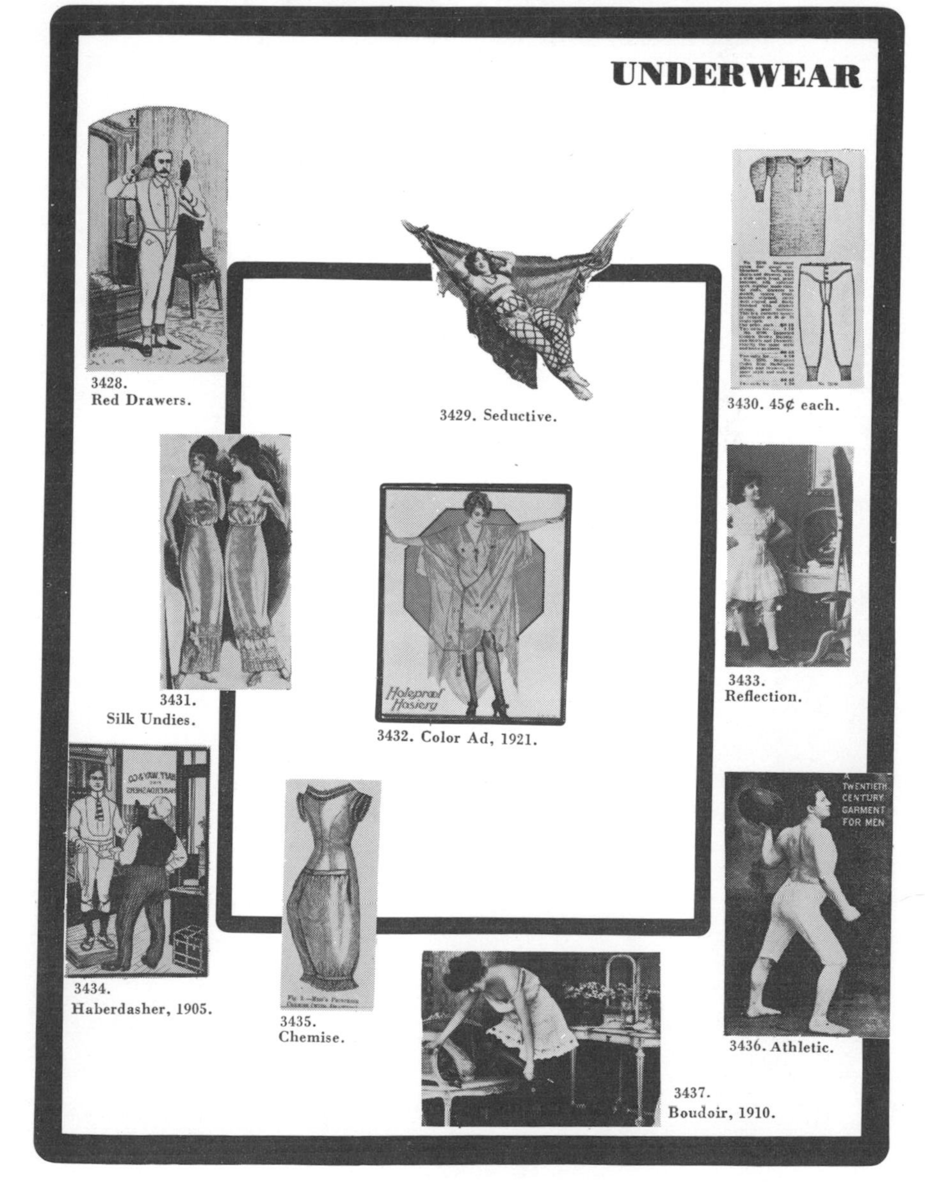

3428.
Red Drawers.

3429. Seductive.

3430. 45¢ each.

3431.
Silk Undies.

3432. Color Ad, 1921.

3433.
Reflection.

3434.
Haberdasher, 1905.

3435.
Chemise.

3436. Athletic.

3437.
Boudoir, 1910.

3438. Belle floating toward Saratoga.

3439. Cook's Office.

3440. French Maid Helps with Packing.

3441.

3442. Too Full.

3443. Arrival at Hotel.

3444. Girl Tourist.

3445. Relaxing on Porch.

3446. Rendezvous.

3447. Porch Talk.

3448. Welcome.

3449. Day at Seaside.

3450. Boardwalk.

3451. In the Swing.

3452. Holiday Flirtation.

3453. Oceanside Hotel.

3454. Ocean View.

Fishing

3455. Serenity.

3456. Great Catch.

3457. Huck Finn.

3458. Homemade Gear.

3459. Outboard Motor.

3460. Fishermen's Camp: Morning.

3461. Bait.

3462.

3463. Catching Blue Fish, Asbury Park.

3464. Beach Hotel, Long Island.

3465. Marquee.

3473.

VENUS

Cabin Roof:
3474.
Guido Reni.

Deck:
3475.
Venus Anadiomene.
3476.
Venus of Milo.
3477.
Cranach.
3478.
Rowlandson.

Ocean:
3479.
Capitoline Venus
3480:
Botticelli: Venus
Boat:
Courtesy: Chris-Craft.

3481. Self-Portrait.

3482. Flight.

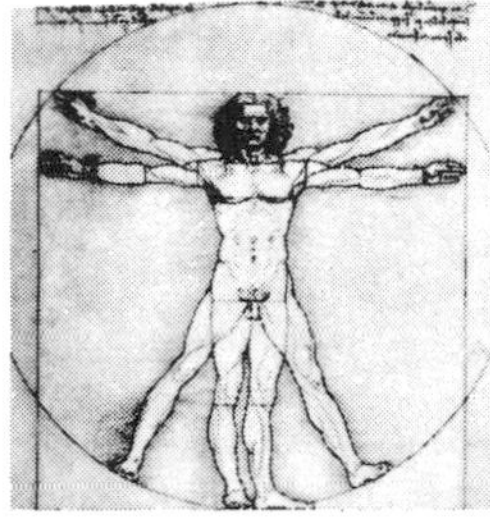

3483. Proportions of Man.

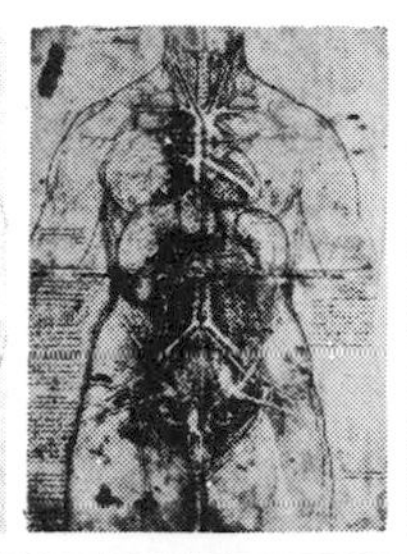

3484. Anatomy.

3485. Mind.

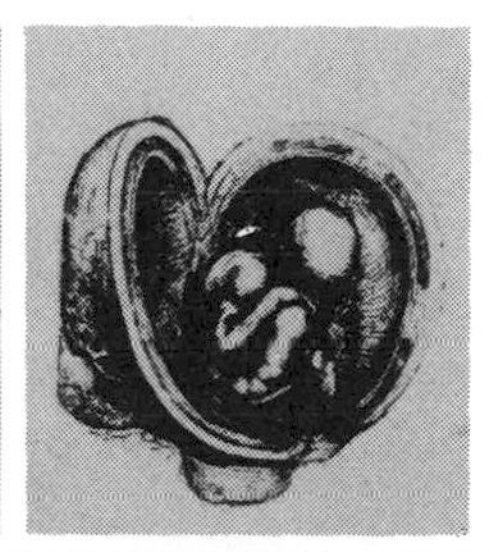

3486. Birth.

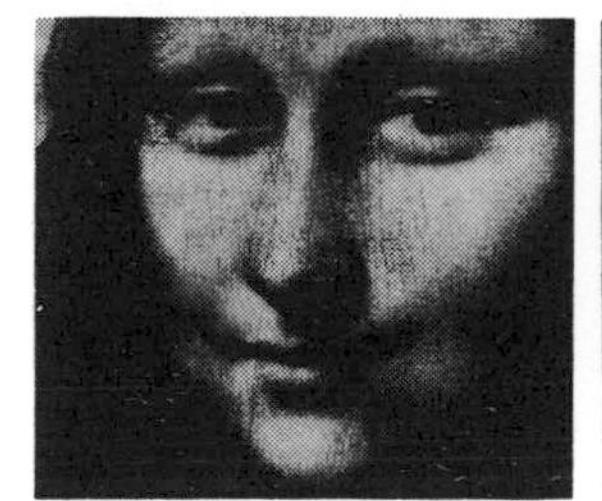

3487. Enigma of Beauty.

3488. Ugliest Woman.

3489. Grotesque.

3490. Equestrian.

3491. Motion Study.

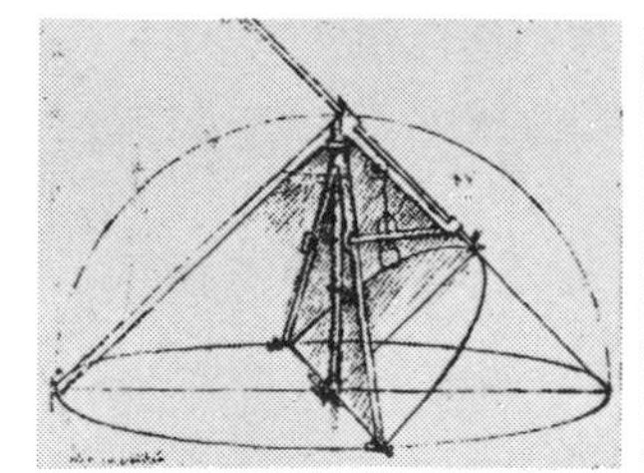

3492. Trigonometry.

3493. Mechanical Lathe.

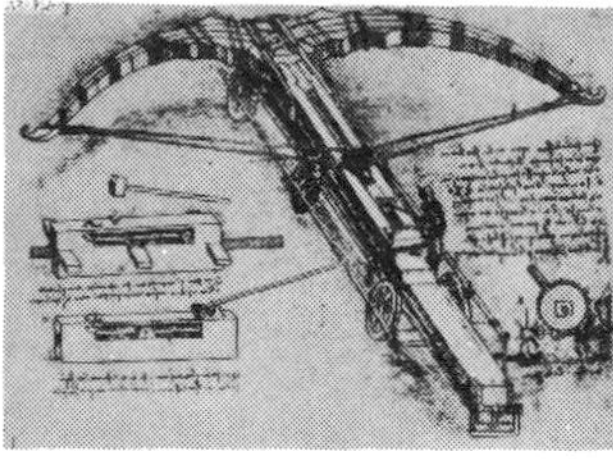

3494. Giant Bow.

3495. Crane.

3496. City Planning.

3497. Water Skis.

3498. Gyroscope.

3499. Life Preserver.

L da Vinci

For complete, analytical subject index turn to page 221.

3500.
Cherry Tree Legend.
3501.
Marriage.
3502.
Mt. Vernon Hunter.
3503.
Statesman.
3504.
Delaware.
3505.
Valley Forge.
3506.
Lafayette.
3507.
Inauguration.
3508.
Reception.
3509.
Martha Washington.
3510.
Country Squire.
3511.
Tombstone.
3512.
Gilbert Stuart (center).
3513.
Overall Frame.

3514. Breakers.

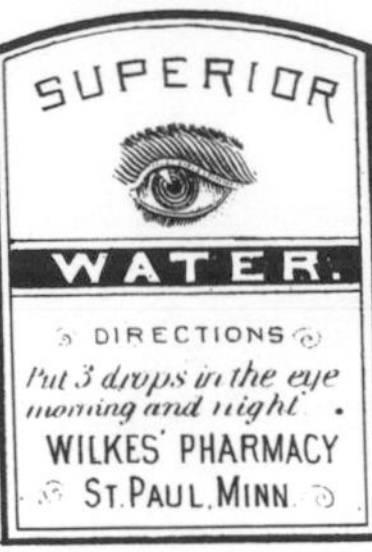

3515.

3516. "The Old Oaken Bucket."

3517. Carrier.

3518. Railroad Water Can.

3519. Waste Disposal.

3520. Archimedean Screw Lifts Water.

3521. Water Carriers, Sudan.

3522. Town Pump.

3523.

3524.

3525. Using the Ladle.

3526. Wooden Pipe.

3527. Garden Fountains.

3528. Farmer.

3529. Laying Water Main.

3530. Wooden Pipes, N.Y.

3531. Fountain of Rome.

3532. Irrigation, China.

3533. Fountain, New York Slums.

WHALING

3534. The Wonderful Whale, 1645.

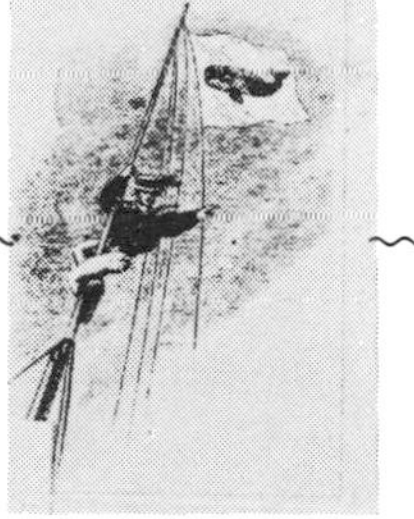

3538. "Thar she Blows."

3535. Moby Dick.

3536. Whaler Isaac Howland, 1750.

3537. Jumping Whale.

3539. Sperm Whale Blowing.

3540. Closing in.

3541. Whaling Boat Overturned.

3542. Whalers' Legend: John Tabor's Ride.

3543. Cutting up a Whale. English, 1658.

3545. Whalers Scrambling for Salt Meat.

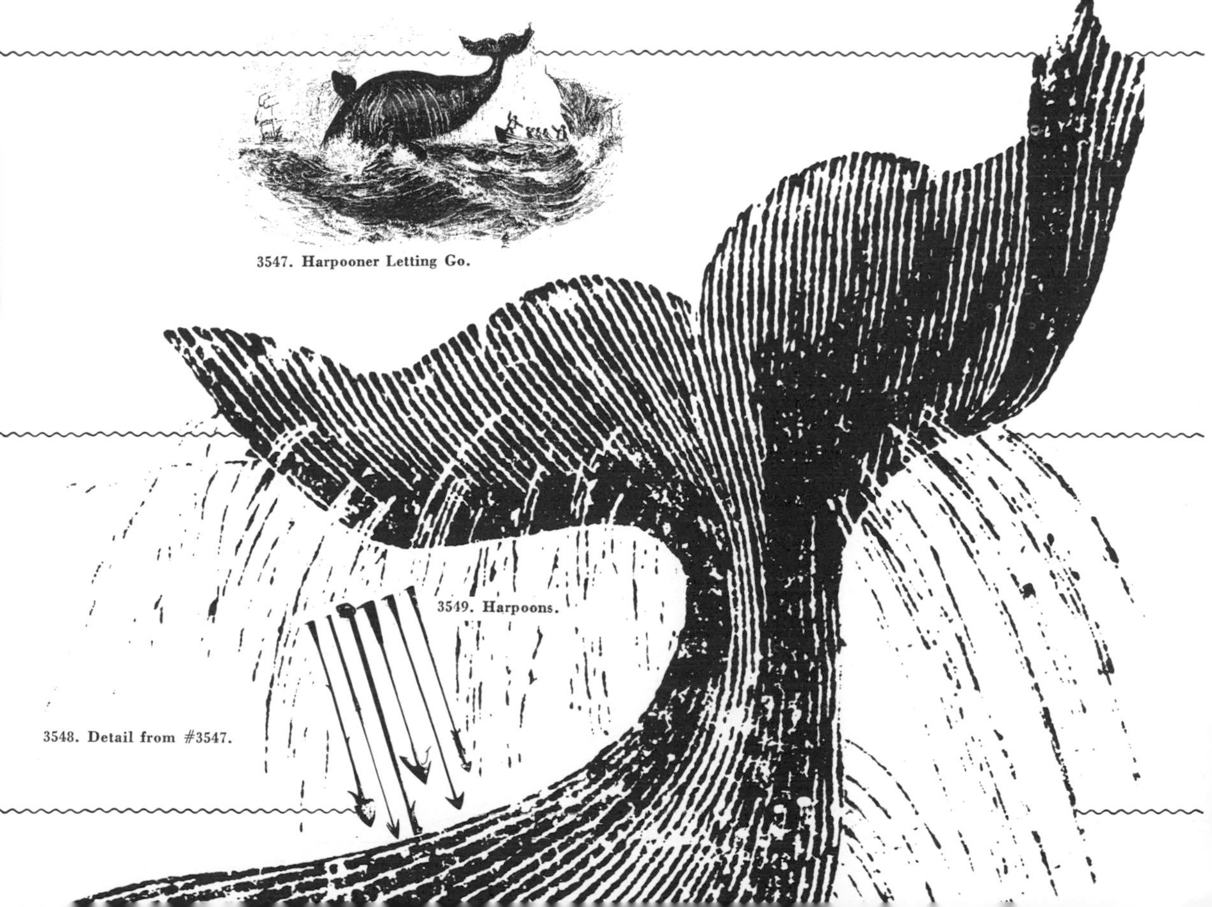

3547. Harpooner Letting Go.

3544. Boiling Blubber.

3546. Whale Oil Wharf.

3548. Detail from #3547.

3549. Harpoons.

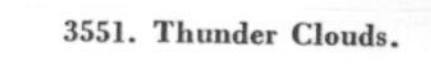

3551. Thunder Clouds.

3550. Electric Rain Maker.

3552. Winds Blowing.

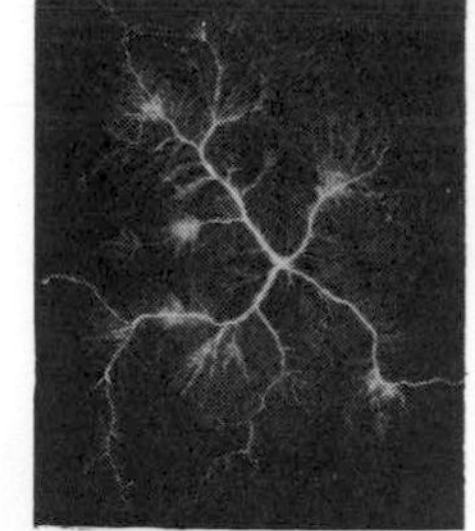

3553. Lightning.

3555. Four Winds.

3554. Aeolus, Wind God.

3556. Meteorologist.

3557. Clouds.

3558. Running from Tornado.

3559. Gusty Day, Paris.

3560. The Blizzard of '88.

Weather Symbols

3561.

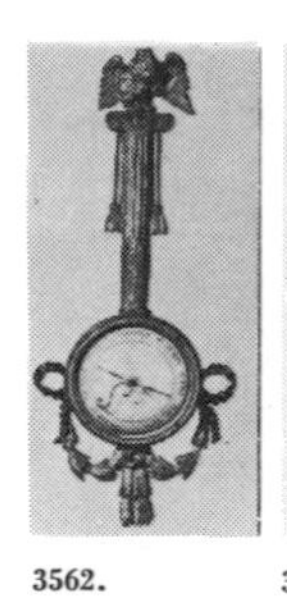

3562.

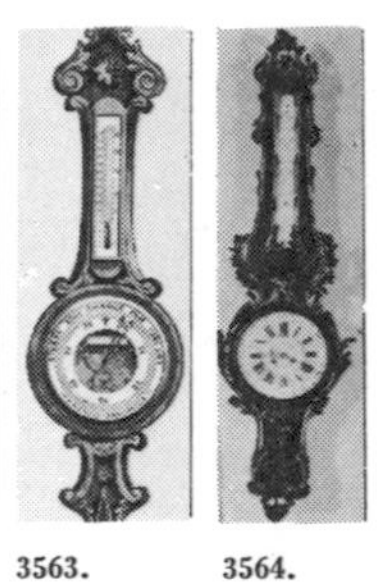

3563. 3564.

3565.

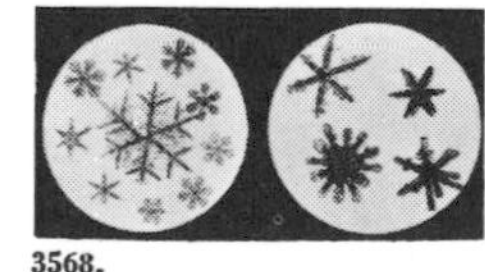

3568.

3566.

3567.

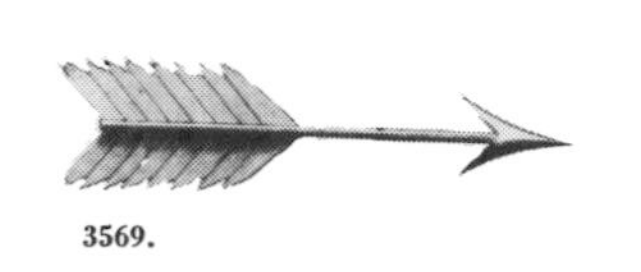

3569.

3570. Explanation of the Optical Basis of Rainbow, 1770.

3571. Lapp Hunters on Skis.

3572. Snowshoe Thompson.

3573. Ski Lift.

3574. Jumper.

3575. Bobsled Crew.

3576. Accident.

3577. Slip.

3578. Suspense.

3579. Lady Alpinist.

3580. Crossing Sea of Ice, Chamonix.

3581. Alpine Guide.

Skating

3582. Hockey Game.

3583. Curling.

3584. Catching up.

3585.

3586. Skating Pond. (Brueghel)

3587.

3588. Central Park.

Sleighs

3589. Reindeer Sleigh.

3590. Rural.

3591. Design. Great Exhibit, 1852.

3592. Family Outing.

3593. Catalogue Page.

3594. Flag-bearer.

3595. Mrs. Cady Stanton and Susan B. Anthony.

3596. Cartoonist's Comment.

3597. Gibson Girls.

3598. Demanding Right to Vote.

3599. Unexpected Effect.

3600. Woman's Inalienable Right.

3601. Headquarters, 1908.

3602. Society Ladies Carrying Posters.

3603. Fifth Avenue Parade.

3604. Four Leaders.

3605. Marshal.

3606. Muscular Feminism Scares Men.

3607. Caught in Winds of Change.

3608. Jane Addams (center) with fellow workers.

3609. Feminist Smokers Shock Parson.

3610. At Last.

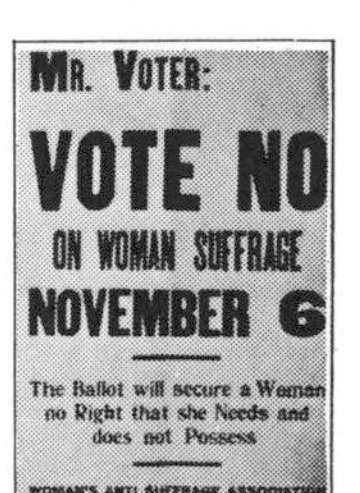

3611.

3612. Arrest of Suffragette, London, 1905.

THE NEW MAGAZINE MACHINE.

This novel application of mechanism, to the purposes of periodical publications, is the invention of an ingenious *litterateur.* The hoppers above being fed with subjects of all sorts, from "Criminal Trials" to "Joe Millers," the handle is turned, and the fountain-pens immediately begin to write articles upon everything.

3613.

3614. Civil War Pictorial Cover.

3615. Babylonian.

3616. Hieroglyphics.

3617. Roman Inscription.

3618. Merovingian Script.

3619. Calligraphic Title Page.

3620. Indian Chronicle.

3621. St. Augustine.

3622. Town Scribe.

3623. Sharpening Quill.

3624. How to hold a quill.

3625. How to sit when writing.

3626.

3627. Signing a Contract.

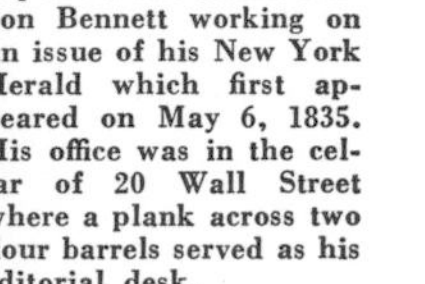

Start of a Great Newspaper Career: James Gordon Bennett working on an issue of his New York Herald which first appeared on May 6, 1835. His office was in the cellar of 20 Wall Street where a plank across two flour barrels served as his editorial desk.

3628.

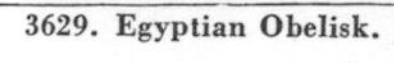

3629. Egyptian Obelisk.

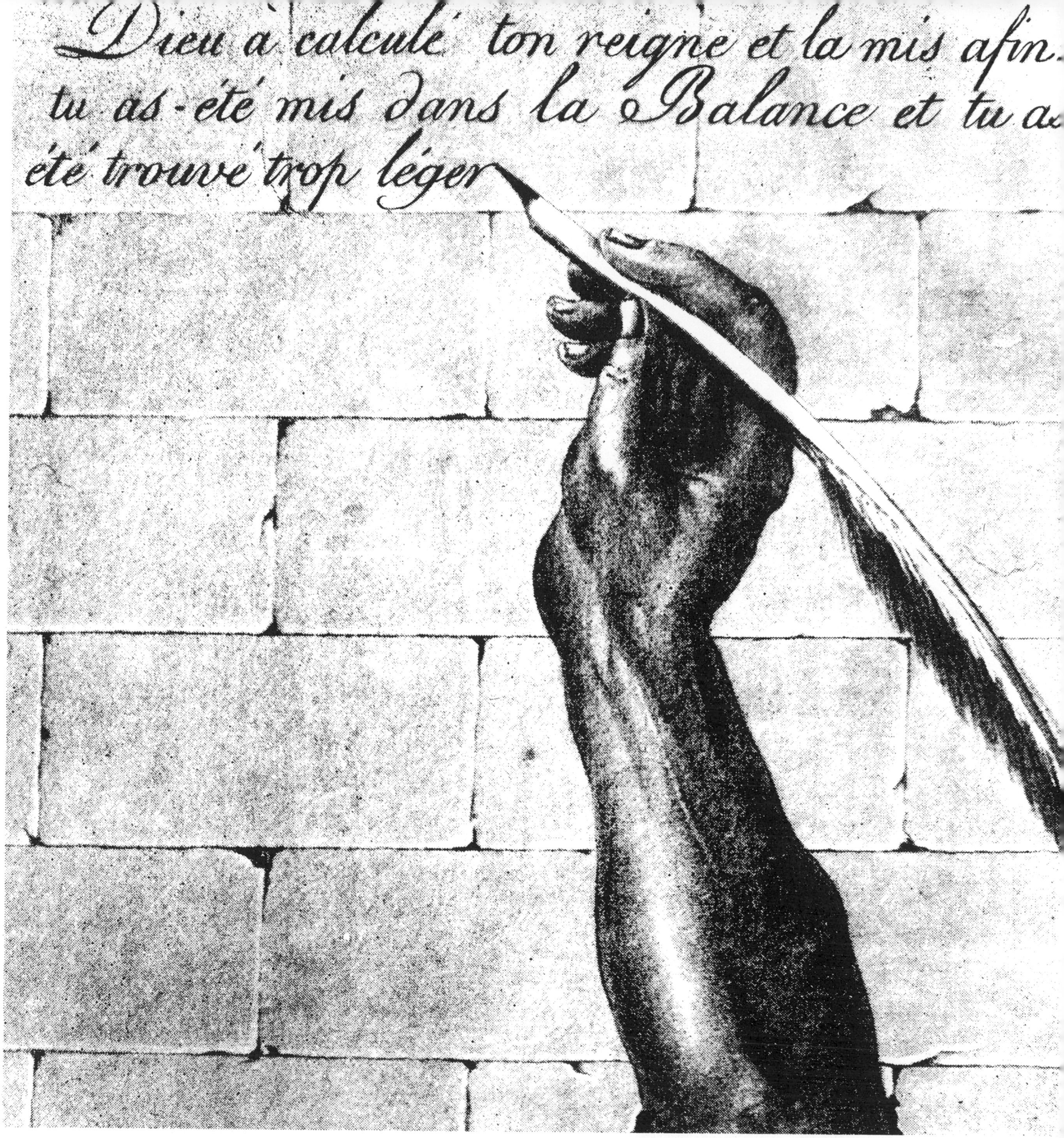

Dieu à calculé ton reigne et la mis afin.
tu as-été mis dans la Balance et tu a
été trouvé trop léger

3630. **Handwriting on the Wall: Symbolical drawing made during the French Revolution pronouncing the condemnation of Louis XVI.**

see also: Astronomy p.18

For complete, analytical subject index turn to page 221.

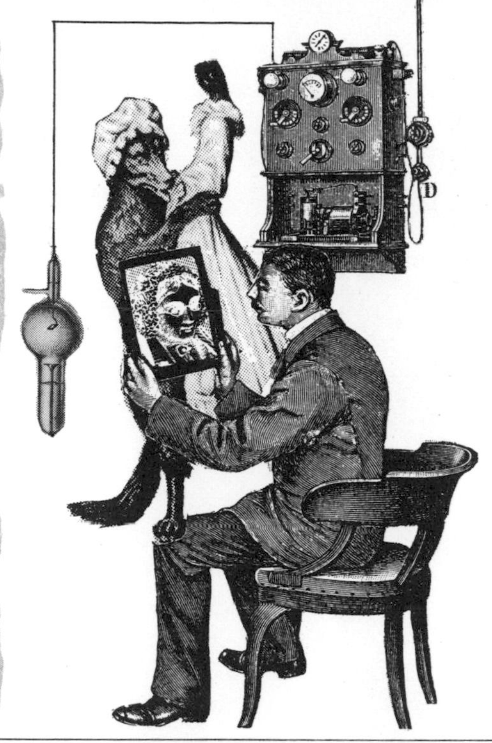

3631. X-ray of wolf's stomach shows Little Red Riding Hood's grandmother.

X-RAY

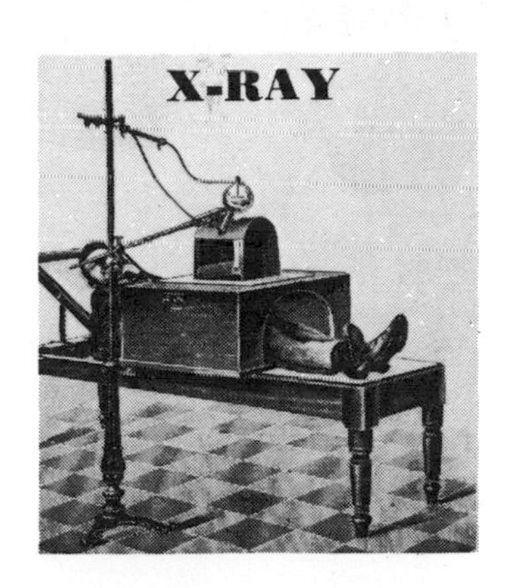

3632. Konrad Roentgen.

3633. Hand, 1895.

3634. U.S. X-ray Pioneers.

3635. X-ray Powered by Battery of Electric Car, 1903.

3636. World War I Medical Corps Truck.

XYLOGRAPHY

3637. Xylographer at Work.

3638. Enlargement from print at left.

YANKEE DOODLE

"Father and I went down to camp Along with Captain Gooding.

There was Captain Washington Upon a slapping stallion.

And then we saw a swamping gun, Large as a log of maple.

It makes a noise like father's gun Only a nation louder"

3640. 3641. 3642. 3643.

The YANKEY's Return from CAMP.

3639.

3644.
Man, the microcosm related to the spheres of the universe: Macrocosm. Illustration from the works of Robert Fludd, XVIIth century London physician and mystic. He revived the ancient theory that the human body was subject to the same cosmic laws as the stars which moved within their prescribed courses, the 12 zodiacal spheres.

3645. Serendipity.

3646. Swallow in Flight.

3647.

3648. Early attempt to analyze bird song.

3649.

3650. Crowned.

3651. Foxy Accountant.

3652.

3653. Animal Love.

3654. Stegosaurus.

3655. Samson and Lion.

3656.

3657.

3658. Brontosaurus Tests Teeth.

3659. Durer: Rhinoceros.

3660. Durer: Walrus.

3661. Noah's Ark.

3662.

3663. Sea Butterfly.

3664. Pompeian Aquarium.

3665.

3666. Izaak Walton: Fisherman's Bible.

3667. Jumping Dolphin.

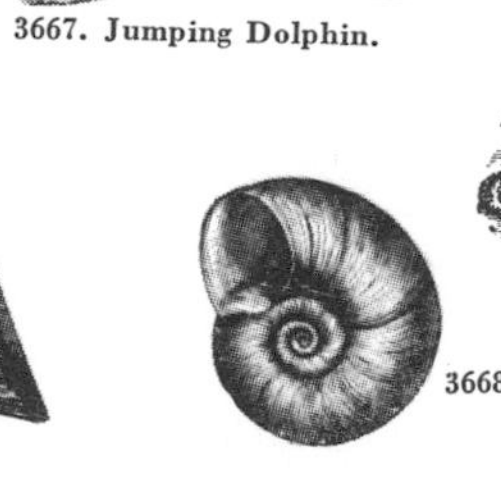

3668.

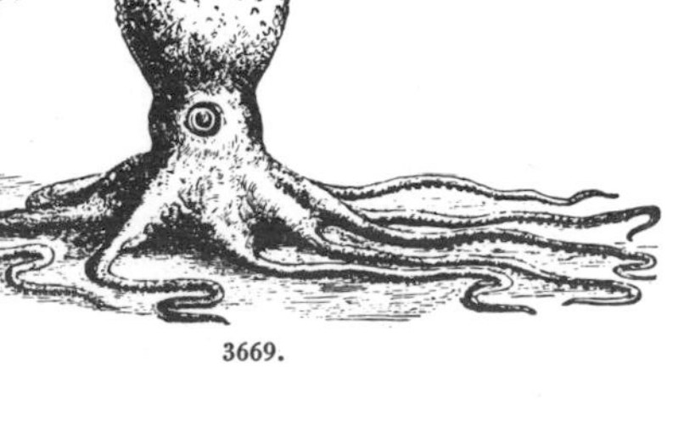

3669.

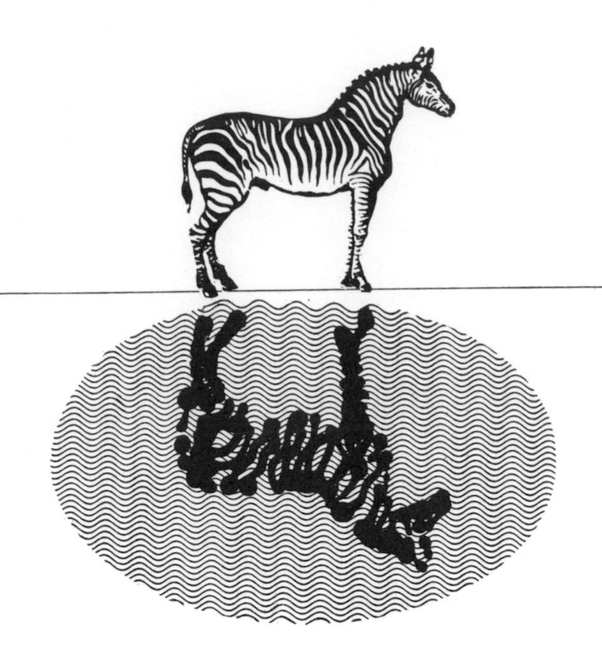

Heavy letters indicate page numbers. Light letters refer to picture numbers.

Heavy letters indicate page numbers. Light letters refer to picture numbers.

Heavy letters indicate page numbers. Light letters refer to picture numbers.

Heavy letters indicate page numbers. Light letters refer to picture numbers.

This book was printed on Mohawk Superfine Paper by The Chaucer Press of Freeport, N.Y.
under the supervision of Edward A. Simmons.